GUIDE TO THE HANNA COLLECTION AND RELATED ARCHIVAL MATERIALS

at the

HOOVER INSTITUTION ON WAR, REVLOLUTION AND PEACE

on the

ROLE OF EDUCATION IN TWENTIETH CENTURY SOCIETY

GUIDE TO THE HANNA COLLECTION AND RELATED ARCHIVAL MATERIALS

at the

HOOVER INSTITUTION ON WAR, REVOLUTION AND PEACE

on the

ROLE OF EDUCATION IN TWENTIETH CENTURY SOCIETY

Compiled by
Fakhreddin Moussavi

Hoover Institution Press
Stanford University
Stanford, California

Hoover Press Bibliographical Series 64
Copyright 1982 by the Board of Trustees of the
  Leland Stanford Junior University

Library of Congress Cataloging in Publication Data

Hoover Institution on War, Revolution, and Peace.
  Guide to the Hanna Collection and related archival
materials at the Hoover Institution on War, Revolution,
and Peace on the role of education in twentieth century
society.

  (Hoover Press bibliographical series ; 64)
  Includes indexes.
  1. Education--History--20th century--Bibliography.
2. Education and state--History--20th century--Bibliog-
raphy. 3. Educational sociology--History--20th century--
Bibliography. 4. Hoover Institution on War, Revolution, and
Peace--Archives--Bibliography. 5. Hanna, Paul
Robert, 1902-   . 6. Hanna, Jean Shuman. I. Moussavi,
Fakhreddin, 1940-   . II. Title. III. Series.
Z5811.H72 1982 (LB7) 081s (016.37019)   82-12131
ISBN 0-8179-2641-0

Manufactured in the United States of America

C O N T E N T S

Foreword   W. Glenn Campbell   vii

Preface   Milorad M. Drachkovitch   ix

Guide Entries to Archives   1

1981 Supplement   201

Notes on Published Holdings   207
  on Education and Society
  in the Hoover Institution Library

Notes on Holdings on Education and   215
  Society in other Stanford
  University Libraries

Index to Guide Entries   221
  Place-names   223
  Topics   231
  Organizations   234
  Personal Names   240

FOREWORD

I am pleased to present this guide to the Hanna Collection, and
other related archival material, on the role of education in
twentieth-century society. It is another in the series of
bibliographic studies published to aid scholars using the Hoover
Institution Library and Archives, which now total over 1.3
million volumes of books, pamphlets, and government documents;
over 30,000 periodical and newspaper titles; and 4,000 archival
and manuscript collections.

For more than a half-century, archivists and curators of the
Hoover Institution have been acquiring materials on the
political, economic, and social aspects of war, revolution, and
peace. Much of this documentation deals with the role of
education in society. In order to focus scholarly attention on
this specialized material and to enhance the collecting effort in
this area, the Hoover Institution in 1976 established the Hanna
Collection on the Role of Education in Twentieth-Century Society.
This guide describes over 600 archival and manuscript collections, relating wholly or in part, to education. It includes
those that constitute the Hanna Collection as well as those
acquired separately or before 1976. These archives, both U.S. and
foreign, treat government educational policy, promotion of peace
through education, propaganda and education in wartime,
international educational programs, education in developing
nations, comparative education, and related topics.

The Hanna Collection is named for Paul and Jean Hanna, who
founded this program and launched it with substantial monetary
and material contributions. Dr. Paul R. Hanna is the Lee L.
Jacks Professor of Education (emeritus) at Stanford University
and Senior Research Fellow at the Hoover Institution. He was
founder and first director of the Stanford International
Development Education Center (SIDEC) and undertook numerous
missions abroad for Stanford, the U.S. Departments of State and
Defense, UNESCO, foreign governments, and private foundations and
agencies. He has participated in U.S. national efforts to create
educational policy. Mrs. Jean S. Hanna was for many years a
teacher of English in this country and abroad and is coauthor and
editor with her husband of several widely acclaimed textbook
series.

Publication of this guide represents another step forward in the
Institution's efforts to make its holdings better known and more
accessible for research purposes.

W. Glenn Campbell, Director
Hoover Institution

PREFACE

The Hanna Collection on Education at the Hoover Institution of Stanford University added a new dimension to the Institution's collecting and research activities. The role of education in society is now a clearly distinguishable subject for research and publication, a specific part relating to the Institution's triad of war, revolution, and peace.

Education--both formal schooling and informal communications-- has always been a powerful instrument in preparing for war, creating and maintaining peace, and achieving national goals. If there is a certainty in our age of uncertainty, it is that the role of education will be enhanced in the future in all the countries of the world.

This guide to twentieth-century archival materials on education lists the holdings acquired by the Hoover Institution through 1980. (Materials received after 1980 will be included in later supplements.) Fakhreddin Moussavi, a native of Iran, who recently earned his doctorate at Stanford University, spent fifteen months examining over 4,000 collections in the Hoover Institution Archives. He identified over 600 that deal in whole or in part with education. Dr. Moussavi prepared short descriptions of these collections, arranged them in alphabetical order by donor's name, and compiled an index.

Most guide entries have two parts. The first, a description of the entire collection, was drawn from The Guide to the Hoover Institution Archives compiled by Charles G. Palm and Dale Reed (Hoover Institution Press, 1980). The second part consists of the compiler's notes on materials relating specifically to education. When the first description of the entire collection sufficiently covers the materials on education, no compiler's notes are provided.

Most materials described in this guide are located in the Hoover Institution Archives. They may be examined in the Archives Reading Room in the Herbert Hoover Memorial Building (courtyard level) by anyone who presents personal identification, completes a registration form, and adheres to rules regarding use. Archives are not available through interlibrary loan. A limited number of photocopies may be purchased in accordance with a reproduction price list and policy statement (available on request). Reference service is provided to reading room users, as well as to persons writing for information. For extensive searches involving detailed research, interpretation, or evaluation of materials, the names of qualified persons who work for a fee can be furnished. Inquiries should be addressed to the archivist.

In addition to archival materials, this guide, in pages 207 through 213, directs the reader to published, nonarchival materials held by the Hoover Institution Library.

In pages 215 through 220, this guide also describes holdings on education and society in Stanford University libraries other than the Hoover Institution.

Milorad M. Drachkovitch
Archivist and Senior Fellow
Hoover Institution
Stanford University

GUIDE ENTRIES TO ARCHIVES

1. ABERNETHY, DAVID B., 1937- .
    Miscellaneous papers, 1949-1964. 2 ms. boxes.
    Professor of Political Science, Stanford University.
    Notes and pamphlets, relating to political, economic,
        cultural, and social affairs in Nigeria.
    Register.
    Gift, D. B. Abernethy, 1972.

    Box 1 -- Notes of interviews with Nigerian leaders and
        citizens; notes from field trip relating to Nigerian Union
        of Teachers; questionnaires given to 1,350 southern
        Nigerian elementary and secondary school students in June
        1964; and pamphlets on Nigerian education.

2. ADAMS, MARIE, 1891-1976.
    Papers, 1887-1946. 4 ms. boxes.
    American Red Cross social worker; internee, Santo Tomas
        concentration camp, Philippine Islands, 1942-1945.
    Correspondence, propaganda leaflets, memorabilia, and
        printed matter, relating to the Santo Tomas
        concentration camp and the Japanese occupation of the
        Philippine Islands during World War II.
    Preliminary inventory.
    Gift, estate of M. Adams, 1978.

    Box 2 -- Newspaper and magazine clippings on schools and
        colleges in the Philippines.

3. AFRICAN REVOLUTIONARY MOVEMENTS COLLECTION, 1962-1972.
    5 ms. boxes, 1 envelope, 3 phonorecords.
    Pamphlets, newspaper clippings, government publications,
        leaflets, and other printed matter, relating to political
        and military efforts of African revolutionary organi-
        zations, including the Popular Movement for the Liberation
        of Angola, Mozambique Liberation Front, and the South-West
        African People's Organization.
    Register.

    Box 5 -- Pamphlets, articles, memoranda, and reports on South
        African Students' Organization, with sections on black
        education and black universities.

4. AID REFUGEE CHINESE INTELLECTUALS.
    Records, 1952-1970. 44 ms. boxes, 3 albums,
        6 envelopes.
    Private U.S. relief organization.
    Correspondence, reports, minutes of meetings, financial

records, and photographs, relating to ARCI relief for
Chinese refugees.
Preliminary inventory.
Gift, Aid Refugee Chinese Intellectuals, 1970.

Box 13 -- Last folder, several letters relating to Overseas
Educational Service.

5. AITCHISON, BRUCE.
Study, 1943. "The Administration of Occupied Enemy Territory
by the British Army in the Middle East."
1 folder.
Typescript (mimeographed).
Major, U.S. Army, and Staff Judge Advocate, U.S. Armed Forces
in the Middle East.

Section on education.

6. "ALEPPO NEWS-LETTER."
Newsletter, 1920. 1 folder.
Typescript.
Newsletter of Near East Relief workers in Aleppo, Syria.
Four issues, June-July 1920, relating to social conditions and
relief work in Syria.

Accounts of the Near East Relief workers' humane assistance to
Syrian orphans, women, and Armenians in that area.

7. ALLEN, BENJAMIN SHANNON, 1883-1963.
Papers, 1910-1967. 3 ms. boxes, 1 cubic foot box,
2 oversize boxes (1 linear foot), 2 envelopes.
American journalist.
Correspondence, press releases, clippings, other printed
matter, and photographs, relating to activities of the
Commission for Relief in Belgium, U.S. Food Adminis-
tration, and U.S. Fuel Administration during World War I
and of the National Committee on Food for the Small
Democracies and Finnish Relief Fund during World War II, to
political conditions in the U.S., and to Herbert Hoover.
Preliminary inventory.
Gift, B. S. Allen, 1954. Subsequent increments.

Box 3 -- Pocket book relating to imprisonment of Ghent
professors, October 1916.

8. ALMOND, NINA, COLLECTOR.
    Collection on the Treaty of St. Germain, 1919-1920.
        1 ms. box.
    Typewritten transcripts of bulletins, reports, and memoranda,
        published in The Treaty of St. Germain: A Documentary
        History of Its Territorial and Political Clauses, with a
        Survey of the Documents of the Supreme Council of the Paris
        Peace Conference, edited by Nina Almond and Ralph Haswell
        Lutz (Stanford: Stanford University Press, 1935).

    Second folder, on condition of peace with Austria, contains
        section on schools and educational establishments.

9. ALTROCCHI, RUDOLPH, 1882-1953.
    Papers, 1900-1945. 4 ms. boxes, 2 envelopes.
    Second Lieutenant, U.S. Army; Director of Oral Propaganda in
        Italy, American Bureau of Public Information, 1918; U.S.
        Army Liaison Service officer, France, 1918-1919.
    Correspondence, office diary, reports, speeches, military
        orders, newspaper clippings, postcards, posters, sheet
        music, and printed matter, relating to U.S. war propaganda
        work in Italy and Lyons, France, 1918-1919.
    Preliminary inventory.
    Gift, Julia G. Altrocchi, 1955. Subsequent increments.

    Box 2 -- Harvard Alumni Bulletin, January 11, 1941, issue,
        with articles on Harvard University, its students, and
        school textbook controversy.

10. AMERICA FIRST COMMITTEE, 1940-1942.
    Records, 1940-1942. 338 ms. boxes, 20 photographs,
        50 posters, 3 motion pictures.
    Private organization to promote U.S. nonintervention in World
        War II.
    Correspondence, minutes of meetings, reports, research
        studies, financial records, press releases, speeches,
        newsletters, campaign literature, form letters, clippings,
        mailing lists, films, photographs, and posters.
    Register.
    Gift, America First Committee, 1942. Subsequent increments.

    Box 25 -- Newspaper clippings on American Youth Congress.
    Box 35 -- News releases, pamphlets, leaflets, and notes
        relating to Youth Committee Against War.
    Box 36 -- Newspaper clippings and bulletins relating to
        Student Defenders of Democracy.

11. AMERICAN CHILDREN'S FUND, 1923-1950.
        Records, 1923-1950. 55 ms. boxes.
        Charitable organization for the promotion of child health and
            welfare in the U.S.
        Correspondence, memoranda, reports, minutes of meetings,
            financial records, and printed matter, relating to funding
            of the Boy Scouts, Girl Scouts, Boys' Clubs of America, and
            other organizations.

        Box 1 -- Article entitled "A Study of Scouts in Camp."
        Box 5 -- Reports and correspondence on black Scout leaders.
        Boxes 8-13 and 39 -- Correspondence, reports, books, and
            pamphlets on Girl Scouts and Girl Scout leaders.
        Boxes 40 and 41 -- Books and pamphlets on Boy Scouts.

12. AMERICAN COMMITTEE ON UNITED EUROPE.
        Records (in French, German, English, and Dutch),
            1949-1959. 7 ms. boxes.
        Conference proceedings, newsletters, pamphlets, reports,
            clippings, and photographs, relating to the activities of
            the European Federalists' Union, the European Movement, the
            European Youth Campaign, and affiliated organizations in
            promoting European political and economic unity.

        Boxes 1 and 2 -- Pamphlets on European Youth Campaign.
        Box 7 -- Memorandum on International University of Europe and
            report on the European University Teachers' Conference,
            1953.

13. AMERICAN COMMITTEE TO KEEP BIAFRA ALIVE. ST. LOUIS
        CHAPTER, COLLECTOR.
        Ephemera, 1967-1970. 4 ms. boxes, 1 envelope, 2 motion picture
            reels, 2 phonorecords.
        Ephemeral publications of private and governmental organi-
            zations, including the U.S. Agency for International
            Development, the Government of the Republic of Biafra, and
            the Government of Nigeria; press releases from the U.S.
            Department of State, U.S. Congressmen, and Markpress,
            Biafran Overseas Press Division; clippings; periodical
            literature; and audiovisual materials, relating to the
            Nigerian Civil War of 1967-1970.
        Preliminary inventory.
        Gift, Eileen L. Mann, 1971.

        Contents are in English and French.
        Box 1 -- Issue of America with article on Catholic colleges
            and universities.

6

14. AMERICAN EMERGENCY COMMITTEE FOR TIBETAN REFUGEES.
Records, 1959-1970. 17 ms. boxes.
Private organization to provide relief for Tibetan refugees in
    Nepal and India.
Correspondence, reports, minutes of meetings, and photographs.
Preliminary inventory.
Gift, American Emergency Committee for Tibetan Refugees, 1970.

Box 16 -- Folder of letters written by Tibetan schoolboys.
    Letters, with photographs attached, describe atrocities of
    Chinese Communists toward Tibetan people and how boys were
    forced to leave Tibet for India.

15. AMERICAN ENGINEERS IN RUSSIA COLLECTION, 1927-1933.
4 ms. boxes.
Correspondence, writings, articles, and answers to
    questionnaires, relating to economic conditions, wages,
    housing, living costs, and relations with Russian
    administrative personnel, of American engineers in Russia.
Register.

Box 3 -- Article on life in Soviet town with information on
    intelligentsia, religion, morality, and youth.

16. AMERICAN INDIVIDUALISM COLLECTION, 1966-1974.
2 ms. boxes, 7 phonotapes.
Correspondence, reports, essays, financial records, notes,
    leaflets, pamphlets, and printed matter, relating to the
    organization and activities of the Libertarian Party in
    California, 1970-1974; other libertarian and conservative
    youth groups; and the First National Convention of the
    Libertarian Party.
Preliminary inventory.

Box 1, Folder 1 -- Alliance of Libertarian activists on
    Berkeley campus.
Box 2 -- Article entitled "Students in Opposition to the
    Proposed Constitution."

17. AMERICAN LAW INSTITUTE, COMMITTEE TO ENCOURAGE DISCUSSION OF
        ESSENTIAL HUMAN RIGHTS.
Report, ca. 1944. "Statement of Essential Human Rights."
    1 folder.
Typescript (mimeographed).

7

Relates to views of legal experts from several Allied
countries regarding human rights.

Sections on education, religion, and freedom of opinion.

18. ANDERS, WLADYSLAW, 1892-1970.
    Papers (in Polish), 1939-1946. (34 linear feet).
    Polish military officer; Commander-in-Chief of Polish Armed
        Forces in the USSR.; Commander-in-Chief of the
        2d Polish Corps in Italy.
    Orders, reports, card files, questionnaires, accounts, Soviet
        government documents and publications, photographs, micro-
        fiche, and printed matter, relating to World War II, the
        Polish Armed Forces in Russia, the Polish 2d Corps in
        Italy, Polish citizens arrested and deported under German
        and Soviet occupations, Polish foreign relations, the
        Polish Government-in-Exile in London, and Polish Jews.
    Preliminary inventory.
    Deposit, W. Anders, 1946.

    Boxes 69, 71, and 72 -- Reports on Soviet propaganda in Iran,
        Iraq, and Palestine.

19. APPLEGARTH, JOHN S., COLLECTOR.
    Collection on Latin America, 1964-1965. 4 ms. boxes.
    Ephemeral publications, propaganda leaflets, newspaper
        clippings, photographs, placards, and a sound recording,
        relating to the riots in the Panama Canal Zone in January
        1964 and to activities of political parties in Mexico and
        Central and South America.
    Register.
    Purchase, J. S. Applegarth, 1964. Incremental purchase, 1965.

    Box 1 -- Issue of Tropical Collegian by students of the Canal
        Zone, and two issues of Parrakeet, publication of Balboa
        High School journalism class in the Canal Zone.
    Box 3 -- Envelope of leaflets and newspaper clippings, largely
        from the Panama Federation of Students.
    Box 4 -- Envelope of documents relating to communist
        activities against Universidad del Valle and U.S. Peace
        Corps.

20. ARGELANDER, FRANK.
    Memorandum, n.d. 1 folder.
    Typescript.
    American teacher and missionary in China, 1919-1931.
    Relates to the 1927 uprising of the Chinese Communist Party.

Based on diaries written during 1926 and 1927 in Kiukiang,
Kiangsi, and concerns takeover of William Nast College and
other American institutions by communist revolutionaries.
Writer was instructor at William Nast College, an American
missionary school, from 1919 until 1931.

21. ARNOLD, JULEAN HERBERT, 1876-1946.
        Papers, 1905-1946. 14 ms. boxes.
        American consular official; Commercial Attache in China,
            1914-1940.
        Diary, correspondence, speeches and writings, reports,
            dispatches, instructions, and memoranda, relating to the
            U.S. Consular Service in China, to economic and political
            developments in China, and to American commercial and
            foreign policy interests in the Far East.
        Register.
        Gift, William M. Leary, Jr., 1973.

        Boxes 1-3, and 9 -- Materials on American cultural relation-
            ships with China; missionary schools and colleges in China;
            educating Chinese in America; training Americans to know
            Asia; Chinese education; and Chinese students.

22. ASHFORD, DOUGLAS E.
        Papers (in English and French), 1955-1972. 25-1/2 ms. boxes.
        American political scientist and author.
        Writings, correspondence, reports, clippings, notes, interview
            transcripts, government publications, other printed matter,
            and teaching aids, relating to the politics, government,
            education, and agriculture of Morocco, Tunisia, Algeria,
            and other Northern African nations.
        Gift, D. E. Ashford, 1977.

        Some contents are in Arabic.
        Boxes 3 and 13 -- Pamphlet and book on education in Morocco.
        Boxes 8 and 24 -- Newsletters, notes, newspaper clippings,
            pamphlets, and reports on education and students in
            Tunisia.
        Box 9 -- Newspaper clippings and reports on development,
            including education in Tunisia and Morocco.
        Box 10 -- Pamphlet on Islamic Replublic of Mauritania, with
            section on education; notes, clippings, and reports on
            education in Morocco.
        Box 18 -- Memorandum from General Union of Algerian Moslem
            Students to Twelfth General Assembly of the United Nations.
        Box 26 -- Book on education in Algeria.

23. ASIA -- MISCELLANEA, 1944-1960.
      1 folder.
      Pamphlets, newsletter, and report, relating to political,
         social, and economic conditions in various Asian countries.

      Monthly report by General Headquarters of Supreme Commander
         for Allied Powers, February 1951, relating to civil
         information and education in Japan.

24. AUSTRIA -- STUDENT ORGANIZATIONS COLLECTION, 1970-1971.
      (In German) 1 folder.
      Leaflets, periodicals, and a handwritten poster, distributed
         at University of Vienna and relating primarily to the
         Osterreichische Studentenunion (Austrian Student Union) and
         university reform.
      Gift, Grete Heinz, 1974.

25. AYAU, MANUEL F.
      Miscellaneous papers, 1980. 1 folder.
      President, Universidad Francisco Marroquin, Guatemala City.
      Speech, delivered at the general meeting of the Mont Pelerin
         Society held at the Hoover Institution on War, Revolution
         and Peace, 1980; a prospectus and miscellany, relating to
         the Universidad Francisco Marroquin.
      Gift, M. F. Ayau, 1980.

      Financial report of Francisco Marroquin University, 1979-1980,
         and list of books published by that university.

26. BABB, NANCY, d. 1948.
      Papers, 1917-1925. 1 ms. box.
      American Relief Administration and American Friends Service
         Committee relief worker in Russia, 1917-1925.
      Correspondence, reports, and memoranda, relating to American
         Relief Administration and American Friends Service
         Committee work in Russia.
      Gift, Elizabeth Baker.

      Fifth annual report of National Circulating Library of
         Students' Peace Posters.

27. BADE, WILFRID ALBERT KARL, 1906- .
      Papers (in German), 1927-1945. 11 ms. boxes, 1 envelope.
      Official of the German Reichsministerium fuer Volksaufklaerung
         und Propaganda during World War II.
      Manuscripts of writing, correspondence, memoranda, printed

matter, and photographs, relating to dissemination of
German propaganda during World War II.
Preliminary inventory.

28. BAILEY, THOMAS ANDREW, 1902- .
Miscellaneous papers, 1947. 1-1/2 ms. boxes.
American historian.
Diaries, correspondence, notebooks, and passport, relating to
conditions in Europe during the summmer of 1947. Used as
research material for the book by T. A. Bailey, The
Marshall Plan Summer (Stanford: Hoover Institution War,
Revolution and Peace, 1978).
Gift, T. A. Bailey, 1977.

Box 1 -- Students' examination papers, War College diary, and
lecture notes, 1946-1947.
Box 2 -- Several examination papers.

29. BAKER, GEORGE BARR, 1897-1948.
Papers, 1919-1932. 14 ms. boxes.
American journalist; a Director of the American Relief
Administration.
Correspondence, photographs, and printed matter, relating to
the American Relief Administration; Commission for Relief
in Belgium; Paris Peace Conference; U.S. presidential
politics and the 1924, 1928, and 1932 presidential
campaigns; Calvin Coolidge; Herbert Hoover; the Republican
party; and the foreign-language press.
Preliminary inventory.
Gift, Mrs. W. Parmer Fuller, Jr., 1955. Incremental gift,
1959.

Box 1 -- Leaflet entitled "An Urgent Message from the
Commission on Church Colleges."
Box 8 -- News bulletins on White House Conference on Child
Health and Protection. First bulletin relates to education
of exceptional children.

30. BALLANTINE, JOSEPH WILLIAM, 1888-1973.
Papers, 1909-1970. 3 ms. boxes.
American diplomat; Special Assistant to the Secretary of
State, 1945-1947.
Memoirs, notes, reports, articles, and printed matter,
relating to American foreign policy in the Far East and to

the foreign policy views of Owen Lattimore.
Register.

Gift, Lesley Frost Ballantine, 1973.

Box 3 -- Report on background of American policy regarding
China, with sections on American missionary education and
American propaganda in that country.

31. BANE, SUDA LORENA, 1886-1952.
    Documentary history, 1943. <u>Organization of American Relief in
    Europe, 1918-1919.</u> 1/2 ms. box.
    Galley proofs (annotated).
    Relates to World War I relief activities of the American
    Relief Administration and U.S. Food Administration. Edited
    by S. L. Bane and Ralph Haswell Lutz. Published at
    Stanford by the Stanford University Press, 1943.

    Chapter VIII -- Report on problems of peace and children's
    relief, dated June 1919.

32. BARBOUR, GEORGE BROWN, 1890- .
    Papers, 1911-1934. 1-1/2 ms. boxes, 1 envelope, 1 motion
    picture.
    American geologist; missionary and educator in China,
    1920-1932.
    Correspondence, photographs, postcards, drawings, and a motion
    picture, relating to political and social conditions in
    China, missionary service in China, and university
    education in China.
    Gift, Ian Barbour, 1973.

    Box 1, Folder 2 -- Letters describing position of students in
    Christian university in China.

33. BARKER, BURT BROWN.
    Papers, 1887-1966. 1/2 ms. box, 4 phonotapes.
    American educator; boyhood friend of Herbert Hoover.
    Correspondence, phonotapes, and school catalogs, relating to
    Herbert Hoover's youth, early schooling, and mining career
    in Australia. Includes correspondence between Herbert
    Hoover and B. B. Barker.
    Gift, B. B. Barker, 1967; KOIN-TV, Portland Oregon, 1968.

    School catalogs of Friends of Pacific Academy containing names
    of the Board of Trustees, Visiting Committee, faculty,
    students, and courses of study.

34. BARRINGER, THOMAS C.
   Papers, 1922-1925. 2 ms. boxes.
   District Supervisor, American Relief Administration in Russia,
      1921-1923.
   Correspondence, reports, memoranda, photographs, and
      clippings, relating to relief operations of the American
      Relief Administration in two famine areas in Russia.
   Gift, T. C. Barringer, 1956.

   Box 1, Folder 1 -- Report on Simbirsk relating to health and
      welfare of children in that area and letters of gratitude
      for Thomas Barringer's services.

35. BASILY, NICOLAS ALEXANDROVICH de, 1883-1963.
   Papers (in Russian and French), 1881-1957. 25 ms. boxes,
      4 envelopes.
   Imperial Russian diplomat; Deputy Director, Chancellery of
      Foreign Affairs, 1911-1914; member, Council of Ministry of
      Foreign Affairs, 1917.
   Correspondence, memoranda, reports, notes, and photographs,
      relating to Russian political and foreign affairs,
      1900-1917; Russian involvement in World War I; the
      abdication of Tsar Nicholas II; and the Russian Revolution
      and Civil War. Includes drafts of N. A. de Basily's book,
      Russia Under Soviet Rule.
   Register.
   Gift, Mrs. N. A. de Basily, 1965. Subsequent increments.

   Boxes 10, 19, and 20 -- Articles and reports on public
      education in Russia.
   Box 18A -- Reports on elementary schools in Russia.

36. BASTUNOV, VLADIMIR J., COLLECTOR.
   Collection on the Russian Imperial Army (in Russian),
      1897-1917. 4 ms. boxes.
   Imperial orders, military orders, personnel rosters, and
      casualty reports, relating to the operations of the Russian
      Imperial Army and its personnel.
   Gift, V. J. Bastunov, 1975.

   Boxes 1 and 2 -- Imperial orders on military educational
      institutions, 1907-1917.

37. BATSELL, WALTER RUSSELL.
   Memorandum, 1925. "Memorandum on the Union of Soviet
      Socialist Republics." 1 folder.
   Typescript.
   American visitor to European Russia, 1925. Relates to

political conditions in the Soviet Union and to Soviet
foreign policy.
Gift, W. R. Batsell, 1926.

Section on communist propaganda in Soviet Union.

38. BEES OF AMERICA.
     Miscellaneous records (in English and French), 1917-1921.
        1 volume.
     Brooklyn children's organization operating under the auspices
        of the Brooklyn Women's War Relief Committee.
     Correspondence, photographs, and miscellanea, relating to the
        provision of relief for Belgian children during World
        War I.

     Letters of thanks to Bees of America for their help and their
        splendid work; booklet about Bees of America and Bees of
        Brussels.

39. BEKEART, LAURA HELENE.
     Study, n.d. "The A.R.A.: Herbert Hoover and Russian Relief."
        1 folder.
     Typescript.
     Gift, L. H. Bekeart, 1965.

     Part 5 -- Sections on false teachings of communism by
        revolutionary leaders of Russia.

40. BELGIUM - UNDERGROUND MOVEMENT.
     Collection (in French, Flemish, and English), 1939-1945.
        1-1/2 ms. boxes.
     Leaflets, press releases, manuscripts of writings, clippings,
        and miscellanea, relating to the Belgian resistance
        movement during World War II.

     Box 1 -- Pamphlet on university students and professors in
        Belgium, 1945.
     Box 2 -- Notes, newspaper clippings, and pamphlet relating to
        Belgian American Educational Foundation, Inc.

41. BELGIUM (TERRITORY UNDER GERMAN OCCUPATION, 1940-1944)
        MILITAERBEFEHLSHABER IN BELGIEN UND IN NORDFRANKREICH.
        PROPAGANDA-ABTEILUNG BELGIEN.
     Records (in German, French, and Flemish), 1939-1944.
        7 ms. boxes.

Propaganda Division of the German occupation government in
    Belgium.
Correspondence, memoranda, and photographs, relating to
    propaganda activities. Includes examples of German and
    Allied propaganda distributed in Belgium and of clandestine
    anti-German propaganda produced in Belgium.
Gift, 1947.

42. BELORUSSIAN LIBERATION FRONT, LONDON.
    Publications, 1955-1969. 1 folder.
    Anticommunist and nationalist emigre group.
    Brochures and printed matter, relating to Belorussian history,
        nationalism, and cartography.
    Gift, Jan Budzich-Bunchuk, 1976.

    Pamphlets, with sections on UNESCO and corruption of
        educational institutions in Belorussia.

43. BENNETT, A. E., COLLECTOR.
    Collection, 1958-1979. 1 ms. box.
    Letters, clippings, leaflets, pamphlets, serial issues, and
        ephemeral printed matter, issued by conservative and
        anticommunist organizations in the U.S., relating to
        international communism and communism in the U.S.

    Pamphlet entitled "American Interest in the Middle East," with
        sections on culture and education in that area; newsletters
        and reports on communism and American colleges.

44. BERLIN. FREIE UNIVERSITAET.
    Leaflets, issued by student protest groups, 1955-1968.
        4 reels microfilm.

45. BERLIN. FREIE UNIVERSITAET. ALLGEMEINER STUDENTENAUSSCHUSS.
        KONVENT.
    Minutes, 1965-1967. 2 reels microfilm.

46. BERLIN. FREIE UNIVERSITAET. INSTITUT FUER POLITISCHE
        WISSENSCHAFT.
    Collection on student protest movements, 1952-1970.
        7 reels microfilm.

47. BERMAN, GEOFFREY, COLLECTOR.
    Miscellany, 1943-1945. 1 folder.

Syllabus for <u>U.S. Army Air Forces</u> aviation cadet training,
   1943, and a letter and order relating to American aerial
   operations in the Pacific Theater during World War II,
   1945.
Gift, Geoffrey Berman, 1949.

48. BERNADINO, VITALIANO.
   Papers, 1966-1977. 12 ms. boxes.
   Member, Philippines Department of Education; Director,
      Southeast Asia Ministers of Education Secretariat.
   Writings and printed matter, relating to education in
      Southeast Asia.
   Gift, V. Bernadino, 1978.

   Boxes 7 and 8 -- Reports, pamphlets, and writings on Southeast
      Asian education.
   Other boxes contain published and unpublished writings,
      reports, and books on public education in the Philippines.

49. BERNDT, ALFRED-INGEMAR.
   Report (in German), 1944. 1 folder.
   Typescript (photocopy).
   Official of the German Ministry of Propaganda.
   Relates to proposals for administration of the World War II
      German propaganda effort.

50. BERNFELD, SIEGFRIED, d. 1953, <u>COLLECTOR</u>.
   Journals (in German), 1903-1919. 2 ms. boxes.
   Typescript (mimeographed) and printed.
   Literary journals of German and Austrian secondary schools.
   Gift, S. Bernfield.

51. BIAFRA STUDENTS ASSOCIATION IN THE AMERICAS.
   Phonorecord, n.d. <u>This is Biafra</u>.
   National anthem and other songs of Biafra, and a speech by
      Colonel Odumegwu Ojukwu, Head of State of Biafra, in 1967.

52. BIENEN, HENRY.
   Papers, 1961-1967. 1 ms. box.
   Professor of Political Science, Princeton University.
   Drafts of unpublished chapter of a book, minutes of meetings,
      reports, pamphlets, and newspaper clippings, relating to
      Tanzania's political development.
   Register.
   Gift, H. Bienen, 1972.

Folder on party and government includes pamphlet on Dar es
Salaam University College and its students, August 1964.

53. BILMANIS, ALFRED, 1887-1948, <u>COLLECTOR</u>.
     Collection on Latvia (mostly in Latvian), 1944-1948.
       1 ms. box.
     Serial issues, mimeographed bulletins, and manuscripts of
       writings, relating to Latvia during World War II and to
       postwar Latvian refugees in Sweden, West Germany,
       Argentina, and the U.S.
     Gift, A. Bilmanis, 1945.

     Four reports on Latvia, with section on education.

54. BISBEE, ELEANOR.
     Papers, 1918-1956. 16 ms. boxes, 4 envelopes, 3 oversize
       photographs.
     Professor, American University, Istanbul.
     Correspondence, drafts of books and articles, speeches,
       memoranda, notes, pamphlets, clippings, and photographs,
       relating to the history and government of Turkey in the
       twentieth century. Includes an interview with Mustapha
       Kemal, 1922, and manuscripts by Eleanor Bisbee, Resat
       Guntekin, Abdulhak Hisar, Yakub Osmanoglu, Milli Partisi,
       and Ahmen Yalman.
     Gift, estate of E. Bisbee, 1956.

     Box 1 -- Paper on significance of Herbert B. Adams in American
       historiography, with sections on his educational background
       and interests.
     Boxes 2 and 3 -- Paper and pamphlet on teaching Turkish
       grammar.
     Box 9 -- Issue of <u>Islamic Literature</u> with article on Iman
       Ghazali, a great Islamic educator, no. 3, March 1954; two
       issues of <u>Asia and the Americas,</u> with articles on
       propaganda and education, 1943 and 1945.
     Box 10 -- Issues of <u>Alumni Bulletins</u>, of Robert College and
       American College for Girls, with sections on education,
       1953 and 1954.
     Box 16 -- Pamphlet on education in new Turkey, 1848.

55. BLACKWELDER, ELIOT, 1880-1969.
     Papers, 1940-1968. 1 ms. box, 1 envelope.
     Professor of Geology, Stanford University, 1922-1945.
     Correspondence, memoranda, research notes, scrapbook of
       published writings, printed matter, and photographs,
       relating to international affairs and cooperation, world

economics, an Atlantic Union, and Herber Hoover's opinion
poll of the Stanford University faculty on foreign policy
of the U.S.
Gift, Martha B. Merk, 1975.

Articles, notes, and correspondence relating to the Conference
on Research and Education in World Government; articles on
school and university.

56. BOHANNAN, CHARLES T. R.
Papers (in Vietnamese and English), 1945-1965. 13 ms. boxes.
Lieutenant Colonel, U.S. Army; Rand Corporation consultant;
counterguerrilla expert.
Reports, memoranda, and writings, relating to the war in
Vietnam, 1961-1965; counterguerrilla operations in
Colombia, 1959-1960, and Southeast Asia, 1961-1965; and
Allied military government in Japan, 1945.
Preliminary inventory.
Gift, C. T. R. Bohannan, 1977.

Boxes 2 and 3 -- Propaganda leaflets.
Box 7 -- Study report by University of Michigan on a rural
Vietnamese community, January 1960. Report has sections on
social stratification, family cults, and education.
Box 9 -- Survey report of secondary school opinion in Kien Hoa
Province.

57. BOLANDER, LOUIS H.
Bibliography, n.d. "Bibliography of Naval Literature in the
United States Naval Academy Library, 1928-1929."
1 ms. box.
Typescript (mimeographed).

Titles of books, pamphlets, and periodicals relating to naval
history, including the lives, service, and educational
backgrounds of American and world naval heroes.

58. BOND, MARSHALL, 1867-1941.
Diary, 1927. 1 ms. box, 1 microfilm reel.
Typescript (mimeographed).
American visitor to Africa.
Relates to general description of Africa. Microfilm of diary,
and addenda entitled "The Economic Conditions and
Commercial Possibilities of Africa," by M. Bond, "The
Racial Problem in Africa," by Charis Denison, "African
Women," by Margaret Davidson, and "The Progress in Africa,"
by J. H. Denison.

Purchase, M. Bond, Jr., 1978.

Two illustrated volumes on social conditions, culture, and
education.

59. BORDEN MERIT AWARD COMMITTEE.
Records, 1958-1963. 2 ms. boxes.
Correspondence, memoranda, and printed matter, relating to the
selection of candidates for the Borden Merit Award. Award
presented by the Borden Company Foundation to scholars for
excellence in publications based on research at the Hoover
Institution on War, Revolution and Peace.
Gift, Borden Merit Award Committee, 1970.

Box 1 -- Stanford University Bulletin, January 5, 1958, with
information on education and Stanford activities.

60. BOTKINE, SERGE.
Papers (in Russian, German, French, and English), 1918-1930.
8 ms. boxes.
Russian refugee in Germany.
Memoirs, correspondence, reports, memoranda, and printed
matter, relating primarily to Russian emigres in Berlin,
elsewhere in Germany, and in other European countries after
the Russian Revolution.
Preliminary inventory.
Gift, S. Botkine, 1930.

Box 2 -- Reports and correspondence on Russian National
Students Fellowship and Russian Patriotic Youth
Association.
Box 7 -- Reports, pamphlets, and newspaper clippings on
Russian emigre schools.

61. BOWEN, THOMAS JEFFERSON, 1814-1875.
Papers relating to missionary work in Nigeria.
1 microfilm reel.

62. BOYNTON, CHARLES LUTHER, 1881- .
Papers, 1901-1967. 10 ms. boxes.
American Baptist missionary in Shanghai, 1906-1948.
Correspondence, diaries, writings, pamphlets, and photographs,
relating to missionary work in Shanghai, the Shanghai
American School, and general conditions in China during
this period.

Boxes 4, 6, and 7 -- Booklets, notes, letters, and magazines
on Christian colleges in China; Philippine youth;
educational exchange; and the Peace Corps.

63. BRADY, R. F.
Papers, 1933-1941. 1 folder.
American missionary in China.
Notes and printed matter, relating to missionary work in
China. Includes a University of Nanking Hospital report
for 1940 entitled, "Ginling College, 1915-1940"; notes and
notices of the Nanking Union Church and Community, 1941;
"Sketches of Nanking," 1933.

64. BRAMHALL, BURLE, COLLECTOR.
Collection on the Petrograd Children's Colony (in Russian),
1973-1976. 1/2 ms. box.
American Red Cross business manager in Siberia, 1919-1920.
Reminiscences of several of the 781 Russian children known as
the "Petrograd Children's Colony," who were sent by their
parents from Moscow and Petrogad in 1918 because of wartime
shortages, were stranded in the Ural Mountains, evacuated
from the war zones via Vladivostok by the American Red
Cross, and restored to their families in 1920 following a
global ocean voyage. Includes a description of the reunion
of American Red Cross staff members and members of the
Petrograd Children's Colony in Leningrad, 1973.
Gift, B. Bramhall, 1977.

65. BRESHKO-BRESHKOVSKAIA, EKATERINA, 1844-1934.
Miscellaneous papers (in Russian and English), 1919-1931.
2 ms. boxes, 5 envelopes.
Russian Socialist Revolutionary Party leader.
Writings, correspondence, biographical data, and photographs,
relating to the life of E. Breshko-Breshkovskaia. Includes
drafts of book by E. Breshko-Breshkovskaia, The Hidden
Springs of the Russian Revolution (Stanford: Stanford
University Press, 1931), a biographical sketch of
E. Breshko-Breshkovskaia by Aleksandr Kerenskii, and three
letters by E. Breshko-Breshkovskaia.
Preliminary inventory.

Box 2 -- Printed note on boys and girls of the world.

66. BRODIN, NILS-ERIC.
Papers (in English and Swedish), 1939-1969. 23 ms. boxes.
Swedish-American educator.

Writings, notes, clippings, bulletins, press releases, and
    printed matter, relating to the welfare state in Sweden;
    U.S. and world politics; student radicalism; and
    conservative political groups in the U.S., book-length
    study, "Power and the Welfare State: Power and Politics in
    Sweden, 1932-1969," 1969.
Gift, Nils-Eric Brodin, 1969. Increment, 1976.

Box 1 -- Writings on new schools and welfare state in Sweden.
Box 2 -- Newletters relating to American Afro-Asian
    Educational Exchange, Inc.
Box 4 -- Pamphlets, newsletters, and leaflets on education and
    communism.
Box 6 -- Newspaper clippings, pamphlets, and notes on
    education and student unrest in Europe.
Box 13 -- Reports, booklets, pamphlets, and newspaper
    clippings on sex education.
Box 14 -- Newsletters on schools and Stanford University.
Box 16 -- Newsletters and leaflets relating to UNESCO.
Box 17 -- Newspaper clippings on Stanford University and its
    academic activities.
Box 23 -- Newspaper clippings and newsletters on Swedish
    education.

67. BRODY, GENERAL.
    Text of a speech (in French), 1920. 1 folder.
    Typescript.
    Delivered at the Ecole des Francs-Bourgeois in Paris,
        July 11, 1920, at a ceremony in honor of the memory of
        former students of the school who had been killed in World
        War I.

68. BROKENSHA, DAVID WARWICK, 1923- , COLLECTOR.
    Collection on Africa, 1960-1970. 1 ms. box.
    Studies, writings, pamphlets, newsletters, and printed matter,
        relating primarily to rural development, agriculture,
        family life, nutrition, education, and various other socio-
        economic aspects of life in Ghana, South Africa, and
        eastern African countries.
    Register.
    Gift, D. W. Brokensha, 1973.

    Fact sheet on Rhodesia with section on education and a social
        survey report on Obuasi, Ashanti, with a section on
        schools.

69. BROWN, WALTER LYMAN.
    Papers, 1917-1932. 1 folder, 2 envelopes, 1 album.
    European Director, American Relief Administration European
        Children's Fund (ARAECF); Director, Rotterdam Office,
        Commission for Relief in Belgium (CRB).
    Photographs, correspondence and writings, relating to ARAECF
        and CRB relief work in Europe during and immediately after
        World War I.
    Gift, W. L. Brown.

    Letters written to Walter Brown by Herbert Hoover relating to
        relief work in Europe and list of American Children's Fund
        personnel in Europe.

70. BROWNELL, SAMUEL MILLER, 1900- .
    Papers, 1954-1956. 1/2 ms. box.
    U.S. Commissioner of Education, 1953-1956.
    Memoranda, reports, correspondence, and statements, relating
        to desegregation of schools in the U.S.
    Gift, S. M. Brownell, December 1980.

    Memoranda and correspondence relating to federal aid to
        land-grant colleges and proposals for permanent
        legislation in federally affected areas.

71. BROWNLEE, ALETA.
    Papers, 1945-1950. 10 ms. boxes.
    Director of Child Welfare in Austria for the United Nations
        Relief and Rehabilitation Administration (UNRRA) and
        International Refugee Organization (IRO), 1945-1950.
    Memoirs and office files, relating to UNRRA and IRO relief
        work for displaced children in Austria at the end of World
        War II.
    Gift, A. Brownlee, 1969.

    Boxes 1-9 -- Reports on child search and tracing in Europe;
        guardianship and adoption; child emigration and resettle-
        ment in U.S., Canada, Sweden, Australia, and New Zealand;
        and letters from parents and children.
    Box 10 -- Psychological problems of displaced children.

72. BRUNTON, DELBERT.
    Dissertation, 1927. "The German National People's Party,
        1918-1920." 1 folder.

Typescript.
Submitted to Stanford University.

Dissertation has section on schools in Germany.

73. BUNESCU, ALEXANDER D., 1895-   .
    Papers (in Romanian and English), 1949-1971. 1-1/2 ms. boxes.
    Romanian industrialist and university lecturer; Assistant
        Secretary for Public Works and Communications, 1938-1939;
        Undersecretary for Reconstruction, 1944-1945.
    Speeches and writings, lecture notes, reports, studies,
        newsletters, pamphlets, and printed matter, relating to
        twentieth-century Romanian history, politics, government
        and foreign relations; Radio Free Europe; the Romanian
        National Committee; and the Assembly of Captive European
        Nations.
    Box 2 is restricted until January 2, 1989.
    Gift, A. D. Bunescu, 1978.

    Box 1 -- Issue of International Peasant Union Monthly
        Bulletins, with article on Albanian youth.

74. BUNN, JOHN, COLLECTOR.
    Collection on athletics in the military, 1945. 1/2 ms. box.
    Manuals and memoranda, issued by various U.S. Army agencies,
        relating to the organization of athletic programs for
        American soldiers in Europe.
    Gift, J. Bunn, 1946.

    Two manuals for athletic instructors and students of Army
        Athletic Staff School, May and July 1945.

75. BUNYAN, JAMES, 1898-1977.
    Papers (in Russian and English), 1917-1963. 2-1/2 ms. boxes.
    Russian-American historian.
    Excerpts from published sources, documents, and notes
        (primarily in Russian), relating to the Ukrainian govern-
        ment, Russia, Siberia, and the Far Eastern Republic during
        the Russian Civil War in 1919, used by J. Bunyan as
        research material for his book, The Bolshevik Revolution,
        1917-1918 (1934); drafts, notes, charts, and printed matter
        (primarily in English), relating to Soviet economic, ad-
        ministrative, agricultural, and industrial organization and
        planning, 1917-1963, used by J. Bunyan as research material
        for his book, The Origin of Forced Labor in the Soviet
        State, 1917-1921 (1967); and drafts of the latter book.
    Gift, J. Bunyan, 1975. Subsequent increments.

Box 1 -- Handwritten notes on education in Russia during civil
war, 1919.

76. BURGESS, J. STEWART AND STELLA F.
Papers, 1920-1935. 1 folder.
American missionaries in China.
Letters, poems, and printed matter, relating to missionary
work of the Young Men's Christian Association in China and
to revolutionary movements in China.

Letter relating to students' first summer conference for
Government College to be held at Wo Fo Ssu (a temple in
Western Hill north of Peking), July 1911, and twelve-page
letter, dated March 13, 1928, on typical mental reaction of
a young Chinese student to present-day social and political
phenomena in China.

77. BURGESS, WARREN RANDOLPH, 1889-1978.
Papers, 1937-1977. 20 ms. boxes.
American banker; Under Secretary of the Treasury, 1955-1957;
Ambassador to the North Atlantic Treaty Organization
(NATO), 1957-1961.
Correspondence, speeches and writings, minutes, memoranda, and
printed matter, relating to international trade and
finance, NATO, the Atlantic Council, the Atlantic Treaty
Association, and U.S. foreign relations with Europe.
Preliminary inventory.
Gift, Helen Burgess, 1980.

Box 12 -- Correspondence, bulletins, newsletters, and
statement relating to National Citizens Committee to Save
Education and Library Funds.
Box 13 -- Correspondence and reports relating to Teachers
College, Columbia University.
Box 20 -- Correspondence relating to Robert College in Turkey.

78. BURNHAM, FREDERICK RUSSELL, 1861-1947.
Papers, 1876-1964. 7 ms. boxes, 1 oversize box.
American explorer; Major and Chief of Scouts, British Army,
during the Boer War.
Correspondence, writings, clippings, other printed matter,
photographs, and memorabilia, relating to the Matabele Wars
of 1893 and 1896 in Rhodesia, the Boer War, exploration
expeditions in Africa, and gold mining in Alaska during the
Klondike gold rush.
Preliminary inventory.
Gift, Ilo Burnham, 1978.

Boxes 2 and 4 -- Correspondence, newspaper clippings, and
    typescript of book on scouting and Boy Scouts.

79. BURR, MYRON CARLOS, 1884-1977.
    Papers, 1927-1938. 1 folder.
    American engineer.
    Correspondence and printed matter, relating to Herbert Hoover,
        the Republican National Convention of 1936, and Stanford
        University; includes two letters from Herbert Hoover to
        M. C. Burrs.
    Gift, Mrs. Jackson Edwards, 1978.

    Issue of The Stanford Illustrated Review, June 1927, with
        sections on Stanford activities and American students in
        France.

80. BUSTERUD, JOHN ARMAND, 1921- .
    Papers, 1972-1977. 22 ms. boxes.
    U.S. Deputy Assistant Secretary of Defense for Environmental
        Quality, 1971-1972; Chairman, Council on Environmental
        Quality, Executive Office of the President, 1972-1977.
    Correspondence, speeches and writings, memoranda, reports,
        studies, and printed matter, relating to international and
        domestic energy and environmental programs.
    Gift, J. A. Busterud, 1977.

    Box 9 -- Memoranda relating to students' challenges of
        regulatory agency procedures.

81. BUTLER, CHARLES TERRY, 1889- .
    Memoirs, 1975. "A Civilian in Uniform." 1/2 ms. box.
    Typescript (photocopy).
    American physician; U.S. Army surgeon during World War I.
    Relates to activities of the Medical Corps of the American
        Expeditionary Forces in France during World War I.
    Gift, C. T. Butler, 1975.

    Sections on Charles Butler's schooling, his college days and
        activities, and his scientific progress.

82. BUTTS, R. FREEMAN, 1910- .
    Papers, 1925-1975. 143 ms. boxes, 1 envelope.
    American educator; Associate Dean for International Studies,
        Teachers College, Columbia University, 1965-1975.
    Writings, correspondence, reports, conference papers and
        proceedings, syllabi, curriculum material, clippings, and

other printed matter, relating to the role of education in
society, education in the U.S., and international
education.
Gift, R. F. Butts, 1980.

Boxes 1-6, 11, 12, 14, 16, 20-22, 24, 30, 32, 33, 36-38, 47,
    63, 65, 75-77, 102, 108, 117, 118, and 130 -- Newspaper
    clippings, reports, notes, correspondence, pamphlets,
    booklets, articles, leaflets, text of speeches, and printed
    matter on education.
Boxes 7, 8, 122-127 -- Notes, articles, newspaper clippings,
    reports, pamphlets, correspondence, newsletters and
    journals, memoranda, questionnaires, and information
    bulletins on education and religion.
Boxes 9 and 10 -- Newspaper clippings, articles, reports, and
    notes on segregation and desegregation in education.
Boxes 15, 17, 18, 19, 23, 25, 29, 86-92, 140-143 --
    Correspondence, reports, notes, newsletters, pamphlets,
    articles, memoranda, periodicals, and leaflets relating to
    various educational organizations.
Boxes 28, 62, 74, 81, 83, 84, 104-106, 138, and 139 --
    Newspaper clippings, articles, correspondence, reports,
    leaflets, notes, bulletins, newsletters, and texts of
    speeches on international education.
Boxes 34, 39, 48, 54, 55-61, and 69 -- Notes relating to
    outlines of courses in education.
Boxes 43-46, 66-68, 80, 131-133 -- Reports, articles,
    pamphlets, booklets, newspaper clippings, newsletters,
    notes, and correspondence on teacher education.
Box 78 -- Newspaper clippings, pamphlets, booklets, and
    reports on education in U.K., USSR., and U.S.
Boxes 82, 107, 111-113, and 115 -- Pamphlets, reports, notes,
    newsletters, booklets, correspondence, periodicals, texts
    of addresses, newspaper clippings, and memoranda on higher
    education.
Boxes 85 and 110 -- Reports on education in Afghanistan.
Boxes 103 and 116 -- Reports, articles, notes, memoranda, and
    periodicals relating to African education.
Box 109 -- Periodical, correspondence, notes, and reports on
    education in Australia and West and Central Africa.

83. C.R.B. EDUCATIONAL FOUNDATION.
    Records, 1921-1956. 7 ms. boxes, 2 envelopes.
    Affiliate of the Commission for Relief in Belgium.
    Reports, minutes of meetings, correspondence, clippings,
        posters, and photographs, relating to U.S.-Belgian exchange
        fellowships sponsored by the foundation, the German
        occupation of Belgium, King Leopold III of Belgium, and the
        1950 Belgian plebiscite on the restoration of the monarchy.

Preliminary inventory.
Gift, C.R.B. Educational Foundation, 1946. Subsequent
     increments.

Boxes 1, 2, and 4 -- Reports on Belgian-American fellows.
Boxes 4-6 -- Reports of CRBEF and documents relating to CRBEF
     agreement with Stanford University.
Box 5 -- Articles and reports of Belgian educational
     organizations.

84. CALDER, ALONZO BLAND, 1892- .
     Papers, 1911-1956. 45 ms. boxes.
     American consular official stationed in China, 1920-1941 and
          1945-1948.
     Memoranda, reports, correspondence, clippings, photographs,
          and pamphlets, relating to U.S. foreign and economic
          relations with China in the interwar period and immediately
          after World War II, and to U.S. foreign and trade relations
          with Russia, Egypt, and Malaya.
     Gift, Mrs. A. B. Calder, 1975.

     Box 7 -- Report of the Eighth Conference of the Institute of
          Pacific Relations, Mont Tremblant, Quebec, Canada, December
          1942, on Soviet Union and Far East, with section on
          cultural development and education.
     Box 28 -- Pocket book entitled: China Through the American
          Window, with sections on Yen-Ching University, Peiping; an
          American Missionary College; the California College in
          China; and the Shanghai American School.

85. CALDWELL, JOHN KENNETH, 1881- .
     Memoirs, n.d. 1 folder.
     Typescript.
     American diplomat; Consul General at Tientsin, China,
          1935-1942; Ambassador to Ethiopia, 1943-1945.
     Relates to U.S. foreign relations and commerce with Japan,
          Russia, Australia, China, and Ethiopia, 1906-1945, and to
          U.S. participation in international narcotics control
          agencies.
     Gift, J. K. Caldwell, 1976.

     Sections on Berea College and its academic regulations; and
          John Caldwell's youth.

86. CALDWELL, OLIVER JOHNSON, 1904- .
     Papers, 1938-1977. 7 ms. boxes.
     American educator; Assistant Commissioner for International

27

Education, U.S. Office of Education, 1952-1964; Dean of
International Services, Southern Illinois University,
1965-1969.
Speeches, writings, memoranda, reports, and correspondence,
relating to international education, U.S. educational
policy, conditions in China prior to World War II, and
operations of the U.S. Office of Strategic Services in
China during World War II.
Preliminary inventory.
Gift, O. J. Caldwell, 1978.

All boxes contain reports on international education.
Box 5 -- Reports on reform in the American university system.

87. CAMPBELL, HANNAH BRAIN, 1880- .
Memoirs, 1945. 1 folder.
Typescript.
American Red Cross worker in Siberia, 1917-1920.
Memoir entitled "Adventure in Siberia," as told to Sarah E.
Mathews, relating to activities of the American Red Cross
in the eastern part of Russia, 1917-1920; and memoir
entitled "Children's Ark," relating to the return of
Russian children by the American Red Cross to their parents
in Russia in 1920.
Gift, S. E. Mathews, 1973.

"Children's Ark" compares the Russian children with those of
U.S. in various aspects.

88. CARR, WILLIAM G.
Letters, 1947. 1 folder.
Typescript (mimeographed).
Adviser to the U.S. delegation to the second general
conference of the United Nations Educational, Scientific
and Cultural Organization held in Mexico City, 1947.
Relates to proceedings of the conference.

Ten personal letters providing day-by-day background information for friends and acquaintances of the writer in the
United States and abroad.

89. CARSON, ARTHUR LEROY, 1895- .
Diary, 1921. 39 ms. boxes, 1 folder.
Typewritten transcript (photocopy).
American missionary and educator; teacher in China, 1921-1926
and 1931-1938; President, Silliman University, Philippine
Islands, 1939-1953.

Relates to journey from Canton to Linchow, China. Includes
     memoir by Edith (Mrs. L. M.) Carson, relating to American
     refugee life in the Japanese-occupied Philippines,
     1942-1944.
Gift, A. L. Carson, 1978.

Box 1 -- Newspaper clippings, bulletins, newsletters,
     correspondence, and printed matter on Peace Corps and adult
     education.
Box 3 -- Unpublished study on education in Philippines and
     report on missionary education in Pakistan, 1953-1954.
Boxes 4 and 5 -- Correspondence, notes, pamphlets, articles,
     reports, and bulletins relating to the Christian Univer-
     sity, the Association of Episcopal Colleges, and Trinity
     College of Quezon City.
Boxes 6, 8, 10, 12-15, and 39 -- Articles, notes, newsletters,
     leaflets, newspaper clippings, bulletins, correspondence,
     and reports on elementary, secondary, and higher education
     in the Philippines.
Boxes 7 and 38 -- Newspaper clippings and reports on different
     educational institutions and student activities in the
     Philippines.
Box 9 -- Reports and texts of addresses on curriculum
     development in the Philippines.
Boxes 35 and 36 -- Writings, texts of speeches, articles, and
     newsletters relating to Silliman University.

90. CARTER, GWENDOLEN.
     Summaries of interviews, 1973. 1 folder.
     Typescript.
     Professor of political science, Northwestern University.
     Interviews held by G. Carter with African scholars and
          leaders, relating to race and political problems in South
          Africa and to possible establishment of a British
          Documentation Center for microfilming or acquisition of
          Southern African archival and library materials.
     Gift, G. Carter, 1973.

     In addition to interviewing African scholars, Professor Carter
          interviewed British scholars and educators on establishment
          of Center.

91. CASAS ARMENGOL, MIGUEL.
     Papers (in Spanish), 1976-1980. 2 ms. boxes.
     Rector, Universidad Nacional Abierta, Caracas.
     Reports, memoranda, organizational manuals, and printed
          matter, relating to the organization and activities of the
          Universidad Nacional Abierta of Venezuela.

Gift, M. Casas, 1980.

Box 1 -- Three pamphlets relating to National University of Venezuela.

92. CENTRAL AND EASTERN EUROPEAN PLANNING BOARD, NEW YORK.
Records, 1942-1943. 1 folder.
Joint committee of the Polish, Czechoslovakian, Yugoslavian, and Greek governments in exile. Reports and minutes of meetings, relating to planning postwar reconstruction.

Report on activities of Central and Eastern European Planning Board from January 1942 to April 15, 1943, with section on education and activities of the Educational Committee.

93. CENTRALNY KOMITET dla SPRAW SZKOLNYCH i OSWIATOWYCH.
Records (in Polish), 1945-1949. 1/2 ms. box.
Polish refugee organization for the administration of schools for Polish displaced persons in Germany after World War II.
Correspondence, reports, and bulletins, relating to Polish refugee education in Germany.
Gift, S. Zimmer, 1949. Incremental gift, 1950.

94. CERF, JAY H., 1923-1974.
Papers, 1940-1974. 4-1/2 ms. boxes.
Director, Foreign Policy Clearing House, 1957-1961; U.S. Assistant Secretary of Commerce, 1961-1963; Manager, International Group, U.S. Chamber of Commerce, 1963-1969.
Correspondence, writings, reports, instructions, and memoranda, relating to U.S. commerical and foreign policy. Includes the Ph.D. dissertation of J. Cerf, "Blue Shirts and Red Banners," 1957, relating to the East German communist youth organization, Freie Deutsche Jugend.
Gift, Mrs. J. H. Cerf, 1976. Incremental gift, 1978.

Box 5 -- Dissertation entitled "Blue Shirts and Red Banners and Control of Students in East Germany."

95. CHADBOURN, PHILIP H. AND WILLIAM H.
Papers, 1915-1929. 2 ms. boxes.
Commission for Relief in Belgium workers during World War I.
Letters, reports, pamphlets, photographs, clippings, and memorabilia, relating to the Commission for Relief in Belgium.

Gift, P. H. Chadbourn, 1963.

Contents are in English, German, and French.
Box 2 -- A.B.C. textbook in French for children and cards of
gratitude from children to relief members.

96. CHAIGNEAU, VICTOR-LOUIS.
Papers (in French), 1910-1949. 5 ms. boxes.
French historian.
Manuscripts of writings, memoranda, political campaign
literature, and clippings, relating to social and economic
legislation in France, particularly during the Vichy
regime, and to French politics. Includes doctoral thesis
of V.-L. Chaigneau, "La Charte du Travail: Loi d'Octobre
1941" (The Charter of Labor: Law of October 1941).

Box 2 -- Articles and reports on education in France.
Box 5 -- Reports on French youth.

97. CHANDLER, ROBERT W.
Study, 1976. "War of Ideas." 1/2 ms. box.
Typescript (photocopy).
Major, U.S. Air Force.
Relates to U.S. propaganda in Vietnam, 1965-1972.
Gift, R. W. Chandler, 1977.

Describes and appraises American use of propaganda in Vietnam
(1965-1972) as an instrument of foreign policy, with
numerous illustrations.

98. CHANG, HSIN-HAI, 1900-1972.
Papers (in English and Chinese), 1936-1976. 19 ms. boxes.
Chinese educator and diplomat; Ambassador to Portugal,
1933-1934; Ambassador to Czechoslovakia and Poland,
1934-1937.
Correspondence, writings, clippings, and printed matter,
relating to Chinese foreign relations with the United
States, 1941-1971; Chinese efforts to gain public support
in the United States, 1941-1945; Chinese history; and World
War II. Includes correspondence of Siang Mei Rosalynde
Chang.
Register.
Deposit, Siang Mei Chang, 1977.

Boxes 9, 12, 13, and 15 -- Materials on Eastern and Western
philosophy and responsibility of American youth.

99. CHAPIN, LELAND T.
        Papers, 1941-1944. 1 ms. box.
        Executive Secretary, Morale Committee on Educational
            Institutions in Hawaii; Civil Affairs Officer, U.S. Navy,
            during World War II.
        Writings, minutes of meetings, radio transcripts, and serial
            issues, relating to the promotion of patriotism in Hawaiian
            schools and within the Oriental community in Hawaii and to
            military government in the Marshall Islands during World
            War II.
        Preliminary inventory.
        Gift, L. T. Chapin, 1969.

        Correspondence relating to University of Hawaii and Punahou
            School.

100. CHAPMAN, FRANK MICHLER, 1864-1945.
        History, 1920. "The American Red Cross in Latin America."
            1 volume.
        Typescript.
        Relates to Red Cross work in Latin America during World War I.

        Services of Red Cross in Latin American countries and
            enthusiasm of adults and schoolchildren in accepting
            membership in it. List of chapters and branches of
            American Red Cross located in South America.

101. CHAPPELL, CHURCH ALLEN, d. 1976.
        Papers, 1925-1953. 1 ms. box.
        Captain, U.S. Navy.
        Diary, correspondence, orders, U.S. naval activities in the
            Philippines, 1935-1937, and at Pearl Harbor, 1941, and to
            the U.S. Naval Academy Postgraduate School.
        Gift, C. A. Chappell, 1974.

        Instructional materials relating to U.S. Naval Academy
            Postgraduate School.

102. CHERINGTON, REED B.
        Papers, 1918-1941. 1 ms. box, 3 albums, 1 envelope,
            1 folder.
        Chaplain, U.S. Army.
        Photographs, memorabilia, chaplain's manual and prayer books,
            and miscellaneous American and German military documents,
            relating to the American Expeditionary Force in France
            during World War I.
        Gift, Mrs. R. B. Cherington, 1945. Incremental gift, 1949.

Training manual with sections on religious training and
educational activities, 1926.

103. CHILDS, JAMES RIVES, 1893- .
Memoirs, n.d. 1/2 ms. box.
Typescript.
American diplomat; American Relief Administration worker in
Russia, 1921-1923; Charge d'Affaires in Morocco, 1941-1945;
Ambassador to Saudi Arabia, 1946-1950; Ambassador to
Ethiopia, 1951-1953.
Relates to relief work and social conditions in Russia, U.S.
foreign relations with Balkan and Near Eastern countries,
diplomacy regarding Morocco in World War II, and the role
of Iran in world politics, especially in relation to
Russia.

Volume entitled Thirty Years in the Near East has sections on
Iranian civilization, westernization, and educational
reforms in that country by Reza Shah.

104. CHINA -- COMMUNIST POSTERS AND RECORDS.
(In Chinese), ca. 1949-1953. 63 posters, 19 phonorecords.
Propaganda relating to Chinese revolutionary history, mutual
aid teams, policy towards minorities and marriage reforms,
Sino-Soviet friendship, Mao Tse-tung, and Lu Hsun.
Preliminary inventory.
Purchase, John W. Powell, 1974.

105. CHINA -- MISCELLANEA, 1922-1952.
1 ms. box.
Collection of intelligence reports, pamphlets, clippings,
bulletins, and notes, relating to Japanese intervention in
China, and to political, social, and economic conditions in
China.

Issue of The Chinese Record, no. 3, March 1930, with section
on religion and education and educational unification.

106. CHRISTIAN, SUTTON.
Papers (in Chinese and English), 1931-1945. 1 ms. box.
Director, Chengtu and Sian Branches, China Division, U.S.
Office of War Information, 1945.
Correspondence, writings, reports, and printed matter,
relating primarily to U.S. propaganda activities in the
communist border areas of China, 1944-1945.
Gift, Nevada Christian, 1978.

107. CHRISTOFF, PETER K.
        Collection (in Russian), 1840-1956. 1 ms. box, 2 envelopes.
        Photocopies of originals located at the Lenin Library, Moscow.
        Correspondence, diaries, and writings of prominent Moscow
            Slavophiles, 1840-1864, and photographs depicting social
            conditions in the Soviet Union, 1931-1956.

        Notes from Iu. F. Samarin's reminiscences about university
            life in Soviet Union.

108. CHURCH, MICHAEL P., COLLECTOR.
        Collection on American youth movements and communism,
            1933-1941. 1-1/2 ms. boxes.
        Writings, notes, clippings, leaflets, and pamphlets, relating
            to American youth movements and communist activities in
            American educational institutions.
        Gift, M. P. Church, 1962. Subsequent increments.

        Box 1 -- Materials relating to Youth Congress and education in
            different states of America.
        Box 2 -- Report from Baldwin-Wallace College, Ohio, on
            American Youth Congress, July 1938.

109. CITIZENS COMMITTEE FOR A FREE CUBA, 1963-1974.
        Records, 1962-1974. 58 ms. boxes.
        Anticommunist organization founded in the United States to
            disseminate information about communism in Cuba and other
            Latin American countries.
        Clippings, newsletters, press releases, reports, conference
            papers, speeches, and printed matter, relating primarily to
            the political, economic, and social effects of communism in
            Cuba, communist subversion in Latin America, U.S. foreign
            policy toward Cuba, and activities of the Cuban emigre
            community.
        Gift, Citizens Committee for a Free Cuba, 1973.

        Box 4 -- Newspaper clippings on U.S.-funded Social Studies
            Center in Bolivia.
        Box 5 -- Newsletter on student disorder in Colombia.
        Boxes 7 and 30 -- Reports, newsletters, and newspaper
            clippings on education and indoctrination in Cuba.
        Boxes 9, 39, and 41 -- Newsletters and newspaper clippings on
            problems at Catholic University, Santiago, Chile, and
            communist students in the country.
        Boxes 11 and 12 -- Newsletters on university crisis and
            student agitation in Dominican Republic.
        Boxes 19 and 40 -- Newsletters on student rioting in Caracas,
            Venezuela.

Box 23 -- Newspaper clippings on Mexican student strikes.
Boxes 24 and 25 -- Newsletter and newspaper clippings on
    student riots and universities in Peru.
Boxes 29 and 56 -- Newspaper clippings, newsletters, and
    reports on student rebellion and education in the U.S.
Box 43 -- Newsletters on student unrest in Brazil.

110. CITIZENS COMMITTEE FOR REORGANIZATION OF THE EXECUTIVE BRANCH OF
        THE GOVERNMENT, 1949-1958.
    Records, 1949-1958.   103 ms. boxes, 1 motion picture film.
    Private organization for promotion of U.S. governmental
        administrative reforms.
    Correspondence, reports, newsletters, press releases,
        clippings, and printed matter, relating to the
        recommendations of the two Hoover Commissions on
        governmental reorganization.
    Preliminary inventory.
    Gift, Citizens Committee for Reorganization of the Executive
        Branch of the Government, 1952. Incremental gift, 1958.

    Box 6 -- Reports by Citizens Committee with some emphasis on
        education and health.
    Boxes 13 and 14 -- Hoover Commission reports with sections on
        education.
    Box 38 -- Report on investigation of G.I. schools and their
        educational and training program.

111. CLAPP, FRANCES BENTON, 1887- .
    Study, ca. 1958. "Kyoto, Fact and Fancy: A Historical Sketch
        and Description of Its Places, Shrines, Temples,
        Institutions and Legends." 1 ms. box.
    Typescript.
    Professor of Music, Doshisha University, Japan, 1918-1957.
    Gift, Charlotte B. DeForest, 1969.

    Chapter 19 describes educational institutions as well as
        elementary, secondary, and higher education in the city of
        Kyoto in Japan.

112. CLARK, ERIK.
    Papers, 1925. 1 folder, 1 envelope.
    Memoirs and photographs, relating to the 1925 student riots in
        China, precipitated by an incident in Shanghai during which
        British and Japanese police killed 21 students.

35

Reaction of Chinese students to atrocities of British and
    Japanese troops.

113. CLARK, GROVER.
        Report, 1932. "Research Needs and Opportunities in China:
        Memorandum for the Director of the Program of Research in
        International Relations of the Social Science Research
        Council." 1 folder.
        Typescript (mimeographed).
        Relates to proposed research topics on political, social, and
        economic conditions in China.

        Section on China's cultural and educational relations with
        other countries.

114. CLARKE, HAROLD A., COLLECTOR.
        Miscellany, 1942-1949. 1 folder.
        Correspondence, newsletters, and printed matter, relating to
        civilian public service performed by conscientious
        objectors in the U.S. during World War II.

        Pamphlet by General Bruce C. Clarke entitled "How to Study and
        Take Examinations," with guidelines for studying in high
        schools and colleges.

115. CLARKE, IONE CLEMENT, 1889- .
        Biography, n.d. "One in a Hundred." 1 folder.
        Typescript (photocopy).
        Relates to Ernest Wilson Clement, an American missionary in
        Japan, 1887-1891 and 1895-1927, and father of
        I. C. Clarke.
        Gift, I. C. Clarke, 1973.

        Chapter 1 -- Account of Ernest W. Clement's childhood and his
        membership in a Christian volunteer movement made up of
        students interested in social service and teaching.
        Chapter 2 -- His teaching career.
        Chapter 3 -- His life in Japan and establishment of his
        boarding school.

116. CLARKE, WILLIAM H.
        Microfilm. 1 reel.
        Memoirs relating to missionary work in Central Africa,
        1854-1858.

117. COBB, JOHN B.
        Letters, 1946-1948. 1 folder.
        Typescript.
        American missionary in Japan.
        Relates to efforts of the Foreign Missions Conference of North
            America to bring relief supplies to Japan. Letters written
            for distribution by the Methodist Board of Missions.
        Gift, J. B. Cobb, 1974.

        Letter 4 -- Christian education in Japan.
        Letter 13 -- Popularity of Christian schools in Japan and the
            Japanese school system.
        Letter 18 -- Night schools and the persistence of Japanese
            students in learning English despite difficulties.

118. COFER, MRS. LELAND E.
        Papers, 1915-1945. 6 ms. boxes, 5 envelopes.
        American relief work administrator in World Wars I and II.
        Correspondence, speeches and writings, reports, postcards,
            photographs, and memorabilia, relating to the adminis-
            tration of relief during and after the two world wars and,
            in particular, to the activities of the New York Committee
            for the Fatherless Children of France. Includes some
            papers of Leland E. Cofer, Health Officer for the Port of
            New York and Assistant Surgeon General, U.S. Public Health
            Service.
        Gift, Mrs. L. E. Cofer, 1950.

        Some notes and newspaper clippings are in French.
        Box 1 -- Issue of Greater New York, August 5, 1923, with
            article on establishment of the Division of Industrial
            Hygiene and Educational Council by Labor Department.
        Boxes 4-6 -- Reports on fatherless children of France, 1916.

119. COLE, BETTY.
        Papers, 1973-1980. 2 ms. boxes.
        Coordinator, Peace Studies Program, Pacific Southwest Region,
            American Friends Service Committee.
        Correspondence, bulletins, minutes, memoranda, questionnaires,
            curriculum material, and printed matter, relating to
            education for peace.

        Box 1 -- General evaluation reports of Peace Studies Program.
        Box 2 -- Questionnaires and course outlines.

120. COLTON, ETHAN THEODORE, b. 1872.
        Papers, 1918-1952. 7 ms. boxes.

American relief worker with the European Student Relief and the Young Men's Christian Association in Russia.

Correspondence, reports, manuscripts of writings, and clippings, relating to European Student Relief activities in Russia and other European countries, 1920-1925, and to social conditions, the educational system, and the status of religion in Russia in the 1920s and 1930s. Includes memoirs of E. T. Colton and 13 antireligious Soviet posters.

Gift, E. T. Colton.

Boxes 1 and 2 -- Reports on European Student Relief of World Student Christian Federation and reports on conditions of professors in universities of Central Europe.

Box 4 -- Articles on Russian emigre youth and students and counterrevolution.

Box 6 -- Articles and newspaper clippings on education in USSR.

Box 7 -- Article by Ethan Colton on high schools and students in USSR.

121. COMMISSION FOR POLISH RELIEF, 1939-1949.
Records, 1939-1949. 51 ms. boxes.
Private organization for provision of relief to Poland during World War II.
Correspondence, reports, memoranda, financial records, and photographs.
Preliminary inventory.
Gift, Commission for Polish Relief, 1948. Subsequent increments.

Box 21 -- Pamphlet entitled "The Truth about Poland," with information on Polish people, Polish education, and universities in Poland.

Box 35 -- News bulletins with information on Polish children and youth and their abuse by German government.

Box 50 -- Two illustrated guides on Poland relating to its social customs, arts, the University of Krakow, and people of Poland.

122. COMMISSION FOR RELIEF IN BELGIUM, 1940-1945.
Records (in English, French, German, and Flemish), 1940-1947. 19 ms. boxes.
Affiliate of the National Committee on Food for the Small Democracies.
Correspondence, memoranda, reports, photographs, and posters, relating to efforts to provide civilian relief to Belgium and Luxemburg during World War II.

Box 2 -- Newspaper clippings and letters on children's
crusade.
Box 3 -- Two letters on orphans and their adoption.
Box 4 -- Newspaper clippings and correspondence on refugee
children.
Box 15 -- Manuals for campus action by the National Student
Executive Committee.

123. COMMITTEE FOR FREE ASIA, COLLECTOR.
Committee for Free Asia collection on China and Taiwan (in
Chinese), 1951-1953. 9 ms. boxes.
Clippings and press releases, relating to political, social,
and economic conditions in China and Taiwan. Includes
clippings from Chinese, Hong Kong, and Chinese-language
U.S. newspapers, and press releases issued by Radio Free
Asia.

Boxes 1 and 2 -- Newspaper clippings and newsletters on
education in China.
Box 3 -- Newsletters on education in Formosa.
Box 9 -- Newsletters and newspaper clippings on social
conditions and students in China.

124. COMMUNIST PARTY OF SOUTH AFRICA.
Issuances (in English and Afrikaans), 1937-1943. 1/2 ms. box.
Pamphlets and leaflets, relating to political conditions, race
relations, the labor movement in South Africa, and the
South African role in World War II. Includes some material
issued by other leftist South African organizations.
Preliminary inventory.

Pamphlet entitled "The Nation's Question Solved," about
women's rights, rights of minorities, and education in
USSR.
Typewritten issue of Youth, official organ of Labor League of
Youth of South Africa, February 1939.

125. COMMUNIST PROPAGANDA.
(In French, Italian, German, and Vietnamese), 1950-1961.
2 ms. boxes.
Posters, leaflets, and election campaign material, consisting
of electoral and other communist propaganda from France,
Italy, Austria, East Germany, and Vietnam. Includes some
electoral propaganda distributed by noncommunist parties in
France and Italy, antimilitarist propaganda from West
Germany, and one anti-American poster from Korea.
Gift, U.S. Library of Congress, 1962.

Box 2 -- Last folder contains notes, newspaper clippings, leaflets, and pamphlet on Vietnam and American intervention in that country.

126. COMMUNIST YOUTH MOVEMENT COLLECTION, 1938.
     1 folder.
     Report and newsletter relating to the strategy of the communist youth movement in the U.S., especially with regard to the American Youth Congress and the Boy Scouts.

     Copy of memorandum on role of Communists in the American Youth Congress; letter from Boy Scouts of America's Chief Executive; confidential information relating to Communists' new attack on Boy Scouts.

127. CONFERENCE OF THE INSTITUTIONS FOR THE SCIENTIFIC STUDY OF INTERNATIONAL AFFAIRS, MILAN, 1932.
     Report, 1932. 1 volume.
     Typescript (mimeographed).
     Conference held under the auspices of the International Institute of Intellectual Cooperation of the League of Nations. Report of the fifth session.

     Issues with which conference dealt included education and the aim and activities of the League of Nations.

128. COOMBS, PHILIP HALL, 1915- . (See also International Council for Educational Development.)
     Papers, 1955-1976. 4-1/2 ms. boxes.
     American educator; U.S. Assistant Secretary of State for Educational and Cultural Affairs, 1961-1962; Director, International Institute for Educational Planning, 1963-1968.
     Speeches and writings, correspondence, and printed matter, relating to international education and education in underdeveloped countries.
     Gift, P. H. Coombs, December 1980.

     Box 1 -- Pamphlets, reports, and texts of speeches on education and television instruction.
     Box 2 -- Philip Coombs's book Fourth Dimension of Foreign Policy, relating to educational and cultural affairs; pamphlets and printed matter relating to UNESCO.
     Box 3 -- Articles and printed matter on educational planning and comparative education.

Box 4 -- Articles and reports relating to International
    Conference on the World Crisis in Education.
Box 5 -- Correspondence and reports on education in
    Bangladesh.

129. COWAN, LAIAN GRAY.
    Papers, 1952-1970. 12 ms. boxes.
    American author and educator.
    Reports, articles, seminar papers, speeches, minutes, and
        printed matter, relating to political, economic, and social
        conditions, education, nationalism, and foreign aid in
        newly independent African states.
    Gift, L. G. Cowan, 1974.

    Box 1 -- Reports, essays, and articles on elementary,
        secondary, and higher education in Africa.
    Box 3 -- Report and essay on education and Overseas
        Educational Service.
    Box 4 -- Pamphlets and questionnaire on education in
        Congo.
    Box 5 -- Pamphlet on education in Ivory Coast.
    Box 7 -- Newsletters and reports on education in Liberia and
        Malawi.
    Box 9 -- Report on education in Nigeria.
    Box 10 -- Report on secondary school dropouts in Kenya, on
        adult education, and on School of Education of Zambia
        University.
    Box 11 - Reports of International Institute for Educational
        Planning.

130. CRAMPTON, FRANK ASBURY, 1888-1961.
    Papers (in English, Chinese, and Korean), 1924-1963. 6 ms.
        boxes, 42 posters and maps, 5 envelopes, 2 album boxes.
    American mining engineer; Adviser to the South Korean Ministry
        of Commerce and Industry, 1953-1954.
    Correspondence, reports, memoranda, speeches, statistics,
        printed matter, posters, maps, and photographs, relating to
        revolution in Canton and Shanghai, 1924-1927, and to relief
        and economic reconstruction, especially mining operations,
        in South Korea after the Korean War.
    Gift, Esther L. Crampton, 1980.

    Boxes 5 and 6 -- Book, newsletters, periodicals, and reports
        on Korean people, culture, 'and education.

131. CROSS, ROWLAND MC LEAN, 1888- .
    Papers, 1921-1963. 1 ms. box.

American missionary in China.

Correspondence, reports, and printed matter, relating to
political and social conditions in revolutionary and
communist China.

Gift, R. M. Cross, 1972.

Pamphlets and reports on education, culture, and students in
China; newsletters with information on Chinese youth.

132. CUTLER, RICHARD L.

Study, 1972. "The Liberal Middle Class: The Maker of
Radicals." 1/2 ms. box.

Typescript.

Professor of Psychology, University of Michigan.

Relates to the causes of radicalism among American middle-
class youth during the late 1960s and early 1970s.

Gift, R. L. Cutler, 1973.

Chapter 10 -- Universities.

Chapter 11 -- Culture and how to subvert it.

133. DAGDEVIREN, HIDAYET, COLLECTOR.

H. Dagdeviren collection on Turkey (in Turkish), 1831-1951.
28 ms. boxes, 22 binders.

Letters, memoranda, reports, proclamations, speeches,
clippings, newspaper issues, and photographs, relating to
political and social conditions in Turkey during the
Ottoman Empire and the early years of the Turkish Republic,
to Turkish military activities during the World War I, to
Turkish foreign relations, and to ethnic minorities in
Turkey.

Preliminary inventory.

Purchase, Saadet Dagdeviren, 1952.

Box 19 -- Pamphlets on American College in Sivas.

Box 20 -- Pamphlets and newspaper clippings on industrial
schools; articles and newspaper clippings on premodern
schools.

Box 27 -- Articles by Hassan Ali Yucel on Turkish education
and articles by Aski Bir Asker on Turkish military schools.

134. DALLIN, ALEXANDER.

Papers (in English, German, and Russian), 1939-1972.
8 ms. boxes, 1 microfilm reel.

American historian and political scientist.

Writings, correspondence, memoranda, reports, orders, interview transcripts, notes, and printed matter, relating to

the German occupation of areas of the Soviet Union during
World War II and to Soviet collaborators and partisans.
Includes photocopies of German military documents.

   Box 5 -- Folder on culture contains notes on family and youth
      in German-occupied Russia.

135. DANIELOPOL, DUMITRU.
      Papers (in English, Romanian, and French), 1940-1973.
         10 ms. boxes, 1 envelope.
      Romanian banker; member of Romanian delegation to Paris Peace
         Conference, 1946.
      Correspondence, writings, reports, and photographs, relating
         to the Paris Peace Conference, 1946, the peace settlement
         with Romania at the end of World War II, and world
         politics, 1964-1973.
      Preliminary inventory.
      Gift, D. Danielopol, 1972. Subsequent increments.

      Box 4 -- Articles on communist countries and youth problems;
         Communists on campus.
      Box 5 -- Article on student riots in international scene.
      Box 6 -- Article on youth and communism.
      Box 7 -- Articles on youth and peace.

136. DANQUAH, JOSEPH BOAKYE, 1895- .
      Studies, 1961-1963. 1 ms. box.
      Typescript.
      Fellow, Ghana Academy of Learning.
      Studies entitled "Revelation of Culture in Ghana," 1961, and
         "Sacred Days in Ghana," 1963, relating to Ghanaian culture
         and the development of the Ghanaian calendar.
      Gift, Gail Kelley, 1967.

      First study -- Texts of lectures and essays on discoveries
         regarding ancient origins of a progressive people.
      Second study -- Section entitled "A Modern School Girl."

137. DAVIS, RICHARD HALLOCK, 1913-1972.
      Miscellaneous papers, 1949-1950. 1 folder, 1 envelope.
      American diplomat; student, Russian Institute, Columbia
         University, 1949-1950; U.S. Deputy Assistant Secretary of
         State, 1960-1972.
      Lecture notes relating to Russian history, government,
         economics, and literature, taken at the Russian Institute
         at Columbia University, course syllabi, and three
         unidentified photographs.

Bibliographical guides on Russian history and teaching of
   Russian history.

138. DAVIS, ROBERT E.
      Reports, 1917-1919. 1 folder.
      Typescript.
      Major, U.S. Army; American Red Cross worker in Kuban area,
         Russia.
      Relates to the work of the American Red Cross and the
         political and military situation in South Russia,
         1917-1919. Addressed to Colonel Robert E. Olds, American
         Red Cross Commissioner to Europe.
      Gift, Earl Talbot, 1973.

      Article in McCall's Magazine entitled "Your Boy and the Great
         Adventure," June 1918.
      Report by Robert Davis entitled "Armenian Notes of a Red Cross
         Scout."

139. DAY, GEORGE MARTIN.
      Papers, 1922-1937. 1/2 ms. box.
      Professor of Sociology, Occidental College, Los Angeles.
      Writings, correspondence, and questionnaires, relating to
         social conditions, education, and religion in the Soviet
         Union and to the adjustment to American society of Russians
         living in the Los Angeles area in 1930.

      Monthly issues of The Russian Student.
      Articles contrasting life in German universities with that in
         Russian universities.
      Essay on Leningrad University.

140. DECKER, BENTON W., 1899- .
      Papers, 1916-1976. 4 ms. boxes, 1 envelope.
      Rear Admiral, U.S. Navy; and Commander, Yokosuka Naval Base,
         Japan, 1946-1950.
      Correspondence, speeches and writings, orders, citations, and
         printed matter, relating to U.S. occupation forces in Japan
         and U.S. foreign relations in the Far East.
      Register.
      Gift, B. W. Decker, 1974. Incremental gift, 1977.

      Box 2 -- Text of speech to Daughters of the American
         Revolution by Admiral Benton Decker entitled "Youth and
         America," 1954.

141. DE CONDE, ALEXANDER, 1920- .
      Thesis, 1947. "Herbert Hoover's Latin American Policy."
          155 pages.
      Typescript (carbon copy).
      American historian.
      Relates to U.S. foreign policy toward Latin America during the
          presidential administration of Herbert Hoover. M.A.
          thesis, Stanford University. Published (Stanford, 1951).
      Gift, Paul B. Ryan, 1979.

      Sections on cultural, educational, and intellectual relations
          between U.S. and Latin America.

142. DE FOREST, CHARLOTTE B., 1879- .
      Papers, 1909-1971. 1 ms. box.
      American missionary at Kobe College, Japan, 1903-1940 and
          1947-1950.
      Correspondence, manuscripts of writings and translations,
          notes, and printed matter, relating to missionary work and
          education in Japan.
      Register.

      Booklets and pamphlets are in Japanese.
      Newsletters and reports on International Christian University
          and Kobe College in Japan.

143. DELAGE, JEAN.
      Papers (in French), 1941-1944. 1 ms. box.
      Chief of Information, Chantiers de Jeunesse.
      Reports, correspondence, memoranda, instructions, programs,
          and printed matter, relating to the operation and purpose
          of youth work camps operated by the Vichy Government in
          France. Includes a chart outlining French social
          organization, 1941.
      Purchase, Thomas D. Walker, 1975.

144. DELAVIGNETTE, ROBERT LOUIS, 1897-1976.
      Papers (in French), 1949-1960. 1/2 ms. box.
      French colonial administrator; Director of Political Affairs,
          Ministere de la France d'Outre-Mer, 1947-1951.
      Letters, periodicals, reprints of articles, newspaper issues,
          and newsletters, relating to economic and social conditions
          in Algeria, independence movements in the African colonies,
          and French colonial policy.
      Gift, William Cohen, 1976.

Pamphlets on Catholics and religious education; newspaper
clipping on child care and education of children.

145. DEUTSCHE FORSCHUNGSGEMEINSCHAFT.
        Correspondence (in German), 1934-1936. 6 ms. boxes.
        German Government organization for promotion of academic
            research.
        Correspondence relating to grant applications for research
            projects. Includes correspondence with the Reichsamts-
            leitung of the Nationalsozialistischer Deutscher Dozenten-
            bund, the Kreisleitungen of the Nationalsozialistesche
            Deutsche Arbeiterpartei, the various police presidents of
            German cities, the Dozentenschaften of the various German
            universities and Technische Hochschulen, and private
            persons.

146. "DIE DEUTSCHE JUNGENDFUEHRUNG IN DER NEUORDNUNG" (The German
            Youth Leadership in the New Order).
        Memorandum (in German), ca. 1945. 1 folder.
        Typescript.
        Relates to the role of the youth movement in post-World War II
            German reconstruction.

        Eight articles on German youth leadership.

147. DODGE, ALICE SINCLAIR, 1876-1965, COLLECTOR.
        Collection on relocation of Japanese Americans, 1942-1946.
            1 ms. box.
        Correspondence, mainly with Roy Nakata, 1942-1946; scrapbooks,
            1942-1944; San Francisco and Palo Alto newspapers and news-
            paper clippings, 1942-1945; and minutes of meetings of the
            Japanese American Citizens League and American Friends
            Service Committee, 1945, relating to relocation and citizen
            rights of Japanese Americans in the U.S. during World
            War II.
        Gift, Mrs. O. Yount, 1970.

        Numerous letters, most relating to Japanese students'
            relocation in West Coast area.

148. DOM POLSKICH DZIECI, OUDTSHOORN, SOUTH AFRICA.
        Records (in Polish), 1942-1947. 3 ms. boxes.
        Polish Children's Home, founded in 1943 for the care of Polish
            war orphans from Russia.
        Correspondence, telegrams, notes, memoranda, clippings,
            accounts, lists, protocols, reports, inventories, and

published materials, relating to the evacuation of the war
orphans from Russia to Oudtshoorn, the establishment and
operation of the Home, and the care and education of the
orphans.
Register.
Gift, Tadeusz Kawalec, 1975.

Historical account of orphaned and deported Polish children in
Russia. In 1943, 500 of these children were sent to South
Africa. Includes correspondence, notes, and reports about
welfare of the children; their religious education,
scouting activities, schooling, and reunification with
their families.

149. DOMINICAN REPUBLIC.
Microfilm. 1 reel, 1965.
Miscellaneous material consisting mostly of correspondence of
Dominican students' associations or religious groups
relating to the revolution of 1965.

150. DOMKE, PAUL C.
Audio-visual materials, 1936-1945. 8 motion picture reels,
1 envelope.
Teacher, Carleton College-in-China, 1937-1939; member, U.S.
Observer Mission to Yenan, 1944-1945.
Films and photographs, depicting missionary schools in China,
1936-1937, the effects of Japanese bombing in China, 1939;
the transport of a giant panda from China to the St. Louis
Zoo, 1939; scenes at Angkor Wat, 1939, the U.S. Observer
Mission to Yenan, 1944-1945; U.S. Army Headquarters in
Chungking, 1945; and various other scenes in China,
1936-1945.
Gift, P. C. Domke, 1978.

151. DONOHOE, CHRISTINE, COLLECTOR.
Miscellany, 1931-1960. 1 ms. box.
Publications, mostly anticommunist, relating to communism in
the U.S. and Spain.

Article by Dorothy Thompson, July 8, 1959, on failure of
American educational system and article by the United
Spanish Youth entitled "A Message to the Youth of Every
Nation."

152. DONOVAN, JAMES BRITT, 1916-1970.
Papers, 1940-1970. 106 ms. boxes.

47

American lawyer and educator; Associate General Counsel,
    Office of Scientific Research and Development, 1942-1943;
    General Counsel, Office of Strategic Services, 1943-1945;
    Assistant to U.S. Chief Prosecutor, Trial of Major German
    War Criminals, Nuremberg, 1945; negotiator of Abel-Powers
    spy exchange with USSR and of the Cuban prisoners exchange
    following the Bay of Pigs; President of the New York City
    Board of Education, 1963-1965.
Correspondence, reports, memoranda, studies, drafts of book
    manuscripts, scrapbooks, notes, photographs, and printed
    matter, relating to the U.S. Office of Scientific Research
    and Development and the Office of Strategic Services during
    World War II, the Nuremberg war crime trials, the Rudolph
    Abel-Gary Powers spy exchange, the Cuban prisoner exchange
    following the Bay of Pigs landing, and the New York City
    Board of Education.
Preliminary inventory.
Access to materials relating to James B. Donovan's
    relationship with his family and his associates in law and
    in business requires the written permission of Mary D.
    O'Connor or John B. Donovan.
Deposit, Mary D. O'Connor, 1972.

Boxes 27 and 28 -- Correspondence, newspapers, and catalogues
    relating to St. Francis College, 1960-1961.
Boxes 55, 60-62, 78, 82, 84, 86, and 87 -- Correspondence,
    newsletters, reports, memoranda, notes, and articles on
    public education, school planning, and boards of education.
Box 56 -- Reports on education in Florida.
Boxes 58, 59, 63-65, and 69 -- Reports, memoranda, notes,
    correspondence, newspaper clippings, and articles on
    integrated education.
Boxes 66-68, 70-73, 77, 80, 81, and 85 -- Reports, minutes of
    meetings, memoranda, notes, correspondence, and texts of
    speeches relating to New York City Board of Education.
Box 85 -- Reports, articles, memoranda, and correspondence on
    vocational education.

153. DOWD, PATRICK.
    Papers, 1968-1971. 3 ms. boxes.
    California State Chairman, Young Americans for Freedom, 1969.
    Correspondence, reports, memoranda, circulars, minutes of
        meetings, and printed matter, relating to political
        activities on college campuses, and to the Young American
        for Freedom.
    Register.
    Gift, P. Dowd, 1973.

Boxes 1 and 3 -- Reports and correspondence on Young Americans
for Freedom.
Box 2 -- Article about students seeking awareness.

154. DRAGNICH, ALEX N., 1912- .
Papers (in English and Serbo-Croatian), 1934-1949.
4 ms. boxes.
American political scientist; Senior Propaganda Analyst, U.S.
Department of Justice, 1942-1944; Research Analyst, U.S.
Office of Strategic Services, 1944-1945; Cultural Attache
and Public Affairs Officer, U.S. Embassy in Yugoslavia,
1947-1950.
Writings, correspondence, reports, historical studies,
memoranda, legal and government documents, diaries, and
newspapers, relating to the history, politics, and
government of Serbia and Yugoslavia, relations between
Croatia and Serbia, activities of the Hrvatski Domobran in
the U.S., the Communist Party of Yugoslavia, and the trial
of Draza Mihailovic.
Gift, A. N. Dragnich, 1977. Incremental gift, 1978.

Box 1 -- Memoranda with sections on propaganda and propaganda
analysis.
Box 2 -- Issues of Yugoslav Fortnightly, with articles on
youth and education in Yugoslavia, 1949.

155. DRAPER, THEODORE, 1912- .
Papers, 1912-1966. 37 ms. boxes.
American historian and author.
Correspondence, clippings, pamphlets, newspaper issues, and
congressional hearings, relating to the revolution led by
Fidel Castro in Cuba, political, social, and economic con-
ditions in Cuba, the 1965 crisis and U.S. intervention in
the Dominican Republic, and the Communist Party, U.S.A.
Preliminary inventory.
Boxes 1-22 are open without restriction. Selected files on
Cuba (boxes 23-26) and the Dominican Republic (box 27) as
well as all files on the Communist Party, U.S.A. (boxes
28-37) may be used only with the permission of Theodore
Draper.
Gift, Theodore Draper, 1967. Incremental gift, 1969.

Box 9, Envelope 14 -- Articles, newspaper and magazine
clippings, and reports by UNESCO on education in Cuba.
Box 17, Envelope 17 -- Newspaper clippings, articles, and
newsletters on U.S. students in Cuba.

156. DUMBACHER, JOSEPH.
        Papers, 1962-1966. 2 ms. boxes.
        Typewritten account by J. Dumbacher of the 1963 SDS national
            convention, as well as pamphlets, bulletins, and reports,
            relating to Students for a Democratic Society (SDS) and
            other organizations of the New Left in the U.S.
        Preliminary inventory.
        Purchase, Myers G. Lowman, 1967.

        Box 1 -- Text of speech by Tom Hayden, "Student Social Action
            at Challenge," University of Michigan, March 1962
        Box 2 -- Reports and bulletins related to National Student
            Association Convention.

157. DUNNER, JOSEPH H., 1908- .
        Study, n.d. "German Under the Hammer and Sickle: The
            Administration of the Soviet Zone of Germany from 1945 to
            1953." 1/2 ms. box.
        Typescript.
        American political scientist.
        Gift, J. H. Dunner, 1977.

        Chapter 12 -- Educational system of Soviet Zone of Germany and
            problems of intellectuals.

158. DYER, SUSAN LOUISE, 1877-1966.
        Papers, 1895-1965. 9 ms. boxes, 1 scrapbook,
            10 envelopes, 1 phonotape.
        Lifelong friend of Herbert and Lou Henry Hoover, American Red
            Cross worker in France, 1918-1919.
        Correspondence, diary, scrapbooks, memorabilia, clippings,
            photographs, tape recording, and printed matter, relating
            to Herbert Hoover, Lou Henry Hoover, Stanford University,
            the Hoover Institution, the Girl Scouts, and the American
            Red Cross in France during World War I.
        Gift, S. L. Dyer, 1960. Subsequent increments.

        Box 4 -- Pamphlets and reports on students, alumni, and
            academic rules of Stanford University.
        Box 9 -- Clippings on Stanford and its academic activities.

159. EGBERT, DONALD DREW, 1902-1973.
        Study, n.d. "Communism, Radicalism and the Arts: American
            Developments in Relation to the Background in Western
            Europe and in Russia from the Seventeenth Century to 1959."
            2 ms. boxes.
        Typescript (photocopy).

American historian.

Relates to the effects of Marxism and communism on American art, and the relationships between works of art and the social, economic, and political beliefs of the artists who produced them, 1680-1959. A revised version of this study was published under the title: <u>Socialism and American Art in the Light of European Utopianism, Marxism and Anarchism.</u> (Princeton, 1967).

Gift, Theodore Draper, 1964.

Description of various ideologies and their impact on youth and education.

160. ELIEL, PAUL.

Miscellaneous papers, 1938. 1/2 ms. box.

Director, Division of Industrial Relations, Graduate School of Business, Stanford University.

Correspondence, pamphlets, propaganda materials, and newspaper clippings, relating to labor legislation, unionism, and communism in California during 1938.

Gift, Jackson Library, Graduate School Business, Stanford University, 1972.

Folder on propaganda relating to Civic Welfare League of San Francisco.

161. ELLIOTT, WILLIAM YANDELL, 1896-1979.

Papers, 1930-1970. 173 ms. boxes.

American political scientist; Staff Director, House Select Committee on Foreign Affairs, 1947-1949; member, Planning Board, National Security Council, 1953-1957; consultant to the Secretary of State, 1958-1970.

Correspondence, writings, speeches, research notes, clippings, and printed matter, relating to U.S. national security and defense, U.S. politics and foreign relations, U.S. military-industrial relations, and U.S. national labor policy.

Personnel files closed until 1997.

Gift, W. Y. Elliott, 1977.

Boxes 5, 23, and 24 -- Pamphlets, notes, reports, and correspondence relating to several schools, colleges, and universities in the U.S.

Boxes 7, 108, 110, and 111 -- Texts of speeches, reports, newsletters, newspaper clippings, correspondence, pamphlets, and memoranda on educational TV and impact of television on education.

51

Box 12 -- Report on Ninth Annual Student Conference on United
    States Affairs, December 1957.
Boxes 15, 59, 118, and 164 -- Reports, correspondence, and
    memoranda on international education and UNESCO.
Box 30 -- Notes, newspaper clippings, articles, and annotated
    bibliography related to American Association of University
    Women; article on private secondary and college education
    in the U.S.
Box 52 -- Memorandum on educational projects.
Boxes 103 and 170 -- Reports, articles, leaflets, pamphlets,
    memorandum, and correspondence on teacher training and
    education about communism.
Box 120 -- Reports on American Overseas Education.
Box 121 -- Report on ranking of states in regard to education.

162. ELTSE, RUTH RICCI.
    Papers, 1935-1942. 1-1/2 ms. boxes, 7 envelopes,
        5 oversize boxes (2 linear feet).
    American volunteer nurse in the Ethiopian-Italian War,
        1935-1936; photographer and journalist in North Africa,
        1936-1939.
    Correspondence, writings, and photographs, relating to the
        Ethiopian-Italian War, to Italian colonization of Libya,
        and to Italian relations in North and East Africa.
        Includes an album of photographs of Benito Mussolini.
    Gift, Ann K. Snow, 1977.

    Box 2 -- Illustrated memoir by Ruth Eltse on conditions in
        Kenya in 1937-1939, with pictures of villages and village
        schools and their students.

163. EMMET, CHRISTOPHER TEMPLE, JR., 1900-1974.
    Papers, 1935-1974. 124 ms. boxes, 5 cubic foot boxes,
        33 phonorecords, 9 envelopes.
    Chairman, American Friends of the Captive Nations; Executive
        Vice-President, American Council on Germany; officer and
        organizer of other anti-Nazi and anticommunist
        organizations.
    Correspondence, memoranda, reports, press releases, writings,
        recordings of radio broadcasts, and photographs, relating
        to anti-Nazi and anticommunist movements in the U.S.,
        U.S. foreign policy during the Cold War, and U.S.-German
        foreign relations.
    Register.
    Gift, estate of C. T. Emmet, 1974.

Box 3 -- Issue of <u>National Review</u> pamphlet, newsletters, and correspondence relating to American Afro-Asian Educational Exchange.

Box 13 -- Memorandum, questionnaire, and notes on American-German Youth Conference, June 1973.

Box 40 -- Report, pamphlets, newsletters, correspondence, and leaflets on exchange programs of the Institute of International Education and on international education.

Box 59 -- Notes on propaganda.

Box 124 -- Radio broadcast transcript on university youth, copy of newspaper clipping on universities and the left.

164. ENGLEMAN, FINIS EWIG, 1895-1978.

Papers, 1956-1978. 8 ms. boxes, 1 envelope.

American educator; Connecticut Commissioner of Education, 1955; consultant, U.S. Department of State Office of Overseas Schools, 1976.

Correspondence, speeches and writings, reports, photographs, and printed matter, relating to the administration of higher education and of international schools, the Association for the Advancement of International Education, the U.S. Department of State Office of Overseas Schools, the American Association of School Administrators, and the Near East/South Asia Council of Overseas Schools.

Gift, Frederick W. Lowe, 1978.

Boxes 1, 2, and 7 -- Printed matter and reports on education and Faculty of Education in Afghanistan and on international education.

Box 3 -- Printed matter on education and report on history of Association for the Advancement of International Education.

Box 4 -- Technical proposal relating to educational skills training in Nepal.

Box 5 -- Booklet on American elementary and secondary schools abroad.

Box 6 -- Reports on international education.

Box 8 -- Article entitled "The Education Renaissance at the Middle of the Twentieth Century."

165. ENKE, STEPHEN, d. 1974.

Reports, 1966-1973. 1/2 ms. box.

Printed.

U.S. Deputy Assistant Secretary of Defense, 1965-1966; Manager, Economics and Special Studies, Technical Military Planning Operation (TEMPO), General Electric Company. Relates to aspects of the U.S. economy and population, especially economic effects of slowing population growth, and to the South Vietnamese economy. Prepared for TEMPO.

Gift, General Electric Company, 1979.

Several reports on family-planning education and welfare.

166. EPSTEIN, JULIUS, 1901-1975.
Papers, 1939-1972. 180 ms. boxes.
American journalist and author.
Correspondence, speeches and writings, clippings, photographs,
and printed matter, relating to World War II, communism,
forced repatriation of Russian prisoners to the Soviet
Union following World War II, the Katyn forest massacre,
unreported deaths of Soviet cosmonauts, and the efforts of
J. Epstein to obtain restricted government documents on
these subjects.
Gift, Mrs. J. Epstein, 1975.

Boxes 4 and 10 -- Newspaper clippings on propaganda.
Box 54 - Newspaper clipping relating to President Roosevelt's
address to delegates of the American Youth Congress,
February 11, 1940.
Box 55 -- Newspaper clipping relating to anti-Nazi textbooks
used in German schools, December 1944.
Box 72 -- Pamphlets, newspaper issues, newspaper clippings,
and newsletters on UNESCO.
Box 136 -- Stanford University news releases, with information
on students and academic activities.

167. ETHNOGEOGRAPHIC BOARD, WASHINGTON, D.C.
Reports, 1945. "Reports on Area Studies in American
Universities." 1 folder.
Typescript (mimeographed).
Agency of the Smithsonian Institution.
Relates to European and Far Eastern area study programs at the
University of California, the University of Chicago,
Harvard University, Cornell University, the Carnegie
Institute of Technology, and Grinnell College. Edited by
William N. Felton.
Gift, Harold H. Fisher, 1945.

Sections on schools, students, teachers, teaching methods, and
academic regulations.

168. EUROPEAN WAR, 1914-1918.
Propaganda, 1914-1918. 1 ms. box.
Propaganda leaflets and broadside, issued by the German
Government, German left socialists, and the Allied Govern-
ments during World War I.

Gift, Robert B. Honeyman, Jr., 1977.

Photos, newspaper clippings, and booklets in German and
French.

169. FAR WESTERN SLAVIC CONFERENCE, STANFORD UNIVERSITY, 1959.
Proceedings, 1959. 7 phonotapes.
Conference of Slavic studies scholars in the Western U.S.
Relates to the history, politics, foreign relations,
economy, society, and literature of the Soviet Union and
Eastern Europe.

Sections on education.

170. FARRAND, STEPHEN M.
Papers, 1943-1945. 3 ms. boxes, 1 scrapbook.
Staff member, Alien Enemy Control Unit, U.S. Department of
Justice, and Prisoner of War Division, Office of the
Provost Marshal General, U.S. Army, 1942-1946.
Bulletins, regulations, correspondence, newsletters, clip-
pings, periodical issues, and photographs, relating to
prisoner of war camps in the U.S. during World War II.
Gift, S. M. Farrand, 1949.

Box 3 -- Report of Prisoner of War Conference, 1944, with
section on education and recreation.

171. FELDMANS, JULES, 1889-1953.
Papers, 1919-1955. 18 ms. boxes, 1 envelope.
Latvian diplomat.
Correspondence, memoranda, and reports, relating to the
Russian occupation of the Baltic states in 1940, displaced
persons in Germany, immigration, and Latvian emigre
organizations after World War II.
Register.
Gift, American Latvian Association in the U.S., 1973.

Boxes 1 and 2 -- Correspondence relating to Foreign Students'
Association in British Zone of Germany and Latvian
students' group at University of Bonn, 1947.

172. FELIZ, FRANK E.
Papers, 1941-1948. 13 ms. boxes, 1 scrapbook.
Director of Information, U.S. War Assets Administration,
during World War II.
Correspondence, memoranda, reports, writings, and printed

matter, relating to labor and production allocations in the
United States during World War II, postwar recovery, and
activities of the War Production Board, War Manpower
Commission, U.S. Employment Service, and War Assets
Administration.
Gift, F. E. Feliz, 1963.

Box 5 -- Pamphlet on training vocational counselors.
Box 10 -- Pamphlet on training womanpower, October 1943.

173. FELLERS, BONNER FRANK, 1896-1973.
    Papers, 1934-1972. 16 ms. boxes.
    Brigadier General, U.S. Army; Director, Psychological Warfare
        Division, U.S. Army, 1943-1945; Chairman, Citizens Foreign
        Aid Committee, 1959-1969.
    Research studies, reports, correspondence, memoranda, and
        operational instructions, relating to U.S. propaganda and
        military activities during World War II, the U.S. economy
        and foreign aid, and the Citizens Foreign Aid Committee and
        Taxpayers Committee to End Foreign Aid.
    Register.
    Gift, B. F. Fellers, 1970. Subsequent increments.

Box 10 -- Reprint from Encyclopedia Britannica on social
    conditions, history, and education in Japan.
Box 11 -- Notes on indoctrination course in psychological
    warfare given by officers of Far Eastern Liaison Office.

174. FERTIG, LAWRENCE, 1898- .
    Papers, 1943-1978. 5-1/2 ms. boxes, 3 oversize boxes,
        9 phonotapes, 2 motion picture reels.
    American economic journalist; Hearst newspaper syndicated
        columnist, 1944-1967.
    Speeches and writings, correspondence, printed matter, sound
        recordings and motion picture film, relating to U.S. and
        international economic conditions, governmental economic
        policy, and laissez-faire economics.
    Preliminary inventory.
    Gift, L. Fertig, 1978.

Box 1 -- Correspondence relating to colleges and universities.
Box 2 -- Correspondence, pamphlets, and newspaper clippings
    relating to the Foundation for Economic Education and New
    York University.
Box 3 -- Correspondence relating to Cornell Alumni Committee
    for Balanced Education.
Box 4 -- Statement on educational policy.

Box 6 -- Report on financing public education in New York state, 1958.

175. FIGHT FOR FREEDOM COMMITTEE.
Records, 1940-1942.   4-1/2 ms. boxes.
Private organization lobbying for U.S. intervention in World War II.
Correspondence, memoranda, press releases, pamphlets, clippings, and printed matter, relating to the interventionist and noninterventionist movements in the U.S. during World War II, the America First Committee, and the activities of Charles Lindbergh and Herbert Hoover in the noninterventionist movement.

Box 1 -- Booklet entitled Norway Does Not Yield, relating to invasion of Nazis and their penetration of schools, churches, and society in Norway.
Box 3 -- Booklet on America, with sections on propaganda and democracy.
Box 4 -- Pamphlet on German youth and Nazi dream of victory.

176. FINN, CHESTER E., JR.
Papers, 1969-1972.   15 ms. boxes.
American educator; Staff Assistant to the President of the U.S., 1969-1970; Special Assistant for Education to the Governor of Massachusetts, 1972.
Speeches and writings, memoranda, reports, correspondence, and printed matter, relating to U.S. educational policy during the presidency of Richard M. Nixon.
Preliminary inventory.
Gift, C. E. Finn, Jr., 1978.

Boxes 1 and 7 -- Correspondence, reports, memoranda, and newspaper clippings on education in Massachusetts.
Boxes 2, 10-12, 14, and 15 -- Memoranda, articles, reports, newspaper clippings, and pamphlets relating to education in U.S.
Boxes 3-5 and 8 -- Memoranda, reports, and newspaper clippings on higher education and campus unrest.
Box 6 -- Reports and memoranda on youth.
Box 9 -- Memoranda and reports relating to Harvard Education Project, nonpublic schools, and teachers' unions.
Box 13 -- Article on education in Argentina; reports and memoranda on research in education.

177. FISHER, HAROLD HENRY, 1890-1975.
Papers, 1917-1974.   32 ms. boxes, 4 card file boxes

(2/3 linear foot), 5 envelopes, 1 album.
American historian; Director, Hoover Institution on War,
    Revolution and Peace, 1943-1952.
Clippings, printed matter, notes, correspondence, pamphlets,
    articles, microfilm, and photographs, relating to the
    Soviet Union, the San Francisco Conference organizing the
    United Nations, the Civil War in Spain, Herbert Hoover and
    the American Relief Administration, and the history of
    Finland.
Register.
Gift, H. H. Fisher.

Box 6 -- Newspaper clippings on education.
Box 13 -- Correspondence, newspaper clippings, notes, reports,
    and leaflets on peace and peaceful change in modern
    society, 1936-1942.
Box 15 -- Newspaper clippings relating to U.N. Conference in
    San Francisco on educational and cultural cooperation.
Box 18 -- Reports on School of Naval Administration,
    1946-1947.
Box 21 -- Newspaper clippings and reports on education in
    Soviet Union.
Box 24 -- Newspaper clippings and notes on Soviet propaganda.

178. FLINT, REBECCA.
    Papers, 1918-1919. 3 ms. boxes.
    Young Men's Christian Association relief worker in France,
        1918-1919.
    Memoranda, pamphlets, photographs, memorabilia, and printed
        matter, relating to Young Men's Christian Association work
        with the American Expeditionary Force in France.
    Gift, Wisconsin State Historical Society, 1959.

    Box 1 -- Small booklet relating to university work in Paris
        for American soldiers.
    Box 2 -- Small booklet by University of Wisconsin on the
        university and the war, May 3, 1977.

179. FOTITCH, KONSTANTIN, 1891-1959.
    Papers (in Serbo-Croatian and English), 1934-1964.
        56 ms. boxes.
    Yugoslav diplomat; Minister and Ambassador to the U.S.,
        1935-1944.
    Correspondence, speeches and writings, diaries, printed
        matter, and photographs, relating to Yugoslav-American
        relations, political and military conditions in Yugoslavia
        during World War II, postwar communism in Yugoslavia, and
        Yugoslav emigre politics.

Closed until August 14, 1989.
Gift, Tatiana Fotitch, 1969. Incremental gift, 1974.

Box 8 -- Reports, correspondence, and notes on Catholic
    University of America and curricula of its College of Arts
    and Sciences.
Box 48 -- Articles on Soviet culture, communist education, and
    deprivation of youth in Soviet Union and pamphlet relating
    to Free Europe University in Exile.

180. FRANCE. COMMISSARIAT GENERAL a la FAMILLE.
    Pamphlets (in French), 1941-1943. 1 ms. box.
    Agency of the Vichy Government of France. Relates to
        encouragement of birthrate increase, promotion of the
        family as a social institution, and discouragement of
        alcoholism.

    Pamphlets, booklets, and leaflets on family education and
        child care.

181. FREDERIKSEN, O. J.
    Letters, 1924. 1 folder.
    Typewritten transcripts.
    Relief worker in Leningrad, 1924.
    Relates to the flood in Leningrad and to the dismissal of
        students from Russian universities.

182. FREE SOCIETY ASSOCIATION.
    Records, 1964-1968. 17-1/2 ms. boxes, 6 phonotapes.
    Conservative American political organization.
    Correspondence, memoranda, speeches, press releases,
        and financial records, relating to American
        politics.
    Preliminary inventory.
    Box 18 closed during the lifetime of William H. Rehnquist.
    Gift, Denison Kitchel, 1980.

    Box 1 -- Letters, newsletters, and application forms
        relating to Americans for Conservative Education.
    Box 15 -- Correspondence and notes on schools and
        universities.
    Box 17 -- Letters and notes relating to Young Americans
        for Freedom.

183. FREEMAN, JOSEPH, 1897-1965.
    Papers, 1915-1965. 222 ms. boxes.

American author; editor and correspondent, New Masses,
   1926-1937; editor, Partisan Review, 1934-1936.
Writings, correspondence, printed matter, notes, and
   photographs, relating to the relation between communism and
   art and literature and to communism in the U.S., Mexico,
   and the Soviet Union.
Preliminary inventory.
Purchase, Charmion von Wiegand, 1980.

Box 134 -- Notes, articles, and newspaper clippings on
   educational television.
Box 204 -- Pamphlet relating to Universidad Obrera de Mexico,
   1937.
Box 206 -- Catalogue of St. John's College in Annapolis,
   Maryland, 1937-1938.

184. FREEMAN, ROGER ADOLF, 1904- .
   Papers, 1950-1974. (Ca. 195 linear feet.)
   American economist; Senior Fellow, Hoover Institution on War,
      Revolution and Peace, 1962-1975; Special Assistant to the
      President of the U.S.; 1969-1970, and other government
      positions.

   Correspondence, memoranda, reports, studies, speeches and
      writings, and printed matter, relating to governmental
      problems in the State of Washington, 1950-1955, fiscal
      problems of Bolivia, 1957, international economic
      development, taxation (federal, state, and local),
      intergovernmental relations in the U.S., public and private
      education from lower schools to university in the U.S. and
      the Soviet Union, public welfare in the U.S., and the
      growth of American government.
   May not be used without permission of R. A. Freeman, the
      Director of the Hoover Institution, or the Director of the
      Domestic Studies Program of the Hoover Institution.
   Deposit, R. A. Freeman, 1975.

   Includes reports and printed matter on curriculum development,
      philosophy of education, international education, adult
      education, vocational education, campus unrest, children,
      and educational tests.

185. FRENCH FIFTH REPUBLIC COLLECTION, 1958-1976.
   (In French) 31 ms. boxes, 21 microfilm reels.
   Miscellaneous election leaflets, posters, pamphlets,
      newspapers, magazines, and government documents, relating
      to political conditions in France under the Fifth Republic.
   Preliminary inventory.

Box 31 -- Leaflets, pamphlets, newspaper clippings, reports, and newsletters on French student groups and their activities.

186. FRENCH STUDENT REVOLT COLLECTION, 1968.
(In French) 5 ms. boxes, 8 phonotapes, 32 posters.
Pamphlets, leaflets, posters, serial issues, and phonotapes of interviews, relating to the French student-worker revolt of 1968.
Preliminary inventory.

Box 1 -- Reports and leaflets on student uprising and student organizations.
Box 2 -- Reports on teachers' unions and students.

187. FRIEDLAND, WILLIAM H., COLLECTOR.
Collection on Tanzanian trade unions, 1929-1967. 10 ms. boxes, 3 envelopes, 4 microfilm reels.
Reports, articles, minutes of meetings, and clippings.
Preliminary inventory.
Gift, W. H. Friedland, 1969.

Box 1 -- Newspaper clippings on education in Tanzania, 1960-1964.

188. FRIEDMAN, MILTON, 1912- .
Papers of Milton Friedman, 1939-1980. 56 ms. boxes, 10 motion picture reels, 10 videotape reels.
American economist; professor of economics at the University of Chicago, 1946-1977; Senior Research Fellow, Hoover Institution, Stanford University, 1977-.
Writings, correspondence, notes, statistics, printed matter, sound recordings, and motion picture file, 1939-1980, relating to economic theory, economic conditions in the U.S., and governmental economic policy.
Closed until 1990.
Deposit, Milton Friedman, 1977. Subsequent increments.

Box 21 -- Pamphlet on Mike Wallace's interview with Robert M. Hutchins, famous educator and former President of the University of Chicago; pamphlet relating to the Foundation for Economic Education.
Boxes 26-28 -- Issues of The Freedom Ideas on Liberty, with articles on freedom, education, and youth.

189. FRIENDS, SOCIETY OF. AMERICAN FRIENDS SERVICE COMMITTEE.
        CIVILIAN PUBLIC SERVICE.
        Records, 1941-1945. 4 ms. boxes.
        American Quaker Associaton.
        Collection of memoranda, bulletins, newsletters, and reports,
            1941-1945, relating to compulsory nonmilitary public
            service, conscientious objectors in the U.S. during World
            War II, and alternative service programs conducted by the
            Friends Civilian Public Service.

        Box 3 -- Memos and notes on education.
        Box 4 -- Handbook for education secretaries.

190. FRILLMANN, PAUL WILLIAM, 1911-1972.
        Papers, 1941-1969. 3 ms. boxes, 1 album, 3 envelopes,
            3 framed certificates.
        American missionary in China, 1936-1941; Chaplain, American
            Volunteer Group ("Flying Tigers"), 1941-1945; U.S. consular
            official in China and Hong Kong, 1946-1950.
        Correspondence, memoranda, orders, notes, and photographs,
            relating to activities of the American Volunteer Group in
            China during World War II, U.S. foreign relations with
            China, 1946-1950, and conditions in China during the civil
            war.
        Register.
        Gift, Mrs. P. W. Frillmann, 1975.

        Box 2 -- Educational records of Paul Frillman.
        Box 3, U.S. Department of State folder -- Instruction
            pamphlets for foreign service officers attending
            universities.

191. FRONTWACHT.
        Records (in Flemish), 1915-1933. 1/2 ms. box.
        Youth organization of the Vlaamsche Front (Partij der
            Vlaamsche Nationalisten), a Flemish nationalist party.
        Correspondence, memoranda, and financial records, relating to
            Flemish nationalism in Belgium in the interwar period.

192. FURLONG, CHARLES WELLINGTON, 1874-1967.
        Papers, 1917-1963. 9 ms. boxes, 8 envelopes.
        Member, U.S. delegation, Paris Peace Conference, 1918-1919;
            member, Tacna-Arica Commission, 1926.
        Correspondence, memoranda, reports, writings, clippings, maps,
            and photographs, relating to Woodrow Wilson, the Paris
            Peace Conference, military, political, and economic
            conditions in the Balkans (particularly relating to Fiume

and Montenegro), the Tacna-Arica dispute between Peru and Chile, and the work of the Tacna-Arica Plebiscitary Commission, 1925-1926.
Register.
Purchase, C. W. Furlong, 1963.

Box 5 -- Issue of Sempre Abanti, January 1922, with article on moral strength of Italian youth; pamphlet on Serbia, April 1920, with section on school system in Serbia.
Box 8 -- Folder on Woodrow Wilson contains issue of Facts, January 1943, with article on English public schools.

193. GADSBY, HENRY FRANKLIN, 1868- .
Papers, 1897-1950. 18 ms. boxes.
Canadian journalist and political satirist.
Writings, correspondence, printed matter, and memorabilia, relating to Canadian and British politics, primarily in the interwar period, and to British Empire war efforts during World War I.
Gift, Clarence V. Blake, Sr., 1978.

Box 12 -- Pamphlet relating to Convocation of the University of Toronto with information on Canadian education, November 1947.
Box 18 -- Pamphlet on the University of Toronto relating to its postwar expansion and its activities.

194. GAHAGAN, G. WILLIAM, 1912- .
Papers, 1941-1954. 9 ms. boxes, 10 motion picture reels.
Information and Public Relations Officer, Office of War Information, San Francisco, 1942-1945.
Photographs, maps, films, and miscellanea, relating to U.S. Office of War Information analysis of Japanese propaganda and preparation of U.S. propaganda during World War II. Includes a few examples of postwar U.S. anticommunist propaganda.
Gift, G. W. Gahagan, 1975.

Boxes 2, 6, and 7 -- Reports on Far Eastern propaganda analyses.

195. GANN, LEWIS HENRY, 1924- .
Papers, 1950-1976. 30 ms. boxes.
Author and historian; Senior Fellow, Hoover Institution on War, Revolution and Peace, 1964- .
Correspondence, typewritten drafts of writings, galley proofs, transcribed interviews, and other material, relating to

Federation of Rhodesia and Nyasaland, German colonialism in
Africa, and Northern and Southern Rhodesia. Includes
drafts of and research materials used for the books by
L. H. Gann and Peter Duignan, Huggins of Rhodesia, A
History of Northern Rhodesia, Colonialism in Africa, and
The Birth of a Plural Society.
Preliminary inventory.
Gift, L. H. Gann, 1972. Subsequent increments.

Boxes 23 and 24 -- Envelopes of handwritten notes on
missionary and African education in Federation of Rhodesia
and Nyasaland.

196. GARDINIER, DAVID E., 1932.
Writings, 1972-1978. 1 folder.
Printed.
American historian.
Relates to education in the states of Equatorial Africa.
Gift, D. E. Gardinier, 1978.

Leaflet on education in French Equatorial Africa.
Essay on schooling in states of Equatorial Africa.
Bibliographical essay entitled "Education in the States of
Equatorial Africa.

197. GARSIDE, BETTIS ALSTON, 1894- .
Papers, 1897-1980. 4 ms. boxes.
American educator; missionary in China relief agencies.
Speeches and writings, correspondence, memoranda, minutes, and
printed matter, relating to mission schools in China, the
life of American missionary Henry W. Luce, communism in
China, and post-World War II relief to China and refugees
from China.
Gift, B. A. Garside, 1980.

Box 1 -- Reports on Boy Scouts and two issues of Cheelo,
alumni magazine of Shantung Christian University, in
English and Chinese.
Box 2 -- Manuscript chapters of book on life at Yale.
Box 3 -- Reports, correspondence, and leaflets on Christian
colleges in China.

198. GAULD, CHARLES ANDERSON, 1911- .
Papers (in English, Portuguese, and Spanish), 1932-1968.
18 ms. boxes.
American historian and author.
Clippings, correspondence, pamphlets, and serial issues,

relating to political, social, and economic conditions in
Latin America, especially Brazil, to Latin America's role
in World War II, to the Castro regime in Cuba, and to
problems of birth control, food production, communism, and
religion in Latin America.
Preliminary inventory.
Gift, C. A. Gauld, 1944. Subsequent increments.

Box 4 -- Issue of The Protestant, with article on German
re-education, March 1945.
Box 16 -- Pamphlet entitled "Latin America and the United
Presbyterians," with information on United Presbyterians'
social work and their assistance to youth in Brazil,
Colombia, Venezuela, Chile, Ecuador, Guatemala, and Mexico.
Statistical report on Latin America, with sections on
elementary school enrollment, illiteracy, and educational
attainment in Latin America.

199. GAVRILOVIC, MILAN, 1882-1976.
Papers (in Serbo-Croatian and English), 1939-1976.
55 ms. boxes.
Yugoslav journalist, politician, and diplomat; Ambassador to
the Soviet Union, 1940-1941; member, Yugoslav Government-
in-Exile, London, 1941-1943.
Correspondence, speeches and writings, office files, and
printed matter, relating to Yugoslav politics and
government, Yugoslavia during World War II, the Yugoslav
Government-in-Exile, Draza Mihailovic and the Chetnik
resistance movement in occupied Yugoslavia, relations
between the Kingdom of Yugoslavia and the Soviet Union,
and the activities of Serbian emigre groups following World
War II.
Preliminary inventory.
Closed until August 21, 1995.
Gift, Milan Gavrilovic, 1975.

Box 42 -- Issues of Information Bulletin by Serbian National
Committee, with sections on education.
Box 45 -- Complete transcript of National Educational
Television's journal.

200. GAY, EDWIN FRANCIS, 1867-1946.
Papers, 1917-1927. 6 ms. boxes, 1 roll of charts.
American economist; Director, U.S. Central Bureau of Planning
and Statistics, 1918-1919.
Correspondence, diary, reports, memoranda, and writings,
relating to U.S. economic mobilization and government
control of the economy during World War I, to activities of

65

the Central Bureau of Planning and Statistics, War
    Industries Board, War Trade Board, Shipping Board, and
    Commerical Economy Board, and to the U.S. delegation at the
    Paris Peace Conference.
Gift, Mrs. Godfrey Davies.

Box 2 -- Printed proposals for social reconstruction affecting
    education, civil rights, and health.

201. GEIGER, THEODOR.
    Memoranda (in German), 1949. 1 folder.
    Typescript.
    Relates to reconstruction of the German educational system
        after World War II.

202. GEORGE PEABODY COLLEGE FOR TEACHERS, NASHVILLE, TENNESSEE.
    Reports, 1958-1962. 8 microfilm reels.
    Typescript (microfilm). Originals located at the George
        Peabody College for Teachers.
    Relates to a project carried out by the George Peabody College
        for Teachers in cooperation with the Government of South
        Korea to provide technical assistance in the training of
        teachers in South Korea.
    Preliminary inventory.
    Purchase, George Peabody College for Teachers, 1978.

203. GEORGE, ROSEMARY, COLLECTOR.
    Textbooks (in Spanish), 1978-1979. 1 folder.
    Printed.
    Cuban elementary and secondary school textbooks, relating to
        the Cuban political system and world affairs.
    Gift, R. George, 1980.

    Books are illustrated and contain pro-Castro propaganda.

204. GERMAN AMERICAN BUND.
    Records (in English and German), 1936-1941. 1/2 ms. box,
        1 envelope.
    Photocopy. Most originals located in the U.S. National
        Archives.
    Fascist organization in the U.S.
    Minutes of meetings of the Executive Committee, translations
        of Fuehrer commands, financial records, propaganda, and
        photographs, relating to activities of the Bund.
    Gift, P. Dunne, 1972.

Folder 6 -- Reports, clippings, and notes dealing with propaganda.

205. GERMAN COMMUNIST ANTI-NAZI PROPAGANDA.
        (In German), ca. 1933-1939. 1 folder.
        Printed.
        Camouflaged anti-Nazi pamphlets, issued by the Kommunistische
           Partei Deutschlands.

206. GERMAN EDUCATION ESSAYS.
        (In German), 1943. 1 folder.
        Holograph.
        School essays, written by German pupils.

207. GERMAN STUDENT PROTEST COLLECTION.
        (In German), 1966-1972. 10 ms. boxes.
        Periodicals, pamphlets, leaflets, and proclamations, issued by
           leftist student groups in West Germany, relating to West
           German and international political issues, including the
           West German emergency laws, the publisher Axel Springer,
           the visit of the Shah of Iran to Berlin in 1967, the
           invasion of Czechoslovakia in 1968, and the Vietnamese War.
        Register.
        Gifts and purchases, various sources, 1970-1974.

        All boxes include materials relating to German Student
           Union and its activities.

208. GERMAN YOUTH MOVEMENT COLLECTION.
        (In German), 1908-1973. 1/2 ms. box.
        Radio broadcast transcripts and published articles relating to
           the German youth movement, the "Wandervogel"-Bewegung,
           1901-1933, and various youth movements after the end of
           World War II.
        Preliminary inventory.
        Purchase, Archiv der deutschen Jugendbewegung, 1974.

209. GERMANY. DEUTSCHE KONGRESS-ZENTRALE.
        Records (in German), 1870-1943. 426 ms. boxes.
        German Government agency regulating all congresses and
           conventions of German and international organizations
           taking place in Germany.
        Correspondence, memoranda, pamphlets, conference proceedings,
           clippings, and newspaper issues, relating to conferences of
           cultural, scientific, social reform, professional,
           business, educational, and other organizations.

Register.

Box 57 -- Notes and correspondence relating to Chinese
   students' unions in Europe.
Boxes 63, 64, 92, 222, 223, 298-301, 337, and 338 --
   Bulletins, pamphlets, booklets, reports, articles,
   correspondence, leaflets, news sheets, and newspaper
   clippings on International Confederation of Students;
   foreign students and their activites.
Boxes 80-84, 194, and 195 -- Pamphlets, articles, reports,
   printed matter, correspondence, and newspaper clippings on
   international education and International Bureau of
   Teachers.
Box 93 -- Correspondence and notes on European youth.
Box 101 -- Correspondence, notes, and pamphlets on Finnish
   students.
Box 127 -- Notes and pamphlets on German education.
Box 144 -- Correspondence, newspapers, notes, pamphlets, and
   leaflets relating to Heidelberg University.
Boxes 166 and 167 -- Correspondence, reports, articles,
   newspaper clippings, pamphlets, and booklets on German
   youth.
Boxes 172 and 173 - Correspondence, notes, newspaper
   clippings, pamphlets, leaflets, and reports related to
   child care, child care organizations, and kindergartens.
Box 288 -- Reports, notes, and booklets on social studies
   education.
Boxes 321 and 322 -- Correspondence, leaflets, pamphlets,
   reports, and newspaper clippings on university women and
   International Federation of Universities.

210. GERMANY. REICHSSICHERHEITSHAUPTAMT. SICHERHEITSDIENST.
   Miscellaneous records (in German), 1935-1944. 1/2 ms. box.
   Lessons, exercises, and other instructional material, relating
      to the training of German police officers in the Sicher-
      heitsdienst in both political and criminal police work.

211. GERMANY - SOCIAL CONDITIONS, 1918-1933.
   Slides, 1919-1933. 2 boxes.
   Depicts social conditions in Germany during the period of the
      Weimar Republic and the first months of Nazi rule,
      including scenes of theater productions, boxing tourna-
      ments, and portraits of military and political figures.

   Depicts German life, including schooling.

68

212. GERMANY - TERRITORY UNDER ALLIED OCCUPATION, 1945-1955.
U.S. ZONE. OFFICE OF MILITARY GOVERNMENT FOR BAVARIA.
KREIS TRAUNSTEIN.
Records (in English and German), 1945-1948. 10 ms. boxes.
Memoranda, reports, correspondence, and office files, relating
to civil administration of Traunstein, including problems
of public health and safety, administration of justice,
allocation of economic resources, organization of labor,
denazification, and disposition of displaced persons.
Includes annual administrative reports for other districts
in Bavaria.
Gift, William G. Marvin.

Boxes 4 and 8 -- Annual historical reports, with sections on
education, June 1947 and July 1948.

213. GHENT. RIJKSUNIVERSITEIT.
Congratulatory letter (in Flemish), 1936, to Harvard
University. 1 folder.
Printed (photocopy).
Relates to the 300th anniversary of the founding of Harvard
University.

214. GITLOW, BENJAMIN, 1891-1965.
Papers, 1918-1960. 17 ms. boxes.
American communist leader; later anticommunist writer.
Writings, correspondence, minutes of meetings, clippings, and
printed matter, relating to communism and socialism in the
U.S. and Europe.
Preliminary inventory.
Purchase, Myers G. Lowman, 1967.

Box 2 -- Two issues of The Educational Reviewer, with sections
on citizenship and democracy.
Box 6 -- Report of meeting of Georgia Commission on Education,
Atlanta, September 1957.

215. GODARD, YVES JEAN ANTOINE NOEL, 1911-1975.
Papers (in French), 1929-1974. 14-1/2 ms. boxes, 1 volume,
1 envelope.
Colonel, French Army; Director of Police in Algeria,
1958-1960; organizer of the Organisation Armee Secrete
(O. A. S.), 1961-1962.
Correspondence, messages, reports, dossiers, maps,
photographs, clippings, and speeches and writings, relating
to military and resistance operations during World War II,
military operations during the Indochinese War, and

69

military, police, and terrorist activities during the
Algerian independence struggle. Includes records of the
Armee Secrete de Haute-Savoie (Secret Army of Resistance
Fighters of Haute-Savoie).
Register.
Purchase, Mrs. Yves Godard, 1976.

Box 3 -- Reports, articles, and newspaper clippings on modes
of life, social instruction, religious fraternities, and
educational achievements in Algeria.

216. GOLDER, FRANK ALFRED, 1877-1929.
Papers (in English and Russian), 1812-1930, 41-1/2 ms. boxes,
1 envelope.
American historian; American Relief Administration worker in
Russia.
Correspondence, diaries, memoranda, articles, pamphlets, and
photographs, relating to Russian history in the late
nineteenth and early twentieth centuries, the Russian
American Company in Alaska, the Russian Revolution, and
American Relief Administration work in Russia.
Preliminary inventory.
Gift, Thomas and Henrietta Eliot and H. M. Hart.

Boxes 12, 18, 22, 41 and 42 -- Articles, reports, and notes on
social conditions, education, religion, students,
university life, teachers, and schools in Russia.

217. GOOD, ALBERT I.
Papers, ca. 1890-1929. 1 folder.
American missionary in Cameroon.
Memoir, entitled "The Church in the Cameroun," relating to
missionary activity in the 1920s, and printed matter,
relating to missionary activity in Africa, 1890-1908.
Gift, Edwin M. Good, 1964.

Chapter on church and education.

218. GOODMAN, ALLAN ERWIN, 1944- .
Papers, 1947-1975. 126 ms. boxes, 2 card file boxes,
3 binders, 16 notebooks, and 7 envelopes.
Consultant on Vietnamese Affairs, U.S. Department of State and
Rand Corporation, 1967-1971.
Writings, reports, correspondence, clippings, notes,
interviews, and printed matter, relating to the Vietnamese
war, the Paris peace talks of 1968-1973, elections in South
Vietnam from 1967 to 1971, the South Vietnamese

legislature, migration to Saigon, urbanization and
political and demographic change in Southeast Asia,
counterinsurgency, and Soviet-U.S. detente.
Register.
User must sign a statement agreeing not to identify any
persons mentioned in unpublished material in the collection
(deceased U.S. citizens may be identified after January 2,
1980). Also, 2-1/2 ms. boxes and 12 notebooks are closed
until 2005.
Gift, A. E. Goodman. Subsequent increments.

Boxes 12, 16, 25, 33, 88, and 121 -- Reports, articles, and
notes on education in Vietnam.
Boxes 14, 22, and 23 -- Reports, articles, notes, and
newspaper clippings on Vietnamese youth, students, and
universities.
Boxes 47, 78, and 81 -- Text of speech, notes, newspaper
clippings, and articles on education and universities
in U.S.
Box 56 -- Newspaper clippings on education in Indonesia.
Box 58 -- Leaflet and notes on education in Kenya.
Box 59 -- Reports on literacy in Laos. Report by Rand
Corporation on student radicalism in Latin America.
Box 75 -- Newspaper clippings and notes on student radical
movements in the world.
Box 96 and 97 -- Pamphlets relating to U.S. AID education in
Vietnam.
Box 112 -- English-Vietnamese and Vietnamese-English
dictionary of educational terms.

219. GRAHAM, MALBONE WATSON, 1898-1965.
Papers, 1914-1956. 15-1/2 ms. boxes.
American political scientist.
Pamphlets, bulletins, writings, memoranda, and clippings,
relating to the League of Nations and to political
conditions and diplomatic relations in Finland, the Baltic
states, and Eastern Europe from the Russian Revolution to
World War II.
Preliminary inventory.
Gift, Gladys Graham, 1967.

Mimeographed book entitled "Hitler's First Foes,"
1936, with section on Catholics and Catholic
education.

220. GRANT, DONALD, 1889- .
Writings, 1920-1935. 1 folder.
British author and lecturer; Director, European Student

Relief, 1920-1925.
Notes, diary entries, letter extracts, and a pamphlet,
relating to social conditions and relief work in Russia and
Eastern and Central Europe, 1920-1922, and to the economic
and social policy of the socialist municipal government in
Vienna, 1919-1934.
Gift, Joseph Jones, 1977. Gift, D. Grant, 1978.

Pamphlet on Vienna, 1919-1934, with section on school reform
in that city.

221. GRAY, EDWARD RUTHERFORD, 1896-1974.
Papers, 1894-1979. 18 ms. boxes.
American economist; Chief, Governments Division, U.S. Bureau
of the Census, 1940-1945.
Writings, correspondence, memoranda, reports, statistics, and
printed matter, relating to finances of federal, state, and
local governments in the U.S. and to post-World War II
economic reconstruction in Europe.
Gift, Virginia Gray, 1980.

Box 3 -- Budget report of U.S. Government for fiscal year
ending June 30, 1951. Report has section on education.
Box 14 -- Report on centralization in United States, 1933-
1939, with section on intergovernmental cooperation in the
provision of educational facilities for youth, December 30,
1939.

222. GREAT BRITAIN. DIRECTOR OF PROPAGANDA IN ENEMY COUNTRIES.
Leaflets (in German), 1918. 1 ms. box.
Printed.
British propaganda leaflets prepared for distribution behind
German lines during World War I.

223. GREAT BRITAIN. FOREIGN OFFICE. POLITICAL INTELLIGENCE
DEPARTMENT.
Microfilm. 2 reels.
Captured German documents issued for propaganda purposes,
partly by the Gestapo and Reichssicherheitshauptamt,
1939-1944.

224. GREAT BRITAIN. FOREIGN OFFICE. WELLINGTON HOUSE.
Issuance, ca. 1914-1918. 36 pamphlet boxes (12 linear feet),
2 ms. boxes.
Printed.
Propaganda section of the British Foreign Office.

Books, pamphlets, and reprints, issued as British propaganda
during World War I.
Preliminary inventory.

Box 1 -- Newspaper clipping with cartoons on Pan-German peace
fantasies and pamphlet of German propaganda.

225. GREAT BRITAIN IN WORLD WAR II COLLECTION, 1939-1945.
11 ms. boxes.
Pamphlets, relating to conditions in Great Britain during
World War II, war aims, civil defense, the wartime economy,
and postwar reconstruction.
Preliminary inventory.

Box 1 -- Booklets on battle training.
Box 2 -- Pamphlet on development of British universities, June
1944.
Box 3 -- Booklet on education in democracy for social
renaissance, 1944.
Box 4 -- Pocket book with 375 questions and answers on
training, 1943.
Box 5 -- Pocket book on principles of army instructions, 1942.
Box 7 -- Booklet on youth problem, 1942.

226. GREECE -- MISCELLANEA, 1945-1947.
1 folder.
Collection of reports, newsletters, pamphlets, and leaflets,
relating to relief activities in Greece during and after
World War II. Includes issuances of Greek War Relief
Association and of American Mission for Aid to Greece, and
a pamphlet on communist atrocities in Greece.

Includes topics on culture, civilization, education, and
social conditions in Greece.

227. GREGORY, THOMAS T. C., 1878-1933.
Papers, 1918-1932. 3 ms. boxes, 1 album, 2 envelopes.
American lawyer; American Relief Administration Director for
Central Europe, 1919.
Correspondence, reports, memoranda, and printed matter,
relating to the work of the American Relief Administration
in Central Europe, the fall of the 1919 Bela Kun communist
regime in Hungary, and the 1928 presidential campaign of
Herbert Hoover.
Register.
Gift, John M. Gregory, 1972.

Box 3 -- Issue of Stanford Illustrated Review, March 1927, and text of address by T. T. C. Gregory relating to Stanford.

228. GREY, BEN, 1893-1980.
Papers, 1919-1979. 1 ms. box.
American journalist and public relations counsel; adviser to President Franklin D. Roosevelt.
Correspondence, memoranda, writings, clippings, printed matter, photographs, and motion picture film, relating to miscellaneous aspects of American politics and foreign relations with Latin America, especially Haiti.
Gift, Naomi Grey, 1980.

Report entitled "An American Contribution," June 1926, related to National Farm School Conference.

229. GRIMM, DAVID DAVIDOVICH, 1864- .
Papers (in Russian), 1919-1934. 4 ms. boxes.
Russian educator, Rector, Petersburg University, 1899-1910; Assistant Minister of Education, Russian Provisional Government, 1917.
Correspondence, memoranda, press reports, and printed and other material, relating to the Russian emigre community in Finland and other parts of Europe and to the Russian Civil War.
Register.
Purchase, Nikita Struve, 1976.

Box 3 -- Article on Russian education during Civil War.

230. GRIVAS (GEORGE) COLLECTION, 1955-1964.
1-1/2 ms. boxes.
Writings, public statements and proclamations, pamphlets, leaflets, and correspondence, relating to the revolutionary activities on Cyprus of the Greek underground organization EOKA, led by G. Grivas, 1955-1959. Includes original manuscript of EOKA's Struggle by G. Grivas.
Gift, Charles M. Foley, 1974.

Box 1 -- Leaflets, postcards, and radio broadcast used as propaganda.
Box 2 -- Writings relating to general strikes and demonstrations by youth.

231. GROSSMANN, KURT RICHARD, 1897-1972.
Papers (in German and English), 1926-1973. 58 ms. boxes, 3 oversize boxes, 1 envelope, 1 motion picture film reel.

German-American author and journalist; President, German
League for Human Rights, 1926-1933.
Writings, correspondence, clippings, and serial issues,
relating to Jewish refugees from Nazi Germany, postwar
German and Austrian restitution payments to Jewish war
victims, German-Israeli relations, the condition of Jews
throughout the world, and civil liberties in the U.S. and
Germany.
Purchase, Elsa Grossmann, 1975.

Box 15 -- Magazine clippings on American students.
Box 27 -- Notes and reports on children and youth.
Box 58 -- Report entitled "Survey of Events in Jewish Life,"
1953, with section on cultural activities and education.

232. GRZYBOWSKI, KAZIMIERZ.
Study, n.d. "Soviet Public International Law Doctrines and
Diplomatic Practice." 2 ms. boxes.
Typescript (mimeographed).
Gift, Robert Turner, 1974.

Box 2, Chapter 9 -- Section on propaganda.

233. GUERARD, ALBERT LEON, 1880-1959.
Papers (in French and English), 1942-1948. 5 ms. boxes.
American educator; broadcaster, U.S. Office of War
Information, 1942-1945.
Radio transcripts, memoranda, reports, correspondence, and
pamphlets, relating to broadcasts of the French section of
the Office of War Information during World War II and to
the activities of the Committee to Frame a World
Constitution.
Register.
Gift, A. L. Guerard, 1956.

Box 2, Sections XXII and XXIII -- Adult education.

234. GUNN, SELSKAR M.
Report, 1934. "China and the Rockefeller Foundation."
1 folder.
Typescript (mimeographed).
Relates to educational, scientific, technical, and cultural
assistance activities of the Rockefeller Foundation in
China and to proposals for future activities.

Based on study about China by Rockefeller Foundation.
Sections on universities; natural sciences; social
sciences; and primary and secondary education in China.

235. HALL, LUELLA J., 1891-1973.
    Papers, 1925-1971.   103 ms. boxes, 3 cubic foot boxes.
    American historian; Dean of Hartnell College, 1938-1953.
    Clippings, notes, writings, and correspondence, relating
       primarily to foreign relations between the U.S. and
       Morocco, 1776-1956, and to post-World War II political,
       social, and economic conditions in Africa, especially North
       Africa. Includes correspondence with Kaiser Wilhelm II
       relating to the World War I war guilt question, and a card
       index bibliography on the history of Morocco.
    Gift, L. J. Hall, 1939. Subsequent increments.

    Boxes 20, 21, 29, and 38 -- Magazine and newspaper clippings
       on African education.
    Box 22 -- Newspaper clippings on U.S. Peace Corps.
    Box 71 -- Newsletters, newspaper clippings, and essay relating
       to Moroccan propaganda in U.S.
    Box 101 -- Newspaper and magazine clippings on education in
       Tunisia.

236. HALLGARTEN, GEORGE WOLFGANG FELIX, 1901-1975.
    Papers (in German and English), 1912-1975. 39 ms. boxes,
       2 microfilm reels.
    German-American historian.
    Correspondence, diaries, speeches and writings, photocopies of
       government documents, propaganda leaflets, and printed
       matter, relating to European diplomacy, imperialism,
       psychology of national socialism and totalitarianism, U.S.
       and German propaganda during World War II, and the arms
       race, 1870-1970. Includes drafts of a study by G. W. F.
       Hallgarten, entitled "Imperialismus vor 1914" (Imperialism
       before 1914.)
    Register.
    Diaries and private correspondence (boxes 30-39) are closed
       until May 22, 2000.
    Gift, Katherine Drew Hallgarten, 1977.

    Box 3 -- Newspaper clippings and leaflets on education.
    Box 7 -- Reports and articles on peace research; handwritten
       notes on Turkish theology students.
    Box 8 -- Handwritten notes on Young Turks.

237. HALLGARTEN, KATHERINE DREW, 1908-1980.
    Papers (in English and Spanish), 1953-1979. 40-1/2 ms. boxes.
    American lawyer; Chairman, Section on Communications,
        Inter-American Bar Association, 1961,
    Reports, conference papers and proceedings, laws and treaties,
        hearing transcripts, correspondence, and printed matter,
        relating to international communications and space law.
    Gift, Viva Drew Adamson, 1980.

    Box 24 -- Issue of United Nations General Assembly, with
        article on role of educational broadcasting in developing
        countries.
    Box 35 -- Pamphlet by Inter-American Association of
        Broadcasters entitled "Communication Media: Instrument of
        Freedom and Culture."

238. HALPERN, JOEL M., COLLECTOR.
    Grant applications, 1968-1969. 3 ms. boxes.
    Photocopy.
    Grant applications to the Southeast Asia Development Advisory
        Group of the Asia Society, relating to proposed research
        projects on Indonesia, the Philippines, Malaya, and other
        parts of Southeast Asia.
    Closed until June 1990.
    Gift, J. M. Halpern, 1976.

    Box 1 -- Reports on rituals and role of women in Macedonian
        village in Yugoslavia, May 1977.
    Box 2 -- Reports on population studies with sections on child
        health and education.

239. HAMILTON, MAXWELL MC GAUGHEY, 1896-1957.
    Papers, 1916-1957. 4 ms. boxes.
    American diplomat; Chief, Divison of Far Eastern Affairs,
        U.S. Department of State, 1937-1943; Ambassador to Finland,
        1945-1947.
    Reports, memoranda, correspondence, lectures, press releases,
        and printed matter, relating to U.S. foreign policy toward
        China, Japan, the Soviet Union, and Finland. Includes
        report and series of interviews with Japanese, Chinese, and
        other government officials concerning economic and
        political conditions in Japan and Manchuria, 1933-1934.
    Register.
    Gift, Mrs. Maxwell M. Hamilton.

Box 2 -- Newsletters on Japan with sections on Japanese education.
Box 4 -- Bulletin on Russia by U.S. State Department, November 1951, with information on educational system of Soviet Union.

240. HANNA, PAUL ROBERT, 1902- .
Miscellaneous papers, 1941-1977. 4 ms. boxes.
American educator; Professor of Education, Stanford University, 1935-1967; Director, Stanford International Development Education Center, 1963-1968; Senior Research Fellow, Hoover Institution on War, Revolution and Peace, 1974- .
Bibliographies, books, periodical articles, and speeches, relating to international education.
Gift, P. R. Hanna, 1977.

Box 1 -- Text of address in response to Distinguished Service Award on occasion of Silver Jubilee of the Philippines Public School Teachers' Association, April 9, 1958.
Box 2 -- Articles on spelling.

241. HARRIS, CHRISTINA PHELPS, 1902-1972.
Papers, 1914-1973. 11 ms. boxes, 1 oversize box.
American historian and political scientist; Middle East Curator, Hoover Institution, 1948-1957; professor, Stanford University, 1951-1967.
Writings, correspondence, lecture notes, printed matter, and photographs, relating to political conditions in the twentieth-century Middle East, European intellectual history, and political science.
Gift, Katherine Harris, 1979.

Box 1 -- Reports on Iran and Iraq with sections on education.
Box 4 -- Guidebooks by the Foundation of Audio-Visual Education and Research relating to production of motion pictures on Iran and Egypt, with emphasis on civilization, culture, and education.

242. HARRIS, DAVID, 1900-1975.
Papers, 1929-1967. 3 ms. boxes, 15 card file boxes (5 linear feet), 4 envelopes, 8 medals.
American historian; Associate Chief, Central European Affairs Division, U.S. Department of State, 1943-1947; Professor of History, Stanford University, 1930-1966.
Correspondence, speeches and writings, reports, research

notes, newsletters, lists, and printed matter, relating to
Emperor Napoleon I of France, the Balkan crisis of
1875-1878, international affairs in Europe during the
interwar period, and reconstruction of Germany and Austria
following World War II.
Register.
Gift, D. Harris, 1967. Incremental gift, Katherine Pinkham
Harris, 1975.

Box 1 -- Article on research in history and how to study it.
Box 2 -- Memoranda, notes, and newspaper clippings relating to
postwar education in Germany.

243. HARRIS, HERBERT.
Reports, 1956. 1 folder.
Typescript (mimeographed).
American public opinion pollster.
Relates to the results of a study of American public opinion
regarding the United Nations.

Interviews with educators and professors of various
universities.

244. HASTINGS, WILLIAM, COLLECTOR.
Newspaper clippings, 1942-1943. 4 ms. boxes.
Clippings from Philippine newspapers, relating to conditions
in the Philippines under Japanese occupation during World
War II.
Gift, W. Hastings, 1970.

All boxes include clippings relating to conditions in other
parts of the world as well as to education, universities,
schooling, and students in the Philippines.

245. HATFIELD, MARK ODOM, 1922- .
Thesis, 1948. "Herbert Hoover and Labor: Policies and
Attitudes, 1897-1928." 1 folder.
Typescript (photocopy).
American politician; Governor of Oregon, 1959-1967; U.S.
Senator from Oregon, 1967- .
Relates to the views of President Herbert Hoover on the labor
movement. Master's thesis, Stanford University.

Section on Herbert Hoover's education and on child labor.

246. HEALY, JAMES AUGUSTINE, 1891-1975, COLLECTOR.
        Collection on Ireland, 1896-1966. 21 ms. boxes,
           24 scrapbooks, 1 motion picture film, 1 envelope,
           1 framed photograph.
        Clippings, pamphlets, correspondence, and newspaper issues,
           relating to political and economic conditions in Ireland.
           Includes a 16 mm film, "The Irish Rising, 1916." produced
           for television by George Morrison, and correspondence
           between Herbert Hoover and J. A. Healy.
        Preliminary inventory.
        Gift, J. A. Healy, 1942. Subsequent increments.

        Box 19 -- Annual report of Commission for Relief in Belgium by
           Educational Foundation, 1920, with information on
           education.

247. HEITMAN, SIDNEY, 1924- .
        Study, 1980. "The Soviet Germans in the USSR Today."
           132 pages.
        Typescript (photocopy).
        American historian.
        Relates to social, political, and economic conditions of, and
           current trends among, Germans in the Soviet Union. Study
           prepared for the U.S. Department of State Office of
           External Research.
        Gift, S. Heitman, 1980.

        Sections on cultural profile of Soviet Germans, with emphasis
           on history, traditions, religion, and education.

248. HERBERT HOOVER ORAL HISTORY PROGRAM.
        Transcripts of interviews, 1966-1972. 315 interviews.
        Typescript.
        Relates to Herbert Hoover, President of the U.S., 1929-1933.
           Recollections of political leaders, businessmen, military
           figures, journalists, writers, physicians, secretaries,
           research aids, friends, and associates of Herbert Hoover.
           Interviews sponsored by the Institute for Social Science
           Research and the Herbert Hoover Presidential Library
           Association on behalf of the Herbert Hoover Presidential
           Library and the Hoover Institution on War, Revolution and
           Peace.
        Register.
        A few transcripts are closed for various periods of time.

        Alphabetical list of all people who were interviewed about
           Herbert Hoover, some of whom were educators.

249. HERBITS, STEPHEN E., 1942-   .
     Papers, 1966-1974. 52-1/2 ms. boxes, 1 binder.
     Special Assistant to the U.S. Assistant Secretary of Defense
          (Manpower and Reserve Affairs).
     Correspondence, writings, reports, memoranda, notes, and
          printed matter, relating to proposals for an all-volunteer
          armed force, congressional action on the proposals, and
          evaluation of the new volunteer system in operation.
     Closed until processed.
     Gift, S. E. Herbits, 1975.

     Box 10 -- Writings on youth in transition.
     Box 15 -- Survey report, newspaper clippings, articles,
          correspondence, and notes on impact of draft on graduate
          students and Selective Service System.

250. HERRON, GEORGE DAVIS, 1862-1925.
     Papers, 1916-1927. 26-1/2 ms. boxes, 16 volumes,
          4 scrapbooks.
     American clergyman and lecturer; unofficial adviser to Woodrow
          Wilson, President of the U.S.
     Correspondence, interviews, lectures, essays, notes, and
          clippings, relating to the League of Nations, territorial
          questions, prisoners of war, and other political and
          economic issues at the Paris Peace Conference.
     Preliminary inventory.
     Gift, G. D. Herron, 1922. Subsequent increments.

     Box 18 -- Issue of The Literary Digest, with sections on
          religion and religious education, October 17, 1900.
     Box 19 -- Issue of The Home Missionary, with article on
          American College and Education Society.
     Boxes 21 and 22 -- Several books on religious education.

251. HERZ, MARTIN FLORIAN, 1917-   , COLLECTOR.
     Propaganda leaflets (in English and Vietnamese), 1967-1969.
          1-1/2 ms. boxes.
     North Vietnamese and Viet Cong propaganda directed at American
          soldiers in Vietnam.
     Inventory.
     Gift, M. F. Herz, 1978.

     Statements by deserters in Vietnamese war to their friends in
          American armed forces in South Vietnam to encourage them to
          stop fighting.

252. HEYWORTH-DUNNE, JAMES, d. 1974.
      Papers (in Arabic, Persian, Turkish, German, French, and
          English), ca. 1860-1949. 7 ms. boxes.
      Senior Lecturer in Arabic, School of Oriental Studies,
          University of London.
      Theses, studies, notes, writings, and correspondence, relating
          to the history, philosophy, literature, education, and
          religion of Egypt, the Arab world, and Turkey.
      Purchase, J. Heyworth-Dunne, 1949.

      Box 4 -- Unpublished master's dissertation entitled "The Arab
          Conception of the Ideal Teacher as Revealed in Arabic
          Pedagogical Literature," December 1938.

253. HIESTAND, JOHN, COLLECTOR.
      Collection on psychological warfare, 1942-1945. 1 ms. box,
          2 scrapbooks.
      Letters, conference proceedings, transcripts of radio
          broadcasts, propaganda leaflets, and printed matter,
          relating primarily to the work of the U.S. Office of War
          Information and the U.S. Army Psychological Warfare Branch
          in the Southwest Pacific, 1944-1945.
      Preliminary inventory.
      Gift, J. Hiestand, 1972.

      Booklet: Selections from the Philippine Hour, with section on
          education in the Philippines under Japan.

254. HIGH, SIDNEY C., JR.
      Papers, 1962-1978. 12 ms. boxes.
      American educator; Director, Career Education Programs, U.S.
          Office of Education.
      Correspondence, writings, studies, reports, memoranda, and
          printed matter, relating to vocational education in the
          U.S.
      Gift, S. C. High, Jr. 1980.

      Box 1 -- Report, pamphlets, and newspaper clippings relating
          to Teacher Education Research Center. Correspondence and
          reports on Experimental Schools Program.
      Boxes 2 and 3 -- Pamphlets, articles, and manual on curriculum
          development and vocational and urban education.
      Boxes 4-7, and 9-12 -- Reports, pamphlets, leaflets, and
          articles on career education and Comprehensive Career
          Education Model (CCEM).

255. HILGER, FRANCES E., COLLECTOR.
  Collection, 1967-1979. 88-1/2 ms. boxes, 2 phonorecords.
  Clippings, periodical issues, leaflets, bulletins, and other
    printed matter, relating to the Vietnamese war, opposition
    to the war in the U.S., and U.S. and international
    politics.
  Gift, Frederick E. Hilger, 1979.

  Box 4 -- Newspaper clippings on propaganda.
  Boxes 7 and 13 -- Issues of The New Republic and The Center
    Magazine, with articles on education, peace, and
    universities.
  Boxes 15, 32, and 33 -- Issues of Friends Journal and The
    Nation, with articles on youth.
  Box 34 -- Issues of Vista, with articles on education.
  Box 76 -- Newspaper clippings on education in U.S. and Canada.
  Box 87 -- Pocket book on education in USSR.

256. HILL, MARGARET E.
  Papers, 1942-1948. 3 ms. boxes, 9 envelopes, 4 motion picture
    reels, 5 phonorecords.
  Executive Secretary, United Nations War Relief Council for
    Southern California.
  Press releases, bulletins, correspondence, pamphlets,
    clippings, brochures, photographs, motion pictures, and
    phonorecords, relating to fund raising in southern
    California for World War II relief activities.
  Gift, M. E. Hill. 1979.

  Box 1 -- Pamphlet on Norway's teachers and Nazi invasion.
  Box 2 -- Pamphlets and booklets on American Relief
    Administration and children of the world.

257. HILL, PAUL ALBERT, 1896-1968, COLLECTOR.
  Collection on Woodrow Wilson, ca. 1919-1959. 18 ms. boxes.
  Letters from famous American and foreign statesmen, authors,
    and scholars, relating to their evaluations of the
    historical significance of Woodrow Wilson, President of the
    U.S., 1913-1921.
  Preliminary inventory.
  Gift, Viola Koch, 1969.

  Box 1 -- Letters from famous people, including George Bernard
    Shaw, Sigmund Freud, Carl Young, and Edvard Benes.
  Box 2 -- Letters from college presidents and professors of
    U.S. universities.

258. HILL, ROBERT C.
Papers, 1942-1978. 178 ms. boxes, 16 oversize boxes,
14 scrapbooks, 4 binders, 4 motion picture reels.
American diplomat; Ambassador to Mexico, 1957-1961, Spain,
1969-1972, and Argentina, 1974-1977; Assistant Secretary of
State, 1956-1957; Assistant Secretary of Defense,
1973-1974.
Speeches and writings, correspondence, reports, clippings,
other printed matter, photographs, motion picture films,
and sound recordings, relating to conditions in the U.S.,
relations with Latin America and Spain, U.S. foreign policy
and domestic politics, and the Republican Party.

Box 32 -- Two letters relating to American School Parent-
Teacher Association.
Box 33 -- Correspondence and newspaper clipping on the
American School Teacher Training Workshop and Mexico City
College, 1959.
Box 76 -- Texts of Robert Hill's speeches at different schools
and educational institutions.
Box 128 -- Reports, correspondence, and leaflets relating to
Rollins College.

259. HOOVER, HERBERT CLARK, 1874-1964.
Papers, 1897-1969. 366 ms. boxes, 92 envelopes, 1 album,
6 microfilm reels, 130 motion pictures, 31 phonorecords,
36 phonotapes.
President of the U.S., 1929-1933.
Appointment calendars, correspondence, office files, speeches
and writings, analyses of newspaper editorials, printed
matter, photographs, motion pictures, sound recordings, and
other material, relating to the administration of relief
during and after the two world wars, Hoover's relationship
with Woodrow Wilson, U.S. politics and government, and the
philosophy and public service contributions of Herbert
Hoover.
Register.
Gift, Herbert Hoover, 1962. Subsequent increments.

Box 24 -- Correspondence and reports related to Boy Scouts of
America.
Boxes 30, 31, 119, 122, 152, 222, 287, 330, and 352 --
Correspondence, notes, texts of speeches, articles,
newspaper clippings, and reports on education.
Boxes 136, 346, and 355 -- Texts of addresses, newspaper
clippings, and pamphlet on youth and American Youth for
Freedom.
Box 138 -- Texts of speeches on American campuses.

260. HOOVER INSTITUTION ON WAR, REVOLUTION AND PEACE. PROGRAM ON
          OVERSEAS DEVELOPMENT.
          Records, 1955-1956. 1-1/2 ms. boxes.
          Program conducted by the Hoover Institution under a contract
              with the U.S. International Cooperation Administration.
              Reports and reading lists, relating to the instruction of
              foreign technicians in matters regarding economic
              development.

          Box 1 -- Lecture texts: "Educating Men for Economic
              Productivity" by Paul R. Hanna, and "Land-grant College and
              Its Place in American Life."
          Box 2 -- Reading checklists on several Asian countries and
              Ethiopia. Checklists include titles on education in
              related countries.

261. HOOVER INSTITUTION ON WAR, REVOLUTION AND PEACE. REVOLUTION AND
          THE DEVELOPMENT OF INTERNATIONAL RELATIONS PROJECT.
          Records, 1948-1952. 69-1/2 ms. boxes, 17 card file boxes
              (3 linear feet).
          Memoranda, correspondence, data sheets, and printed matter,
              relating to the comparative study of social, political, and
              economic development in various countries during the
              twentieth century, especially to the comparative study of
              political and military elites in various countries.
          Preliminary inventory.

          Box 4 -- Proposals, memoranda, and correspondence on public
              education.
          Box 7 -- Proposals on adult education.
          Box 10 -- Course outlines and notes on propaganda.
          Box 12 -- Issues of For a Lasting Peace, for a People's
              Democracy, with articles on peace and peace promotion.
          Box 15 -- Preliminary report on leadership and society's
              vulnerabilities to propaganda.

262. HORNBECK, STANLEY KUHL, 1883-1966.
          Papers, 1900-1966. 532 ms. boxes, 41 envelopes, 8 oversize
              photographs.
          American diplomat; Chief, Division of Far Eastern Affairs,
              U.S. Department of State, 1928-1937; Adviser on Political
              Relations, U.S. Department of State, 1937-1944; Ambassador
              to the Netherlands, 1944-1947.
          Correspondence, writings, reports, studies, dispatches and
              instructions, printed matter, memorabilia, and photographs
              relating to U.S. foreign relations in China, Japan, and
              other areas of the Far East, political conditions in China,
              Japan, and other areas of the Far East, political

conditions in China and Japan, and U.S.-Dutch relations. Register.
Gift, Mrs. S. K. Hornbeck, 1967.

Boxes 5, 7, 196, and 214 -- Correspondence, reports, pamphlets, notes, and newspaper clippings relating to activities of educational organizations.
Boxes 11, 120, 142, 143, 176, 354, 357, 426, 427, 446, and 449 -- Reports, newspaper clippings, correspondence, pamphlets, leaflets, articles, and notes relating to some American universities and their activities.
Box 22 -- Report on political relations between U.S. and Australia, with section on education in Australia.
Box 51 -- Article in the Saturday Evening Post on student government, June 4, 1927.
Boxes 56, 74, 87, and 114 -- Reports, articles, pamphlets, correspondence, notes, and newspaper clippings on Chinese education.
Box 60 -- Pamphlet relating to Chinese students in U.S., September 1918.
Boxes 70 and 104 -- Reports and articles on Chinese students and their movement.
Box 113 -- Correspondence, reports, and articles on China and U.S. cultural relations, with information on education.
Box 136 -- Correspondence, newsletters, bulletins, pamphlets, and article on U.S. cultural relations and international education.
Boxes 153 and 154 -- Newspaper clippings, correspondence, articles, pamphlets, booklets, leaflets, and reports on education in U.S.
Boxes 229 and 251 -- Pamphlets, text of speech, and article relating to segregation of Japanese students by school authorities in San Francisco and education in Japan.
Box 236 -- Newspaper clippings and article on education in Japan and Japanese textbooks.
Box 270 -- Articles on Korean educational problems; issue of Korean Student Bulletin, May 1930.
Box 405 -- Newspaper clippings on Latin American students and American higher education.
Box 451 -- Correspondence, newspaper clippings, newsletters, leaflets, and memoranda relating to Young Americans for Freedom.

263. HUDSON, RAY M.
Papers, 1922-1957. 6 ms. boxes.
Chief, Division of Simplified Practice, U.S. Department of Commerce, 1926.
Letters, pamphlets, clippings, and other printed matter, relating to U.S. industry, simplification of industrial

practice, and public life of Herbert Hoover, and the 1928,
1932, and 1936 presidential campaigns.
Preliminary inventory.
Gift, R. M. Hudson, 1962.

Box 1 -- Newspaper clippings, pictures, and pamphlets on
    Herbert Hoover, his youth, and his education.
Boxes 2 and 3 -- Pamphlets on youth and industry.

264. HUNT, EDWARD EYRE, 1885-1953.
    Papers, 1914-1949. 83 ms. boxes, 1 envelope.
    American economist; relief worker in Europe during World
        War I; Secretary, President's Emergency Committee for
        Employment, 1930-1931.
    Reports, memoranda, writings, and printed matter, relating to
        relief and reconstruction in Europe during and after World
        Wars I and II (especially in Belgium, France, Germany,
        Italy, and Poland), the Commission for Relief in Belgium,
        the American Red Cross, Herbert Hoover and the presidential
        campaign of 1920, and U.S. economic questions between the
        two world wars.
    Register.
    Gift, Mrs. E. E. Hunt, 1956. Subsequent increments.

    Boxes 11 and 12 -- Reports, correspondence, and pamphlets
        relating to Belgian-American Educational Foundation.
    Box 19 -- Issues of The Journal of the National Education
        Association, nos. 7 and 8, 1933.
    Box 29 -- UNESCO reports.

265. HUSTON, JAY CALVIN.
    Papers (in English and Russian), 1917-1931. 14 ms. boxes,
        2 envelopes.
    American consular official in China, 1917-1932.
    Writings, pamphlets, leaflets, and clippings, relating to
        cultural, political, and economic conditions in China and
        to communism and Soviet influence in China.
    Preliminary inventory.
    Gift, Payson J. Treat, 1935.

    Box 4 -- Pamphlet on problems confronting the Christian
        movement in China, April 1927, with section on education;
        booklet on National Christian Council of China, 1926-1927,
        with section on religious education.

266. HUTCHINSON, JOHN RAYMOND.
    Papers, 1918-1961. 5 ms. boxes, 2 cubic foot boxes,

2 envelopes, 5 phonorecords.
American educator; educational and pictorial specialist, U.S.
    Office of War Information, during World War II.
Correspondence, film scripts, printed matter, photographs, and
    filmstrips, relating to the production of U.S. propaganda
    films by the Office of War Information for distribution in
    China during World War II and to the history of television
    in the U.S.
Preliminary inventory.
Gift, J. R. Hutchinson, 1952. Incremental gift, 1969.

Box 2, Section E -- Teacher's manual on use of film strips.
Box 5, Section G -- Miscellaneous notes and reports on Thomas
    Jefferson High School, Elizabeth, New Jersey, where John
    Hutchinson taught.

267. ILIFF, JOHN L., <u>COLLECTOR</u>.
        Slides, 1936. 1 ms. box.
        Depicts the Caucasus region and the reconstruction of Moscow.
            Used in a Russian seventh-grade class.
        Gift, J. L. Iliff, 1945.

        Educational slides used in USSR for teaching Russian and
            Soviet history.

268. INDONESIA -- INFORMATION BULLETINS, 1948-1952.
        1/2 ms. box.
        Press releases and newsletters issued by the Dutch and
            Indonesian Governments, relating to the independence of
            Indonesia, Indonesian foreign relations, and the
            government, economy, and culture of Indonesia.

        Information relating to universities and education, in
            Indonesia's weekly newspapers.

269. INGLIS, JOHN AND THEODORA.
        Papers, 1898-1902. 1 ms. box.
        American missionary at An Ting Hospital, Peking, China,
            1898-1900.
        Memoirs, correspondence, and clippings, relating to the Boxer
            Rebellion and the siege of Peking.
        Preliminary inventory.
        May not be quoted without permission of Helen Stote.
        Gift, H. Stote, 1973.

Letters describe poor condition of children in China. Issue
of Presbyterian Banner, with sections on religious
education, April 11, 1901.

270. INNIS, HAROLD ADAMS, 1894- .
Memoir, 1946. "Ottawa to Moscow." 1 volume.
Typescript.
Canadian delegate to the 220th anniversary celebration of the
founding of the Akademiia Nauk SSSR, Moscow, 1946.

Relates to the visit of Western scholars to the celebration.

Includes names of American and English delegations.

271. INSTITUT ZUR STUDIUM DER JUDENFRAGE, COLLECTOR.
Propaganda (in German), 1883-1939. 1 ms. box.
German anti-Semitic propaganda, including clippings, leaflets,
and posters.

272. INSTITUTE OF CURRENT WORLD AFFAIRS.
Memorandum, 1926. 1 folder.
Typescript.
Relates to aims and organization of an Institute of Current
World Affairs for the study of international relations.

Includes academic regulations of the Institute.

273. INSTITUTE OF PACIFIC RELATIONS. AMERICAN COUNCIL.
Records, 1925-1960. 21 ms. boxes, 1 album, 1 envelope.
Correspondence, reports, memoranda, study papers, press
releases, printed matter, and photographs, relating to the
study of political, social, and economic conditions in the
Far East and of U.S. foreign policy in the Far East by the
American Council of the Institute of Pacific Relations.
From the papers of Ray Lyman Wilbur, president of the
American Council of the Institute of Pacific Relations.
Register.
Gift. R. L. Wilbur.

Box 18 -- Publications and study materials on effects of
Sino-Japanese conflict on American educational and
philanthropic enterprises in China.

Box 19 -- Outline of course in Pacific relations for secondary schools.

Box 20 -- Brief summary of report on status of Far East in curricula of schools and colleges in U.S.; summary of legislation concerning public control of private schools and teaching of religion in public schools in U.S.

274. INSTITUTE OF PACIFIC RELATIONS. SAN FRANCISCO BAY REGION DIVISION.
Records, 1944-1947. 26 ms. boxes, 1 card file (1/6 linear foot).
Private organization for the study of the Far East and of U.S. foreign policy in the Far East.
Correspondence, reports, memoranda, studies, and printed matter, relating to the study of political, social, and economic conditions in the Far East and of U.S. foreign policy in the Far East.
Register.
Gift, Mrs. Frank Gerbode, 1955.

Box 14 -- Pamphlets, correspondence, and reports on activities of American Association of University Women.
Box 22 -- Notes, correspondence, and reports on the Far East Teachers' Seminar.
Box 25 -- Notes, correspondence, and reports relating to Teachers' Seminar on Reconstruction in Asia.

275. INTER-AMERICAN CONFERENCE, 6th, HAVANA, 1928.
Records, 1928. 1-1/2 ms. boxes.
Sixth International Conference of American States.
Reports, memoranda, correspondence, reprints, and clippings, relating to economic, social, legal, educational, scientific, and cultural aspects of Pan-American cooperation and to U.S. foreign policy in Latin America.

Box 1 -- Reports of Committee on Intellectual Cooperation, with sections on education.

276. INTERNATIONAL COUNCIL FOR EDUCATIONAL DEVELOPMENT.
Records, 1969-1980. 421 ms. boxes.
American institution for the international promotion of education.
Reports, studies, conference papers, minutes, correspondence, memoranda, pamphlets, health, and family planning in underdeveloped countries.
Gift, Philip H. Coombs, December 1980.

Contents are in different languages.

Collection assembled by Philip Coombs, Director of
   International Council for Educational Development,
   1963-1968.

Boxes 22 and 23 -- Pamphlets and reports on formal and
   nonformal education in Afghanistan.
Boxes 24-26 -- Bulletins, reports, and articles on formal and
   nonformal education in Africa.
Boxes 27-30, 51, 210-212, 214, 215, 218, 224, 329-333, and
   339 -- Newspaper clippings, reports, and leaflets on
   international education.
Boxes 31-43 -- Pamphlets, booklets, reports, notes, corre-
   spondence, and questionnaires relating to formal and
   nonformal education in Bangladesh.
Boxes 44 and 45 -- Pamphlets, booklets, and reports on formal
   and nonformal education in Brazil.
Boxes 46 and 47 -- Reports and pamphlets on education in
   Cameroon.
Box 48 -- Pamphlets, periodicals, and reports on education in
   China.
Box 49 -- Articles, reports, and pamphlet on education in
   Cuba.
Box 52 -- Pamphlets and reports on instructional television
   and educational reform in El Salvador.
Boxes 53-57 -- Reports and pamphlets on formal and nonformal
   education in Ethiopia.
Boxes 58 and 59 -- Reports and pamphlets on education in
   Ghana.
Box 60 -- Reports on education in Guatemala.
Box 61 -- Reports on education in Honduras.
Boxes 62-71 and 265 -- Correspondence, notes, pamphlets,
   brochures, leaflets, booklets, reports, periodicals, and
   articles on formal and nonformal education in India.
Boxes 72-84, 157-165, 172-175, 186, 193, 194, 228, 253, and
   356 -- Reports, pamphlets, booklets, notes, articles,
   newsletters, and memoranda on different aspects of
   education.
Box 85 -- Reports, booklets, pamphlets, and articles on formal
   and nonformal education in Iran.
Box 86 -- Reports and pamphlets on education and educational
   reform in Ivory Coast.
Boxes 87 and 88 -- Reports and notes on Jamaican education.
Boxes 89-93 -- Reports, pamphlets, booklets, and journal on
   formal and nonformal education in Kenya.
Boxes 94-100 -- Booklets, pamphlets, reports, periodicals,
   leaflets, notes, and newspaper clippings on education in
   South Korea.
Box 101 -- Pamphlets, booklets, and reports on education in
   Latin America.

Boxes 102 and 103 -- Reports, pamphlets, booklets, notes, and guidebooks on education in Malawi.

Boxes 104 and 105 -- Books and reports on education and youth in Malaysia.

Boxes 106 and 107 -- Reports, pamphlets, and periodicals on education in Mali.

Box 108 -- Reports on education in Mauritius.

Boxes 109 and 110 -- Reports and notes on education in Mexico.

Box 111 -- Reports and pamphlet on education and literacy in the Middle East.

Boxes 112 and 113 -- Reports and pamphlets on education in Nigeria.

Boxes 114 and 115 -- Reports on education and training in Pakistan.

Boxes 116-125 -- Reports, booklets, periodicals, books, pamphlets, leaflets, and correspondence on education and literacy in the Philippines.

Boxes 126 and 127 -- Reports on education in Senegal.

Boxes 128-130 -- Reports, pamphlets, periodicals, and notes on education and youth in Sri Lanka.

Boxes 131-138 -- Reports, pamphlets, booklets, and notes on education in Tanzania.

Boxes 139 and 140 -- Reports, pamphlets, newspaper clippings, periodicals, and books on Kenya and Tanzania.

Boxes 141-149 -- Pamphlets, reports, booklets, notes, and newsletters on formal and nonformal education in Thailand.

Box 150 -- Pamphlets and reports on education in Uganda.

Boxes 151 and 152 -- Reports, pamphlets, and notes on education in Upper Volta.

Box 153 -- Periodicals and reports on education in Venezuela.

Box 154 -- Reports on education in Western Europe.

Boxes 202-205, 220-222, and 249 -- Books, booklets, reports, pamphlets, periodicals, memoranda, and notes on youth.

Boxes 207, 313, and 314 -- Reports, pamphlets, and newsletters on formal and nonformal education in Asia.

Boxes 213, 217, 229-231, 234-237, 241, 242, 276, 282-286, 303, 307, 315, 340, 341, and 355 -- Reports, bulletins, pamphlets, booklets, and newsletters relating to educational organizations and their activities.

277. INTERNATIONAL POLITICAL SCIENCE ASSOCIATION. 5th WORLD CONGRESS, PARIS, 1961.
Conference papers (in English and French), 1961.
1 ms. box.
Typescript (mimeographed).
Relates to political behavior and to political problems regarding civil-military relations, technocracy, nuclear administration, and poly-ethnic states.

Includes the following papers: "Child's Political World" and
    "Technology and the Role of Experts in Government in
    Israel," with section on education and schools.

278. INTERNATIONAL SOCIALISTS.
    Issuances, 1967-1976. 5 ms. boxes.
    American socialist organization.
    Internal resolutions, reports, and discussion material,
        relating to socialist political activity in the U.S.
    Preliminary inventory.

    Box 1 -- Issues of Forum, with sections on schools and higher
        education.
    Box 4 -- Notes on high school caucus.

279. INTERNATIONAL UNION OF STUDENTS.
    Posters, n.d. 1 oversize box (1 linear foot).
    Propagates left-wing and revolutionary causes throughout the
        world, particularly in Latin America, Africa, and Asia.

280. IRVINE, DALLAS D.
    Memorandum, 1939. "An American Military Institute."
        1 folder.
    Typescript (mimeographed).
    Relates to the founding of the American Military Institute to
        promote the study of American military history.

    Memorandum describes purpose of establishing Institute as
        educational, literary, and patriotic.

281. IRWIN, WILLIAM HENRY, 1873-1948.
    Papers, 1890-1942. 6 ms. boxes, 2 vols.
    American journalist and author.
    Correspondence, writings, and printed matter, relating to
        Herbert Hoover and political and social conditions in the
        U.S. Includes drafts of fictional and other writings by
        W. H. Irwin, and correspondence with Herbert Hoover.
    Register.
    Gifts, Inez Haynes Irwin, 1948, and William Hyde Irwin, 1965.

    Box 1 -- Articles on adolescents and child health.
    Box 2 -- Book on youth.
    Box 5 -- Book on propaganda and news.

282. ITALY - PROPAGANDA.
    1917-1918. 1 folder.
    Italian propaganda leaflets, pamphlets, and newspaper issues,
        directed at Czechs, Poles, Hungarians, Romanians, and
        Croats in the Austro-Hungarian Army during World War I.
    Preliminary inventory.
    Gift, Alfred Lane, 1958.

283. JACKSON, FLORENCE, COLLECTOR.
    Miscellany, 1925-1919. 1/2 ms. box.
    Clippings, leaflets, and miscellanea, mostly relating to
        relief work in World War I.
    Gift, F. Jackson, 1934.

    Notes and newspaper clippings relating to Smith College Relief
        Unit and article about assistance of American women to
        French women and their children.

284. JACOBS, JOSEPH EARLE, 1893-1971.
    Papers, 1925-1951. 1-1/2 ms. boxes.
    American diplomat; Political Adviser to the U.S. Commanding
        General in Korea, 1947-1948; Ambassador to Czechoslovakia,
        1948-1949; Ambassador to Poland, 1955-1957.
    Writings, correspondence, reports, and printed matter,
        relating to reconstruction in Korea after World War II, the
        Italian communist movement, the Philippine independence
        movement, and the Shanghai riot of May 30, 1925.
    Preliminary inventory.
    Gift, J. E. Jacobs, 1969.

    Box 1, Folder C -- Typewritten article entitled "What Is a
        Korean National Youth?"

285. JACOBS-PAUWELS, F. MARGUERITE.
    Papers (in French), 1914-1964. 11 ms. boxes, 1 cubic foot
        box, 2 binders.
    Director, Foyer des Orphelins (Orphanage), Charleroi, Belgium,
        1914-1923.
    Correspondence, reports, financial records, and photographs,
        relating to relief in Belgium during World War I and to the
        operations of the Foyer des Orphelins during and after the
        war.
    Gift, F. M. Jacobs-Pauwels, 1965.

286. JELINEK, JAMES JOHN, 1915- .
    Speeches and writings, 1948-1979. 19 ms. boxes.

American educator.
Published writings and sound recordings of lectures, relating
    to education.
Gift, J. J. Jelinek, 1980.

Box 11 -- Handbook of standard terminology for curriculum and
    instruction in local and state school systems and newspaper
    clippings relating to education.
Boxes 12-19 -- Articles, reports, pamphlets, newspaper
    clippings, and handwritten notes on different aspects of
    education.

287. JENKINS, GEORGE D.
        Papers, 1903-1969. 24 ms. boxes, 1 box of data cards
            (1/3 linear foot), 23 microfilm reels.
        American political scientist.
        Writings, notes, correspondence, minutes of meetings,
            ordinances, pamphlets, clippings, and data cards, relating
            to politics in Nigeria and particularly to the government
            of Ibadan, Nigeria. Includes drafts of a book, The Price
            of Liberty by Kenneth W. J. Post and G. D. Jenkins.
        Preliminary inventory.
        Obisesan diaries may not be used without permission of
            G. D. Jenkins.
        Deposit, G. D. Jenkins, 1969.

        Box 12 -- Newspaper clippings, notes, pamphlets, and reports
            on education in Nigeria.

288. JENNY, ARNOLD E., 1895-1978.
        Papers, 1917-1953. 4-1/2 ms. boxes, 2 envelopes.
        Young Men's Christian Association worker in Siberia,
            1919-1920, and in Germany, 1945-1946.
        Correspondence, diary, reports, memoranda, and printed matter,
            relating to relief work in Siberia during the Russian
            Revolution and among displaced persons in Germany at the
            end of World War II.
        Register.
        Gift, A. E. Jenny, 1973.

        Box 1 -- L'Ecole Superieure de Guerre, alumni bulletins, with
            sections on school activities and students, 1965.
        Box 2 -- Report by United States Military Academy, 1972.
        Box 3 -- Biography entitled "All In a Lifetime," with section
            on education in those days.
        Box 4 -- Folder on war and peace with issue of The World
            Tomorrow, with article on students and national defense,
            October 1926.

289. JOB, MARTHA.
        Papers, 1920-1941. 1/2 ms. box, 3 envelopes.
        Young Women's Christian Association worker in China,
            1919-1929.
        Diary, maps, posters, photographs, clippings, and booklets,
            relating to the Young Women's Christian Associations in
            China, flood relief, the University of Peking, and internal
            problems in China from 1920 to 1928.
        Gift, M. Job, 1974.

        Writings on women students in China in 1926, as seen by YWCA
            secretary Eleanor MacNeil, and writings on students' social
            problems.

290. JONES, HARDIN B., 1914-1978.
        Papers, 1964-1972. Ca. 75 ms. boxes.
        Professor of Medical Physics and Physiology, University of
            California, Berkeley.
        Correspondence, reports, minutes of meetings, clippings,
            leaflets, pamphlets, and other materials concerning campus
            unrest, particularly at the University of California,
            Berkeley, and the reaction to it by university adminis-
            trators and faculty.
        Restricted until processed.

        Boxes 3, 9, and 68 -- Notes, newspaper clippings, articles,
            reports, pamphlets, and leaflets on campus unrest.
        Boxes 5, 11, 12, 19, 20, 23, 26, 57, 66, 72, and 75 --
            Articles, reports, pamphlets, memoranda, minutes of
            meetings, notes, correspondence, and leaflets on student
            activism, education, draft opposition, and professors at
            the University of California.
        Box 13 -- Article on turmoil in higher education.
        Boxes 22, 27, 28, 31-33, 35, 37, 52, 58, and 72 -- Newspaper
            clippings, minutes of meetings, reports, pamphlets,
            articles. Notes on student unions, student mobilization,
            student protest, student unrest, and student governance.
        Box 34 -- Article on liberal education.
        Box 36 -- Newspaper clippings and notes on educational reform.
        Boxes 41 and 42 -- Newspaper clippings relating to Stanford
            University and its students.
        Box 50 -- Newspaper clippings, articles, notes, and pamphlets
            on graduate students at Harvard University.
        Box 67 -- Newspaper clippings on University of California
            campus, U.S. and foreign universities.
        Box 74 -- Newspaper clippings on "The Richmond Schools."

291. JONES, HOWARD PALFREY, 1899-1973.
   Papers, 1934-1973. 98 ms. boxes, 2 card file boxes
      (1/3 linear foot), 12 phonotapes, 5 envelopes, 1 motion
      picture.
   Director, Berlin Element for U.S. High Commissioner for
      Germany, 1950-1951; Chief of Mission, U.S. Economic Aid
      Mission to Indonesia, 1954-1955; U.S. Deputy Assistant
      Secretary of State for the Far East, 1955-1958; U.S.
      Ambassador to Indonesia, 1958-1965.
   Writings, correspondence, reports, research files, studies,
      and printed matter, relating to public finance and postwar
      reconstruction in Germany, 1945-1951, and to U.S. foreign
      relations with Indonesia and other areas of East Asia.
   Register.
   Gift, Mrs. H. P. Jones, 1974.

   Box 22 -- Text of speech entitled "Education for Tomorrow in
      Asia and the Pacific," September 1966.
   Box 45 -- Note on Professor Paul R. Hanna's contributions to
      education in U.S. and the world.
   Box 49 -- Text of speech on youth and the world's future,
      January 1970.
   Box 54 - Article on adult education in Mainland China.
   Box 56 - Articles on education and social values; several
      reports and articles on education in Thailand.
   Boxes 62 and 64 -- Reports, articles, newspaper clippings, and
      notes on education in Indonesia.
   Boxes 70 and 74 -- Notes and bulletin on student unrest in
      Indonesia and the Indonesian Students Association in the
      United States.
   Box 75 -- Leaflets, articles, and reports on international
      education.
   Box 76 -- Memorandum on communist strategy in Japan, with
      sections on youth and student movement.
   Box 80 -- Proposal on peace and peace education.
   Box 90 -- Reports, newspaper clippings, and memorandum on
      U.S.-Japan cultural and educational cooperation and
      American Peace Corps.

292. JORDAN, DAVID STARR, 1851-1931.
   Papers, 1814-1947. 77 ms. boxes, 4 envelopes, 5 scrapbooks,
      8 posters.
   American educator and pacifist; President, Stanford
      University, 1891-1913; Chancellor, Stanford University,
      1913-1916.
   Correspondence, writings, pamphlets, leaflets, clippings, and
      photographs, relating to pacifism and the movement for
      world peace, disarmament, international relations, U.S.
      neutrality in World War I, U.S. foreign and domestic

policy, civil liberties in the U.S., problems of minorities
in the U.S., and personal and family matters.
Register.
Boxes 70-77 are closed until processed.
Gift, Jessie Knight Jordan.

Boxes 44, 49, and 50 -- Articles, newspaper clippings, and
notes on peace and education for peace.
Box 51 -- Newspaper clippings on youth adventure.
Box 53 -- Article on the teacher and war.
Boxes 59 and 67 -- Notes, booklets, pamphlets, articles, and
newspaper clippings relating to Cornell and Stanford
universities and their students.
Box 60 - Newspaper clippings on Boy Scouts; articles on
education for promotions of world peace.

293. JUENGER, ERNST, 1895- .
Essay (in German), 1944. "Der Friede: Ein Wort an die Jugend
Europas, Ein Wort an die Jugend der Welt" (Peace: A Word to
the Youth of Europe, A Word to the Youth of the World).
1 volume.
Typescript.
Relates to post-World War II reconstruction.

294. JUNGSOZIALISTEN.
Issuances (in German), 1972-1973. 1 ms. box.
Youth organization of the Sozialdemokratische Partei
Deutschlands.
Press releases, bulletins, position papers, resolutions, and
periodicals, relating to socialist youth movements in West
Germany, especially to the 1973 Jungsozialisten national
congress.
Gift, Ralph Mendenhausen, 1979.

Newsletters and reports on youth activities.

295. KARCZ, GEORGE F., 1917-1970.
Papers, 1917-1970. 37 ms. boxes, 4 card files boxes
(2/3 linear foot), 1 phonotape.
American agricultural economist; professor, University of
California, Santa Barbara.
Correspondence, writings, research notes, statistical surveys
and reports, and miscellanea, relating to Soviet and East
European agriculture and economics.
Register.
Purchase, Irene Karcz, 1971.

Box 1 -- Bulletin of American Association of Teachers of
    Slavic and Eastern Languages, September 15, 1951.
Box 10 -- Reports on graduate study in Soviet Union, August
    1960.
Box 15 -- Article on student morality.
Box 29 -- Report by CIA on school enrollment in USSR,
    1950-1975.

296. KARSKI, JAN, 1914-   .
    Papers (in Polish), 1939-1944. 7 ms. boxes, 24 envelopes,
        27 microfilm reels.
    Liaison officer and courier of the Polish Government-in-Exile
        (London) to the Polish underground, 1939-1943; author,
        Story of a Secret State (1944).
    Correspondence, memoranda, government and military documents,
        bulletins, reports, studies, speeches and writings, printed
        matter, photographs, clippings, newspapers, periodicals,
        and microfilms, relating to events and conditions in Poland
        during World War II, the German and Soviet occupations of
        Poland, treatment of the Jews in Poland during the German
        occupation, and operations of the Polish underground
        movement during World War II.
    Preliminary inventory.
    Gift, J. Karski, 1946.

    Box 5 -- Two issues of Youth Magazine, with articles in both
        Polish and English.
    Box 7 -- Statistical atlas of Poland.

297. KATZ, FRIEDRICH, COLLECTOR.
    Collection on world affairs (in German), 1919-1945.
        173 pamphlet boxes (43 linear feet).
    Clippings, notes, and pamphlets, relating to international
        relations, international economic conditions, the oil
        industry, domestic conditions in Croatia, Croatia's role in
        international relations, the history and condition of Jews
        throughout the world, and military operations during World
        War II.
    Preliminary inventory.

    Most of the contents relate to youths, education, and social
        conditions in different countries of the world.

298. KEFAUVER, GRAYSON NEIKIRK, 1900-1946.
    Papers, 1943-1946. 38 ms. boxes.
    American educator; U.S. representative to Preparatory
        Commission for establishing the United Nations Educational,

99

Scientific and Cultural Organization.
Correspondence, reports, memoranda, speeches and writings,
minutes, and printed matter, relating to international
educational reconstruction after World War II and the
United Nations Educational, Scientific and Cultural
Organization.
Gift, G. N. Kefauver, 1947.

Boxes 2-6, 8, 10, 11, 16, and 36 -- Reports, correspondence,
and notes on international education.
Boxes 7, 12, 14, 15, 18-22, 27-31, 34, and 35 -- Correspon-
dence, memoranda, articles, and press releases relating to
UNESCO.
Boxes 9, 17, 23-26, 37, and 38 -- Correspondence, reports,
booklets, leaflets, texts of speeches, articles, and notes
on education and educational organizations in U.S.
Boxes 32 and 33 -- Printed matter relating to the Catholic
Educational Association and religious education.

299. KELLOGG, VERNON LYMAN, 1867-1937.
    Papers, 1914-1921. 1-1/2 ms. boxes, 1 oversize certificate.
    American zoologist; officer in relief organizations in Europe
        during World War I. Writings, printed matter, photographs,
        drawings, and certificates, relating to relief work in
        Belgium during World War I, the relief activities of
        Herbert Hoover, and the world food problem.
    Gift, Charlotte Hoffman Kellogg, 1956.

    Box 1 -- Typewritten notes on children of Warsaw by Vernon
        Kellogg. Folder no. 10 includes illustrated article on
        universities' part in war.

300. KERR, GEORGE H., 1911- .
    Papers, 1943-1951. 7 ms. boxes.
    American historian; Vice-Consul, Taipei, Formosa, 1945-1947.
    Reports, notes, press summaries, clippings, and writings,
        relating to political and economic conditions in Formosa
        under Japanese rule, transferral of Formosa's sovereignty
        to China in 1945, Formosan rebellion against Chinese rule
        in 1947, U.S. foreign policy toward Formosa, and political
        and ecomonic conditions in Okinawa and the Ryukyus after
        World War II.
    Gift, G. H. Kerr.

    Box 1 -- Chart on Japanese education in Japanese, 1937.
    Box 2 -- Handwritten notes on education in Taiwan.

301. KERR, MARGARET ANN.
        Papers, 1918-1963. 1-1/2 ms. boxes.
        Secretary-Manager, Better America Federation of California.
        Reports, speeches, letters, membership lists, bulletins,
            minutes, printed matter, and miscellany, relating to com-
            munist and other radical movements in California and to the
            Better America Federation, an anticommunist organization.
        Gift, Ann Speth, Mary Evans, and David Burton, 1980.

        Box 1 -- First- and second-grade Russian textbooks, 1935.
        Box 2 -- Correspondence of American Women, Inc., relating to
            preservation of American home, school, church, and state.

302. KEY, KERIM KAMI.
        Dissertation, 1950. "The Ottoman Intellectuals and the Young
            Turk Reformation of 1908." 1 folder.
        Typescript.
        Relates to the role of intellectuals in the Young Turk move-
            ment and the resurgence of Turkish nationalism.

        Sections on Islamic culture and education and the influence of
            Islam in Turkey.

303. KILPATRICK, WYLIE, 1896-1965.
        Writings, 1922-1965. 10 ms. boxes.
        American economist; Social Science Analyst, U.S. Bureau of the
            Census, 1940-1947; Executive Director, Florida Citizens Tax
            Council, 1956-1957.
        Reports, studies, articles, and books, relating to finances of
            state and local governments in the U.S., especially
            Florida.
        Gift, Mary H. Kilpatrick, 1980.

        Box 2 -- Manuscript of book on higher education in Florida.
        Box 7 -- Report on state and local government finance in
            Florida, with sections on financing of public education.

304. KIRBY, GUSTAVUS T.
        Papers, 1914-1941. 2 ms. boxes.
        Member, Executive Committee, Friends of Belgium.
        Reports, correspondence, clippings, map, and card file,
            relating to relief in Belgium during World Wars I and II,
            exchange of Belgian and American Fellows through the C.R.B.
            Educational Foundation, and charitable and goodwill efforts
            of the Friends of Belgium.
        Preliminary inventory.
        Gift, Mrs. Thomas M. Waller, 1956.

305. KITAGAWA, KAY I., <u>COLLECTOR</u>.
    Collection on the Japanese Army, 1943-1944. 2 ms. boxes,
        2 swords, 1 rifle, 1 bayonet.
    Military manuals, syllabi, and exercises, used by the U.S.
        Military Intelligence Service Language School at Camp
        Savage, Minnesota, relating to the organization of the
        Japanese Army and to the study of the Japanese language.
        Includes four Japanese weapons.
    Preliminary inventory.
    Gift, K. I. Kitagawa.

    Box 1 -- Testing materials, notes, and syllabi relating to
        Japanese language.
    Box 2 -- HEIGO textbooks in English and Japanese.

306. KITTREDGE, TRACY BARRETT, 1891-1957.
    Papers, 1910-1957. 51 ms. boxes, 6 envelopes.
    Captain, U.S. Navy; member, Commission for Relief in Belgium,
        1914-1917.
    Correspondence, reports, writings, notes, and clippings,
        relating to the Commission for Relief in Belgium,
        1914-1924; Paris Peace Conference, 1919; controversy
        between Admiral W. S. Sims and Navy Secretary Josephus
        Daniels, 1919-1920; League of Red Cross Societies,
        1920-1931; and U.S. Navy in World War II.
    Preliminary inventory.
    Gift, Eleanor H. Kittredge, 1960.

    Box 7 -- Several issues of <u>California Alumni Fortnightly</u>, with
        sections on education and students, 1920.

307. KNOWLTON, LUCERNE H.
    Papers, 1922-1953. 1/2 ms. box, 1 envelope.
    American missionary in China.
    Letters, typewritten history, and printed matter, relating to
        missionary work in China, including reports of Hwa Nan
        College, newsletter from Foochow, and reports on Methodist
        Women's Work Conferences at Foochow.

    Typewritten report entitled "One Hundred Years of Methodism in
        China."

308. KOCH, HOWARD, JR.
    Study, 1973. "Permanent War: A Reappraisal of the Arab-
        Israeli Conflict, 1948-1967." 1 folder.
    Typescript.
    Gift, H. Koch, Jr., 1973.

Study was undertaken immediately after June 1967 war between
Egypt and Israel. Includes information on customs,
culture, and education in the Arab world.

309. KOENIGS, FOLKMAR, 1916- , COLLECTOR.
(In German), 1967-1979. 3 ms. boxes.
Flyers, leaflets, and serial issues, distributed at the
Technishche Universitaet Berlin, issued by a variety of
student groups, mostly radical, relating to West German and
world politics and West German universities.
Purchase, F. Koenigs, 1980.

310. KOHLBERG, ALFRED, 1887-1960.
Papers, 1937-1960. 224 ms. boxes.
American business executive; National Chairman, American
Jewish League Against Communism; Chairman, American China
Policy Association; and member of the board, Institute of
Pacific Relations.
Correspondence, newsletters, clippings, and printed matter,
relating to communist influence in the U.S., China, and
other parts of Asia and to anticommunist movements in the
U.S.
Preliminary inventory.
Closed until May 1, 1991.
Gift, Ida Jolles Kohlberg, 1961.

Boxes 24, 36, 77, 97, 162, and 170 -- Correspondence, reports,
articles, notes, leaflets, and newspaper clippings relating
to American universities and their academic activities.
Boxes 33, 211, and 217 -- Correspondence, articles, reports,
newspaper clippings, and notes on education in China.
Boxes 34, 42, 65, and 130 -- Correspondence, newsletters,
newspaper clippings, notes, reports, and leaflets relating
to educational organizations.
Boxes 52 and 160 -- Newsletters, notes, leaflets, and reports
relating to Sons and Daughters of the American Revolution.
Box 59 -- Reports, newspaper clippings, and lettergrams on
communist influence and education.
Box 145 -- Reports and newspaper clipping on propaganda.
Box 169 -- Correspondence, reports, newspaper clippings, and
notes, relating to Taiwan University.
Box 190 -- Reports, notes, correspondence, and newspaper
clippings relating to UNESCO.
Boxes 191 and 192 -- Reports and correspondence relating to
the United States National Student Association.
Box 209 -- Newspaper clippings and articles on education in
Burma.

Box 214 -- Newspaper clippings and reports on education in
    Japan and Korea.
Box 218 -- Newspaper clippings, reports, and pamphlets on
    education in Middle Eastern countries.

311. KRAMER, HOWARD D.
    Papers, 1942-1957. 2 ms. boxes.
    Acting Chief, U.S. Office of War Information Psychological
        Warfare Branch in the Southwest Pacific, 1945; Acting
        Chief, U.S. Information Service in the Philippines,
        1945-1946.
    Transcripts of radio broadcasts, posters, leaflets,
        correspondence, printed matter, and photographs, 1942-1957,
        relating to U.S. and Japanese propaganda activities in the
        Philippines during World War II. Includes a photocopy of
        the Ph.D. dissertation of H. D. Kramer, "History of the
        Public Health Movement in the U.S., 1850-1900."
    Gift, Mrs. H. D. Kramer, 1976.

    Pamphlet entitled "Education for One World," with reports on
        foreign students in the United States, 1953-1954.

312. KRAMER, JACK.
    Papers, 1968-1969. 1 ms. box.
    American journalist in Eritrea.
    Correspondence, writings, printed matter, photographs, and a
        tape recording, relating to the Eritrean Liberation Front
        and the movement for Eritrean independence.

    Text of Constitution of Eritrea, with sections on education
        and welfare, July 1952.
    Memorandum submitted to U.N. Secretary General in 1962 by the
        Eritrean University Student Union in Western Europe.

313. KRUPENSKII, ALEKSANDR NIKOLAEVICH.
    Papers (in Russian, French, and Romanian), 1918-1935.
        9 ms. boxes.
    Marshal of Bessarabian Nobility; President, Bessarabian
        Provincial Zemstvo; Bessarabian delegate to the Paris Peace
        Conference, 1919-1920.
    Correspondence, memoranda, lists, extracts, summaries,
        reports, appeals, protests, protocols, press analyses,
        maps, forms, notes, drafts, clippings, newspaper issues,
        journals, bulletins, and pamphlets, 1918-1935, relating to

104

the Bessarabian question, to relations between Russia,
Romania, and Bessarabia, to the occupation and annexation
of Bessarabia by Romania, 1918, and to the Paris Peace
Conference.

Box 2 -- Correspondence and note on education and students.
Box 3 -- Articles on schools.

314. KWIATKOWSKI, ANTONI WINCENTY, 1890-1970.
        Papers (mainly in Polish and Russian), 1917-1969.
          45 ms. boxes, 1 album, 4 envelopes.
        Polish scholar.
        Writings, correspondence, reports, memoranda, research and
          reference notes, clippings, and photographs, relating to
          Marxism-Leninism, dialectical and historical materialism,
          communism and religion, and the Communist International.
          Includes an autobiography and biography.
        Register.
        Gift, Annemarie Buschman-Brandes, 1971.

        Box 11 -- Research notes and newspaper clippings on
          progaganda.
        Boxes 13 and 14 -- Reports and notes relating to psychology,
          logic, philosophy, Marxism, and Leninism.
        Box 16 -- Reports and notes dealing with Marxism and Leninism
          in higher education.
        Box 18 -- Notes and newspaper clippings relating to teachings
          of Lenin, Stalin, and Khrushchev on peaceful coexistence.

315. LARSEN, E. S. COLLECTOR.
        Collection on the Far East, 1942-1951. 11 ms. boxes.
        Clippings, reports, and pamphlets, relating to political
          events in the Far East.
        Preliminary inventory.

        Boxes 3 and 4 -- Newspaper clippings, leaflets, reports, and
          pamphlets on culture and education in India.
        Box 6 -- Newsletters, journals, newspaper clippings, and
          reports on education in Indonesia.

316. LASERSON, MAURICE, 1880- .
        Papers (in English, French, German, and Russian), 1920-1949.
          1-1/2 ms. boxes, 1 envelope.
        Russian finance, commerce, and law expert.
        Correspondence, writings, reports, government documents,
          printed matter, and photographs, relating to life in Russia
          prior to the 1917 Revolution, the persecution of Jews in

Russia and their emigration to Germany, 1904-1906, Soviet
financial and commercial policy, 1918-1925, the purchase of
600 locomotives by the Soviet Government from Sweden, 1920,
and the German socialist Karl Liebknecht.
Gift, M. Laserson, 1948.

Box 1, Green folder -- Reminiscences of Karl Liebknecht by
Dr. Laserson describing persecution of Jewish students and
restrictions on their admission into Russian universities.

317. LATVIAN REFUGEE SCHOOL CERTIFICATES
(In Latvian and English), 1945-1947.
Printed and handwritten. 1 folder.
Certificates of completion of elementary school by students in
Latvian refugee schools in Germany.

Each certificate includes subject matters and grades
and each certificate is signed by people responsible for
education of the children.

318. LAU, KENNETH, COLLECTOR.
Propaganda (in Chinese), 1947. 1 folder.
Nationalist Chinese propaganda distributed at student
demonstration in Peking.

Slogans were used in student demonstration by pro-Nationalist
government factions in Peiping, China,
March 14, 1947.

319. LAUNAY, JACQUES de, 1924- .
Papers (in French), 1914-1960. 5-1/2 ms. boxes,
4 phonotapes.
Belgian historian.
Correspondence, writings, taped interviews, printed matter,
and clippings, relating to Romania and Belgium during World
War II; the Little Entente; the relationship between Adolf
Hitler and Lord Rothermere, 1933-1939; the Walloon Legion,
1941-1945; and education in Europe. Includes sound
recordings of interviews by J. de Launay with General T.
Bor-Komorowski, 1960; A. Francois-Poncet, 1958; G. Bonnet,
1957; and J. Moch, 1959.
Register.
Purchase, J. de Launay, 1975. Incremental purchase, 1978.

Box 1 -- Notes and reports on future of professional education and youth in Europe, 1959.
Box 4 -- Booklet on Catholic universities of Europe.
Boxes 5 and 6 -- Reports, newsletters, and periodicals on European and world youth.

320. LA VARRE, WILLIAM, 1898- .
Papers, 1957-1978. Ca. 12 ms. boxes.
American author and journalist; Chief, American Republics Unit, U.S. Department of Commerce, 1941-1943; editor-in-chief, American Mercury, 1957-1958.
Memoirs, letters, memoranda, clippings, periodical issues, lists, notes, and financial records, relating to political development in Latin America, especially in the 1930s; U.S. relations with Latin America, 1933-1945; American Mercury; international communist subversion; and international affairs.
Memoirs on American Mercury closed until January 1984.
Gift, W. LaVarre, 1977. Subsequent increments.

Box 1 -- Article from Harvard Magazine entitled "He Wanted to Be a Professor," November 1920.
Boxes 7-11 -- Issues of American Mercury with articles on education, teachers, peace, and youth.

321. LAWRENCE, JOHN HUNDALE, 1904- .
Papers, 1965-1979. 2-1/2 ms. boxes.
American physician; Director, Donner Laboratory, University of California, Berkeley; Regent, University of California.
Correspondence, writings, minutes of meetings, memoranda, reports, and printed matter, relating to administration of and student radicalism at the University of California and to American medical aid to South Vietnam.
Gift, J. H. Lawrence, 1980.

Box 2 -- Correspondence and notes on student participation in department meetings and the University of California crisis, 1964.

322. LEAGUE OF RED CROSS SOCIETIES.
Miscellaneous records, 1919-1922. 1-1/2 ms. boxes.
International relief organization.
Correspondence, telegrams, reports, and minutes of meetings, relating to the founding of the League of Red Cross Societies and to relief operations in Europe.
Preliminary inventory.
Gift, American National Red Cross, 1928.

Box 1 -- Reports on child health fund.

Box 2 -- Red Cross information circulars and newsletters on founding of ARC Museum and Library in Washington and child welfare.

323. LEFEVER, ERNEST WARREN, 1919- .
Papers, 1956-1969. 26 ms. boxes, 1 album, 2 envelopes.
American political scientist; Senior Fellow, Brookings Institution.
Writings, correspondence, reports, interviews, notes, pamphlets, newspaper clippings, and printed matter, relating to political conditions in Zaire, Ethiopia, and other African nations.
Register.
Gift, E. W. Lefever, 1973.

Box 1 -- Pamphlets, notes, and newspaper clipping on education and teaching profession in Congo, 1958.

Box 4 -- Pamphlets, correspondence, and newspaper clippings relating to International Police Academy.

Box 17 -- Newspaper clippings, correspondence, and reports on education for peace; newspaper clipping on education for foreign policy.

Boxes 23 and 25 -- Correspondence, notes, and articles on National Student Council of YMCA-YWCA and social education.

324. LEMARCHAND, RENE.
Papers (in French and English), 1920-1972. 3 ms. boxes.
Director, African Studies Center, University of Florida.
Government reports, ephemeral publications, interviews, correspondence, notes, and printed matter, relating to the political development of Zaire, Burundi, and Rwanda.
Register.
Purchase, R. Lemarchand, 1972.

Box 3 -- Contains typescript of book entitled "The African Monarchies," with sections on education in the countries mentioned above.

325. LERNER, DANIEL, COLLECTOR.
Collection on World War II Allied and German propaganda (in English and German), 1943-1949. 71 ms. boxes.
Reports, correspondence, pamphlets, leaflets, and radio transcripts, relating to Allied propaganda in Europe during

World War II, analysis of German propaganda, evaluation of
wartime German morale, and German public opinion during the
postwar Allied occupation. Includes reports of interro-
gations of German prisoners of war.
Gift, D. Lerner, 1946. Subsequent increments.

Box 27 -- Guide to Allied Military Government in Liguria
    Region, with section on education.
Box 65 -- Pamphlet entitled "Germania," with information on
    education, public welfare, and cultural institutions, no.1,
    March 1945.
Boxes 66 and 68 -- Civil affairs information handbooks on
    Japan, Italy, and Germany, with sections on education.
Box 70 -- Guidebook for regional officers of Piedmonte Region,
    with section on education.

326. LETTRICH, JOSEPH, 1905-1969.
    Papers, 1940-1969. 33 ms. boxes.
    Czechoslovakian statesman; President, National Slovak Council
        and Slovak Democratic Party, 1945-1948; and founder,
        Council of Free Czechoslavakia (Washington, D.C.).
    Correspondence, appointment books, speeches and writings,
        reports, memoranda, clippings, newsletters, printed matter,
        and photographs, relating to political developments in
        Czechoslavakia, the anti-Nazi resistance movement in
        Czechosloakia during World War II, communism in Czecho-
        slovakia, and anticommunist emigre organizations in the
        U.S.
    Gift, Irene Lettrich, 1976.

    Box 28 -- Issue of the bimonthly review of activities of the
        Assembly of Captive European Nations with article on
        communist propaganda.

327. LINDGREN-UTSI, ETHEL JOHN, 1905- .
    Papers, 1924-1941. 4 ms. boxes, 1 motion picture reel.
    British anthropologist.
    Journals, relating to anthropological field trips in
        Manchuria, 1929-1932; notes, relating to the literature of
        anthropology; and a film of domesticated reindeer in
        Manchuria.
    Gift, E. J. Lindgren-Utsi, 1979.
    May not be used without permission of E. J. Lindgren-Utsi.
    For five years after death may not be used without permission
        of her executors.

    Notes on anthropology and pattern of culture and notes on
        Chinese customs, education, and social life in China.

328. LOCHNER, LOUIS PAUL, 1887-   , COLLECTOR.
Collection on Germany (mainly in German), 1934-1946.
9 ms. boxes.
Correspondence, writings, reports, and printed matter,
relating to the Nazi Party, domestic conditions in Germany
and German foreign policy before and during World War II,
postwar occupation of Germany, denazification efforts, and
communist party activities in Germany. Includes correspondence of Joachim von Ribbentrop.
Preliminary inventory.
Gift, 1946. Subsequent increments.

Box 4 -- Article against Western imperialism, supplied to
students of the English Seminary of Berlin University under
Soviet domination.
Box 7 -- Manuals and bulletins relating to troop information
and education.

329. LOEWA, JOACHIM.
Letters (in German and English), 1913-1925, to Raymond Royce
Willoughby. 1 folder.
Holograph and typescript.
German student.
Relates to social conditions in Germany and to personal
matters.

Newspaper clippings, letters, and notes containing information
on psychological difficulties of youth in Germany because
of adult interference in their affairs.

330. LOEWENBERG, PETER.
Study, ca. 1969. "Unsuccessful Adolescence of Heinrich
Himmler." 1 folder.
Typescript (photocopy).
Professor of History, University of California at Los Angeles.
Analyzes the adolescent personality and behavior of Heinrich
Himmler, Reichsfuehrer SS and Chef der Deutschen Polizei
(Reich Leader of the SS and Chief of the German Police) of
the German Third Reich, based on his diaries, 1914-1924.
Gift, P. Loewenberg, 1969.

Article on Heinrich Himmler's youth and his aspirations.

331. LOEWENTHAL, ALFRED MAX, 1916-1980.
Papers, 1932-1980. 35 ms. boxes, 2 oversize boxes.
American labor leader; Assistant to the President,
International Union of Electrical, Radio and Machine

Workers, 1965-1967; Assistant to the President, American
Federation of Teachers, 1970-1979.

Correspondence, memoranda, reports, minutes, serial issues,
and other printed matter, relating to trade unions in the
U.S. and abroad, and to socialism, communism, and
Trotskyism in the U.S.

Gift, Eleanor Loewenthal, 1980.

Box 9 -- Transcript of book on history of the American
Federation of Teachers, with section on AFT program for
education during the Depression.

Box 23 -- Pamphlet entitled "A Federal Department of
Education," with articles on education and reform of
education.

Box 25 -- Correspondence, newspaper clippings, articles, and
reports on education in the U.S.

Box 26 -- Reports of International Federation of Free
Teachers' Union.

Box 31 -- Issues of Anvil, socialist student magazine, and of
International Teachers News.

Box 33 -- Pamphlet on Lenin and youth.

332. LOVESTONE, JAY, 1899- .

Papers, 1906-1976. 634 ms. boxes.

General Secretary, Communist Party, U.S.A., 1927-1929, and
Communist Party (Opposition) 1929-1940; Executive
Secretary, Free Trade Union Committee, American Federation
of Labor, 1944-1955; Assistant Director and Director,
International Affairs, American Federation of Labor-
Congress of Industrial Organizations, 1955-1974.

Correspondence, reports, memoranda, bulletins, clippings,
serial issues, pamphlets, other printed matter, and
photographs, relating to the Communist International, the
communist movement in the U.S. and elsewhere, communist
influence in U.S. and foreign trade unions, and organized
labor movements in the U.S. and abroad.

Published materials are opened. All other materials are
closed until five years after death of J. Lovestone.

Donative sale, J. Lovestone, 1975.

Boxes 8, 11, 34, 86, 101, 162, 167, 184, 229, 232, 270, and
587 -- Pamphlets, journals, reports, news releases, texts
of lectures, and outlines of courses relating to labor,
education, and workers' education.

Boxes 26, 559, and 578 -- Reports, correspondence, leaflets,
newsletters, and newspaper clippings relating to students
and United Student Alliance.

Box 29 -- Pamphlet on detection and management of emotional
disorders in children; pamphlet on education for community

psychiatry in university medical center.

Boxes 46 and 82 -- Pamphlet on communist external propaganda; book on the art of propaganda.

Boxes 52, 130, 176, 449, and 523 -- Pamphlets, reports, and newspaper clippings on public schools and education in the U.S.

Box 64 -- Report on education and world affairs.

Boxes 73, 94, 178, 188, 374, 395, 584, and 588 -- Pamphlets, leaflets, newspaper clippings, reports, and correspondence on youth and communism and world youth.

Box 78 -- Pamphlet on education in Scotland; booklet on working-class education.

Box 100 -- Pamphlet relating to textbooks in India.

Box 397 -- Correspondence, newspaper clippings, and proposal on African education.

Box 431 -- Newspaper clipping and note on education in China.

Box 445 -- Report and newsletter on education in Czechoslovakia.

Box 491 -- Newspaper clippings and leaflets relating to Iran and Iranian Students Association in New York.

Box 569 -- UNESCO reports.

333. LOWDERMILK, WALTER CLAY, 1888-1974.

Papers, 1914-1968. 14 ms. boxes, 3 envelopes.

American agronomist and forester; conservation consultant in China, 1922-1927; Assistant Chief, U.S. Soil Conservation Service, 1939-1947.

Correspondence, writings, printed matter, and photographs, relating to land use and soil and water conservation, primarily in China and Japan.

Register.

Gift, W. C. Lowdermilk, 1970.

Box 2 -- Report on the China-United States Agriculture Mission, with section on education and research.

Box 14 -- Issue of The China Weekly Review, with article on efficient farming education.

334. LOWENKOPF, MARTIN, 1928- .

Papers, 1952-1973. 2 ms. boxes.

American political scientist and author.

Reports, memoranda, notes, press releases, and press summaries, relating to U.S. aid to Liberia, Liberian economic conditions and labor relations, and politics and movements for independence in Uganda and Tanganyika during the 1950s.

Gift, M. Lowenkopf, 1974.

Box 1 -- Report on Webbo District Fundamental Education
project, August-September 1955.
Box 2 -- Report on education in Uganda.

335. LOWMAN, MYERS G.
Papers, 1920-1966. 93 ms. boxes, 3 motion picture reels,
80 phonotapes, 11 envelopes.
Executive Secretary, Circuit Riders, Inc.
Correspondence, memoranda, pamphlets, photographs, and
clippings, relating to communism and other leftist
movements, the civil rights movement, and anticommunism,
primarily in the United States.
Register.
Purchase, M. G. Lowman, 1967.

Box 1 -- Pamphlet, newsletter, and memorandum on academic
freedom.
Box 2 -- Monthly bulletin relating to American-Asian
Educational Exchange; pamphlets and leaflet on American
Association for Economic Education.
Box 5 -- Correspondence and memorandum relating to the
American Institute of Patriotic Education.
Boxes 7, 12, 20, 83, and 84 -- Reports, notes, pamphlets,
leaflets, correspondence, and newspaper clippings on Young
American Youth Council, Young Pioneers, and Young Communist
League.
Boxes 27 and 28 -- Newsletters, reports, pamphlets, booklets,
and leaflets relating to education and communist education;
schools and colleges.
Box 40 -- Bulletins relating to Friends of Public Schools.
Box 79 -- Newspaper clippings, reports, leaflets, and articles
relating to UNESCO.

336. LUBECK, PAUL.
Papers, 1957-1969. 4-1/2 ms. boxes.
American sociologist.
Writings, reports, clippings, and notes, relating to the trade
union movement in Africa, primarily during the 1960s.
Gift, P. Lubeck, 1975.

Box 1 -- Text of address, newspaper clippings, and reports on
education in various African countries.
Box 2 -- Newspaper clippings on education in Ghana.

337. LUNDEEN, ERNEST, 1878-1940.
Papers, 1900-1940. 344 ms. boxes, 10 envelopes.
U.S. Representative from Minnesota, 1917-1919 and 1933-1937;
U.S. Senator from Minnesota, 1937-1940.

113

Correspondence, speeches and writings, clippings, and printed
matter, relating to U.S. politics, U.S. neutrality in World
Wars I and II, military conscription in the U.S., New Deal
social and economic legislation, the "court-packing scheme"
of 1937, the Progressive movement in the U.S., and the
Minnesota Farmer-Labor Party.
Preliminary inventory.
Gift, Mrs. Rufus C. Holman, 1950.

Box 56B -- Pamphlets and newsletters relating to Student
Patriot League.
Box 116 -- Correspondence and pamphlets relating to youth and
Youth Act.
Boxes 335-337 -- Personal notes and correspondence with
information on schools and education.
Box 343 -- Issue of Pan American, April-June, 1940, with
articles on student exchange; "The American School on the
Air"; and higher education.

338. LYLE, ANNIE G.
Papers, 1928-1932. 3 ms. boxes.
American physician; Republican campaign worker.
Correspondence, clippings, and campaign literature, relating
to Herbert Hoover and the U.S. Presidential elections of
1928 and 1932.

Box 1 -- Four issues of Stanford Illustrated Review, 1931,
1932, with sections on students and education.

339. MC CARRAN, MARGARET PATRICIA, SISTER.
Writings, 1968-1969. 1 ms. box.
Daughter of Patrick A. McCarran, U.S. Senator from Nevada.
Photocopy of study (typewritten), entitled "The Fabian
Transmission," relating to Fabian socialist societies in
Great Britain and the U.S.; and biographical sketches
(printed), relating to Senator McCarran.
Gift, M. P. McCarran, 1973.

Book I, Chapter IV -- Relates to education of the Fabians.

340. MC CONNELL, PHILIP C.
Papers, 1937-1963. 3 ms. boxes.
American petroleum engineer; Vice-President, Arabian American
Oil Company.
Diaries, correspondence, notes, reports, brochures, printed
matter, maps, and photographs, relating to operations of
the Arabian American Oil Company in Saudi Arabia and

114

elsewhere in the Middle East and to Arab customs.
Gift, P. C. McConnell, 1962.

Box 1 -- Pamphlets by Aramco, with information on schools and
    social conditions in Saudi Arabia.
Box 2 -- Handbooks by Aramco describing Arab culture and
    education in Saudi Arabia.

341. MC GRATH, EARL JAMES, 1902- .
        Speeches and writings, 1949-1953. 2 ms. boxes.
        Typescript (photocopy).
        American educator; U.S. Commissioner of Education, 1949-1953.
        Relates to education in the U.S. and U.S. government policy
            concerning it.
        Gift, E. J. McGrath, 1980.

        Both boxes include texts of addresses and correspondence on
            elementary, secondary, and higher education, vocational
            education, and parent-teacher cooperation in promoting
            education.

342. MAKERERE UNIVERSITY.
        Slides, 1969. 4 boxes.
        Illustrates the history of Christianity in East Africa.
            Prepared by the Department of Religious Studies and the
            Audio-Visual Aids Center of Makerere University, Kampala,
            Uganda.
        Preliminary inventory.
        Purchase, 1972.

343. MALAYAN COMMUNIST PARTY.
        Propaganda, 1950-1951. 1/2 ms. box.
        Propaganda leaflets and bulletins and translations of
            propaganda leaflets and bulletins (mimeographed), issued by
            the Malayan Communist Party, relating to the communist-led
            independence movement in Singapore.

        MCP propaganda and educational documents.

344. "MANCHURIAN MANIFESTO."
        Press release, 1946. 1 folder.
        Typescript (mimeographed).

Protests Soviet influence in Manchuria. Signed by a number of
American anticommunists.

Essay entitled "Manchuria Manifesto," with section on
students' protest against USSR aggression.

345. MARAWSKE, MAX, <u>COLLECTOR</u>.
Collection on World War I (in German), 1890-1918.
34 ms. boxes.
Clippings from German newspapers and periodicals, relating to
World War I.
Register.

Box 27 -- Newspapers and magazine clippings on youth in
Germany.

346. MARBURGER HOCHSCHULGESPRAECHE, 1946.
Report (in German), 1946. 1 folder.
Typescript.
Summarizes proceedings of the Marburger Hochschulgespraeche, a
conference of German and foreign scholars held at Marburg,
concerning academic studies in Germany.

347. MARLAND, SIDNEY PERCY, JR., 1914- .
Papers, 1943-1978. 7 ms. boxes.
American educator; U.S. Commissioner of Education, 1970-1972;
Assistant Secretary of Health, Education and Welfare,
1972-1973.
Speeches and writings, reports, correspondence, memoranda,
photographs, and printed matter, relating to education in
the U.S., U.S. Government educational policy, and the
career education movement.
Gift, S. P. Marland, 1979.

Boxes 1 and 2 -- Reports and speeches on higher education.
Boxes 3 and 4 -- Reports, speeches, and articles on career
education.
Box 5 -- Report of Princeton University Conference on urban
schools.
Box 7 -- Annual reports relating to education.

348. MARLOWE, SANFORD STRATTON, 1917-1977.
Papers, 1943-1977. 1-1/2 ms. boxes.
U.S. Information Agency officer; Deputy Director, U.S. Joint
Public Affairs Office, South Vietnam, 1965-1966; Public
Affairs Officer and Consul, Hong Kong, 1967-1971.

Speeches and writings, correspondence, printed matter,
memorabilia, and photographs, relating to the U.S.
diplomatic service.
Gift, Margaret A. Marlowe, 1979.

Box 2 -- Issues of Current Scene relating to developments in
Mainland China, with articles on education.

349. MARQUARDT, FREDERIC S., 1905- .
Papers, 1977-1979. 2 ms. boxes.
American journalist; senior editor, Arizona Republic.
Conference papers delivered at the Seminar on Land Policy
and Land Taxation in Commemoration of the Centennial of
Henry George's Writing of Progress and Poverty, Taipei,
1977; and correspondence, writings, press releases,
newspaper issues, and printed matter, relating to the 6th
Conference of Heads of State of Government of Non-Aligned
Countries, Havana, 1979.
Gift, F. S. Marquardt, 1979.

Box 1 -- Pamphlet entitled "Introduction to Cuba," with
section on education.

350. MARVIN LIEBMAN ASSOCIATES, 1958-1969.
Records, 1950-1969. 108 ms. boxes, 3 envelopes.
New York public relations firm. Office files, correspondence,
printed matter, press releases, campaign material,
photographs, and reports, relating to lobbying activities
of U.S. conservative and anticommunist organizations
involved with Asian and African affairs.
Register.
Gift, Marvin Liebman Associates, 1969.

Boxes 5-6 and 43-60 -- Correspondence, reports, articles,
newsletters, and pamphlets relating to American Afro-Asian
Educational Exchange, Inc., 1962-1968.
Box 8 -- Correspondence, newsletters, and reports, relating to
American Affairs Public Educational Fund, Inc., 1965.
Box 24 -- Correspondence, newsletters, reports, and leaflets,
relating to Student Committee on Free China, 1963-1968.
Box 33 -- Correspondence relating to National Schools
Committee for Economic Education, 1967.
Boxes 51-56 -- Correspondence, newspaper clippings, and
newsletters relating to American-Asian Educational
Exchange, 1960-1969.

351. MASON, JOHN BROWN, 1904- .
        Papers, 1935-1945. 1/2 ms. box.
        American educator and author; Chief, Training Division, U.S.
            Foreign Economic Administration, 1944-1946.
        Reports, memoranda, syllabi, and organization charts, relating
            to the training of U.S. Foreign Economic Administration
            personnel for service in occupied Germany and Austria at
            the end of World War II and to living conditions for U.S.
            consular officials around the world.
        Gift, J. B. Mason, 1945. Subsequent increments.

        Information on education in Mexico, Morocco, Panama, Peru,
            Portugal, Turkey, Uruguay, and Venezuela.

352. MATHEWS, FORREST DAVID, 1935- .
        Speech transcripts, 1975-1976. 1/2 ms. box.
        Typescript (photocopy).
        U.S. Secretary of Health, Education and Welfare, 1975-1977.
            Relates to U.S. social welfare policy.
        Gift, F. D. Mathews, 1977.

        Three volumes of major speeches by Forrest Mathews on health,
            education, and welfare.

353. MATTHEWS, HAROLD S., 1894- .
        Papers, 1936-1968. 3 ms. boxes.
        American missionary in North China, 1922-1942; Secretary,
            American Board of Commissioners for Foreign Missions,
            1944-1953.
        Writings, correspondence, reports, and printed matter,
            relating to Christian missionary work in China and Japan
            and to the communist movement in China.
        Register.
        Gift, H. S. Matthews, 1970. Subsequent increments.

        Box 3 -- Writings of Harold Matthews on Christianity in China,
            Christian education, and the story of three church leaders.

354. MATTOX, ELMER L.
        Papers, 1905-1966. 2 ms. boxes.
        American missionary in Hangchow, China.
        Correspondence, writings, pamphlets, and photographs, relating
            to missionary work in Hangchow, to Hangchow Christian

College, and to social conditions in China.

Box 1 -- Papers relating to Chinese Christian Educational
    Association and bulletins of the National Christian
    Council, with information on education.

355. MAURIN, JOAQUIN, 1896-1973.
    Papers (mainly in Spanish), 1920-1973. 24 ms. boxes,
        1 oversize box (1/3 linear foot).
    Spanish politician, journalist, and author; Secretary-General,
        Partido Obrero de Unificacion Marxista.
    Correspondence, writings, newspaper and magazine clippings,
        photographs, and printed matter, relating to communism and
        socialism in Spain, the Spanish Civil War, and the American
        Literary Agency.
    Purchase, Jeanne Maurin, 1977.

    Box 15 -- Essay on social ideas and university for workers.

356. MAYERS, HENRY, 1894- .
    Papers, 1930-1966. 7 ms. boxes, 1 scrapbook.
    American advertising executive; member, Committee for Freedom
        for All Peoples; chairman, Cold War Council.
    Correspondence, speeches and writings, and printed matter,
        relating primarily to the Cold War Council.

    Box 2 -- Writing related to the Private Freedom Academy, with
        section on educational gap in the cold war.
    Box 6 -- Issue of Intercom with sections on education in
        Southeast Asia.

357. MAYO, SEBASTIAN.
    "La Educacion Socialista en Mexico: El Asalto de la
        Universidad Nacional." 1 microfilm reel.

358. MEI, I-CH'I, 1892-1962.
    Papers (in Chinese and English), 1949-1956. 1 ms. box.
    President, Tsinghua University, 1931-1953; Minister of Educa-
        tion of Taiwan, 1958-1961.
    Diaries and correspondence, relating to education and
        political conditions in Taiwan.
    Gift, Mrs. Mei I-ch'i, 1972.

    Includes printed note about life of Mei I-ch'i and his
        contributions to education in Taiwan.

359. MELROSE, PAUL C.
    Papers, 1906-1949. 1/2 ms. box.
    American missionary in China.
    Reports, newsletters, and notes, relating to missionary work
        in China, including the Hainan mission newsletter, 1914-
        1949, and the Hainan mission annual reports, 1906-1948.

    Newsletter and reports include sections on education.

360. MICHIGAN. LEGISLATURE. JOINT COMMITTEE ON REORGANIZATION OF
        STATE GOVERNMENT.
    Reports, 1950-1953. 3 ms. boxes.
    Typescript (mimeographed).
    Relates to the reorganization of various state agencies and
        departments.
    Gift, Frank Andrews, 1958.

    Box 2, Volume 3 -- Section on Michigan's educational agencies
        and their activities.

361. MIKOLAJCZYK, STANISLAW, 1901-1966.
    Papers (in Polish and English), 1938-1966. 137 ms. boxes,
        19 cubic foot boxes.
    Polish politician; Prime Minister, Government-in-Exile
        (London), 1943-1944; Second Vice-Premier and Minister of
        Agriculture, 1945-1947; President, International Peasant
        Union, 1950-1966.
    Correspondence, speeches and writings, reports, notes,
        newsletters, clippings, photographs, tape recordings, and
        printed matter, relating to communism in Eastern Europe and
        Poland, agriculture in Poland, Polish politics, especially
        during World War II, Polish-Soviet relations, the Inter-
        national Peasant Union, the Polskie Stronnictwo Ludowe, and
        Polish emigre politics.
    Consult archivist for restriction.
    Purchase, Marian Mikolajczyk, 1978.

    Box 91 -- Volume 4 of a series of reports, with section on
        education and youth.

362. MITCHELL, ANNA V. S.
    Papers, 1920-1944. 6 ms. boxes, 9 envelopes, 4 medals.
    American relief worker. Correspondence, memoranda, reports,
        clippings, memorabilia, and photographs, relating to World
        War I relief work in France, 1915-1920, and relief work
        with Russian refugees in Istanbul, 1921-1936.
    Register.

Gift, John Davis Hatch, 1967. Incremental gift, 1975.

Box 2 -- Correspondence relating to International Student
Service, 1928, and National Russian Students' Christian
Association in U.S.A., 1924.

363. MITCHELL, RICHARD PAUL, 1925- , COLLECTOR.
Collection on the Muslim Brotherhood (mainly in Arabic), ca.
1953-1963. 6 ms. boxes, 6 oversize boxes, 10 volumes.
Writings, newspapers, magazines, journals, books, and other
printed matter, relating to the activities of the Muslim
Brotherhood, Islamic culture and political movements, and
conditions in Islamic countries.
Preliminary inventory.
Gift, R. P. Mitchell, 1977.

Boxes 1 and 2 -- Several educational books in Arabic.

364. MOLEY, RAYMOND, 1886-1975.
Papers, 1912-1969. 246 ms. boxes, 3 envelopes.
American political scientist and journalist; adviser to
Franklin D. Roosevelt, 1932-1933; U.S. Assistant Secretary
of State, 1933; contributing editor, Newsweek, 1937-1968.
Correspondence, diaries, reports, memoranda, speeches and
writings, notes, and printed matter, relating primarily to
politics in the U.S., particularly the presidential
campaign of 1932; the administration of President Franklin
D. Roosevelt; and Today and Newsweek magazines.
Register.
Correspondence with Richard M. Nixon is closed during the
lifetime of the latter.
Donative sale, R. Moley, 1968.

Boxes 4, 196, 198, and 201 -- Correspondence and notes
relating to colleges and universities.
Box 119 -- Pamphlets, reports, and articles on education.
Box 161 -- Newspaper clippings on academic freedom at Columbia
University, 1917.
Box 203 -- Notes, correspondence, and newspaper clippings
relating to National Student Leadership Conference.
Boxes 207 and 208 -- Leaflets, correspondence, and notes
relating to regulations and curriculum of Barnard College,
Columbia University, 1927.

365. MONAGAN, WALTER E., JR.
Papers, 1945-1948. 8 ms. boxes.
Legal adviser, U.S. Military Government in Korea, 1945-1948.

Reports, ordinances, proclamations, and legal opinions,
    relating to political, economic and legal aspects of
    government administration in Korea and to repatriation of
    Japanese in Korea.
Preliminary inventory.
Gift, W. E. Monagan, Jr., 1972.

Box 2, Volumes 1 and 2 -- Sections on Korean education, YWCA,
    and Ewha Women's University.
Box 3, Volume 1 -- Sections on education in Korea.
Box 4, Volume 10 -- Information on education in Korea.

366. MONDAY, MARK.
    Papers, 1961-1974. 2 ms. boxes, 2 envelopes, 3 motion-
        picture reels.
    American journalist; Phoenix American reporter.
    Writings, correspondence, booklets, reports, newspaper clip-
        pings, photographs, and films, relating to Minutemen,
        Secret Army Organization, and other right-wing paramilitary
        groups, and to infiltration of the Minutemen by M. Monday.
    Preliminary inventory.
    Gift, M. Monday, 1974.

    Box 1 -- Booklets and writings relating to training courses of
        Secret Army Organization.

367. MONTGOMERY, JOHN DICKEY, 1920- .
    Papers, 1946-1959. 15 ms. boxes.
    American political scientist and author.
    Writings, reports, notes, interview summaries, and printed
        matter, relating to U.S. aid to South Vietnam and other
        Southeast Asian countries, economic conditions in these
        countries, Japanese and German public opinion regarding the
        purge of wartime leaders after World War II, and political,
        social, and economic effects of the purge on Japan and
        Germany.
    Register.
    Gift, J. D. Montgomery, 1975.

    Magazine, Burma, 1959 (vol. 4, no. 2), published by Burmese
        government, describes education (1957-1958) and medical and
        military training. Thai material traces beginning of
        Western education in Thailand and analyzes elementary,
        secondary, and higher education, vocational training, and
        special educational projects. Vietnamese materials pro-
        vide brief historical analysis of Vietnamese educational

122

system and concentrate on problems of elementary, secondary, and higher education, vocational training, and construction of school buildings in 1956-1958.

368. MOORE, FRANKLIN.
Papers (in English and French), 1960-1978. 40-1/2 ms. boxes.
American educator; representative of the Ford Foundation in Asia; U.S. Agency for International Development official. Reports and memoranda, relating to the study of education in South America, Africa, and Asia.
Gift, F. Moore, 1978.

Boxes 1, 2, 25, 28, 33, and 41 -- Reports, memoranda, and correspondence relating to formal and nonformal education in developing countries.
Box 3 -- Reports on formal and nonformal education in Cuba.
Box 4 -- Reports on different aspects of education.
Boxes 5 and 6 -- Reports and memoranda on education in Central America.
Boxes 7, 8, 10, 15, 16, 18, 23, 24, 35-37, and 39 -- Reports, memoranda, newsletters, and notes on international education.
Boxes 9, 11, 14, and 19 -- Reports and periodicals on education in Asia.
Boxes 13, 20, 27, 29-31, 38, and 40 -- Reports, memoranda, correspondence, and notes on formal and nonformal education in Africa.
Boxes 17 and 34 -- Reports on education in the Democratic Republic of the Congo.
Boxes 21 and 32 -- Reports and memoranda on education in Botswana.
Box 26 -- Reports on education in Kenya.

369. MOORE, WILLIAM C., 1904- , <u>COLLECTOR.</u>
Miscellany, 1914-1917. 1 volume.
Photographs, clippings, a pamphlet, cartoons, and poems, relating to the outbreak of World War I, military life during the war, and the First Boy Scout International Jamboree in London, 1920.
Gift, W. C. Moore, 1977.

Note on establishment of Boy Scout movement in London and participation of U.S. group in the Boy Scout International Jamboree in London in 1920.

370. MORAN, HUGH ANDERSON, 1881- .
Papers, 1916-1933. 2 ms. boxes.

American clergyman; Young Men's Christian Association worker in Siberia and China, 1909-1918.

Correspondence, writings, clippings, maps, posters, and photographs, relating to the Russian Civil War, political and economic conditions in Siberia and Manchuria, and relief work in Siberia and Manchuria, especially in the prisoner of war camps, during the Russian Civil War.

Preliminary inventory.

Box 2 -- Writings and correspondence on the Ukraine: its culture, its social conditions, and the establishment of Ukrainian University in Prague.

371. MORELAND, WILLIAM DAWSON, JR., 1907- .

Papers, 1949-1965. 6 ms. boxes, 8 envelopes.

American diplomat and consular official; U.S. Consul, Dakar, Senegal, 1949-1951.

Correspondence, reports, dispatches, newspapers, clippings, other printed matter, and photographs, relating to political, economic, and social conditions in West Africa.

Preliminary inventory.

Gift, W. D. Moreland, Jr., 1959. Incremental gift, 1969.

Box 3 -- Pamphlet, report, newsletters, and newspaper clippings on education in West Africa.

372. MOSHER, CLELIA DUEL, 1863-1940.

Papers, 1898-1937. 7 ms. boxes.

American physician and educator; Red Cross worker in France, 1917-1919.

Correspondence, writings, office files, photographs, and postcards, relating to relief work of the Red Cross in France from 1917 to 1919 and to the promotion of health education for women in the U.S. Includes correspondence with Lou Henry Hoover.

Box 4 -- Report by American Red Cross on childrens' situation in France, August 1917.

373. MUNGER, HENRY W., 1876- .

Diary, 1942-1945. 1 vol.

Typescript.

American missionary in the Philippines. Relates to conditions in Japanese prison camps in the Philippines during World War II.

Information on his religious and educational activities.

124

374. MUNICH. UNIVERSITAET - STUDENTS.
        Leaflets (in German), 1931. 1 folder.
        Printed.
        Relates to Allgemeiner Studentenausschuss (AStA) elections and
            party politics in Germany, Leaflets distributed at the
            University of Munich.
        Gift, Dorothea Swanson, 1977.

375. MUNRO, DANA CARLETON, 1866-1933.
        Papers, 1908-1923. 4 ms. boxes.
        U.S. Inquiry investigator, Paris Peace Conference, 1919;
            Research Assistant, Committee on Public Information,
            1917-1918.
        Reports, correspondence, leaflets, and notes, relating to
            political and economic conditions in Turkey, Zionism,
            relief work and the conduct of German occupying forces in
            Belgium during World War I, U.S. neutrality in World War I,
            war propaganda, and proposals for world peace.

        Box 2 -- Pamphlet on Korea, with section on education, April
            1919. Bulletin of the American College for Girls at
            Constantinople, 1921-1922. Pamphlet relating to
            niversity of Budapest and its activities, 1923.

376. MURAVEISKII, S.
        Translation of pamphlet, n.d. "Data on the History of the
            Revolutionary Movement in Central Asia: Result of a Brief
            Study of the Soviet Party Schools and Political Primary
            Schools." 1 folder.
        Typescript.
        Translation by Xenia J. Eudin, of Ocherki po Istorii
            Revolutsionnogo Dvizheniia v Srednei Azii: Opyt Kratkogo
            Posobiia dlia Sovpartshkol i Shkol Politgramoty, published
            in Tashkent in 1926.

377. MURPHY, ROBERT DANIEL, 1894-1978.
        Papers, 1963-1977. 54 ms. boxes, 3 oversize boxes,
            memorabilia.
        American diplomat and business executive; President's personal
            representative in North Africa, 1942; Political Adviser to
            Supreme Headquarters, Allied Expeditionary Forces,
            1943-1949; Ambassador to Belgium, 1949-1952, and Japan,
            1952; Deputy Under Secretary of State, 1953-1959; chairman,
            Commission on the Organization of the Government for the
            Conduct of Foreign Policy, 1973-1975.
        Correspondence, memoranda, speeches and writings, and printed
            matter, relating to American foreign policy, business

enterprises, and humanitarian organizations.
May not be used without written approval of depositors.
Deposit, Mildred Murphy Pond and Rosemary Murphy, 1978.

Box 50 -- Book on Russell H. Conwell and his work as a lawyer,
editor, minister, educator, and founder of Temple
University. Describes his days in school and university,
and his contributions to education.

378. MURRA, WILBUR FIM, 1910- .
Papers, 1943-1974. 1 ms. box.
American educator.
Correspondence, writings, printed matter, and photographs,
relating to comparative and international education.
Gift, W. F. Murra, 1978.

Reports and writings on education in Canada, the United
Kingdom, Western Samoa, and New Zealand.

379. NATHAN, RICHARD P.
Papers, 1957-1979. 63 ms. boxes, 1 oversize box,
5 binders.
Assistant Director, U.S. Office of Management and Budget,
1969-1971; Deputy Under Secretary of Health, Education and
Welfare, 1971-1972.
Correspondence, memoranda, reports, studies, and printed
matter, relating to U.S. politics and intergovernmental
relations and to domestic policy under the presidency of
Richard M. Nixon, especially welfare and revenue-sharing
programs.

Box 3 -- Reports by Nixon-Agnew Campaign Committee, October
1968, with sections on education.
Box 7 -- Newsletters with sections on education and welfare.
Box 11 -- Newspaper clipping on higher education.

380. NATIONAL COMMITTEE ON FOOD FOR THE SMALL DEMOCRACIES, 1940-1942.
Records, 1939-1945. 124 ms. boxes.
Private American charitable organization.
Correspondence, office files, pamphlets, and serial issues,
relating to attempts in the U.S. to organize and secure
international agreement for a civilian relief program for
Norway, Finland, the Netherlands, Belgium, and Poland
during World War II.

Preliminary inventory.

Boxes 59-64 -- Correspondence, newspaper clippings, notes,
    newsletters, leaflets, and pamphlets relating to National
    Student Committee, and Student Defenders of Democracy.
Box 74 -- Pamphlet by Red Cross on child welfare in Finland.

381. NATIONAL COUNCIL FOR PREVENTION OF WAR.
        WESTERN OFFICE, SAN FRANCISCO, 1921-1954.
        Records, 1921-1943.   3-1/2 ms. boxes.
        American pacifist organization.
        Leaflets, pamphlets, press releases, and serial issues,
            relating to movements for peace, disarmament, preservation
            of U.S. neutrality during World War II, and opposition to
            conscription and military training in educational
            institutions.
        Gift, Northern California Service Board for Conscientious
            Objectors, 1943.

        Box 1 -- Pamphlet on California Congress of Parents and
            Teachers, Inc., relating to educating for world
            citizenship.
        Box 2 -- Pamphlets on military training at schools, colleges,
            and universities.
        Box 3 -- Pamphlets on youth and international education.

382. NATIONAL-DEMOKRATISCHE PARTEI DEUTSCHLANDS (Germany, East).
        Syllabus (in German), 1949.   1 folder.
        Typescript.
        Relates to the curriculum of the National Democratic Party
            School for National Politics in Buckow, East Germany,
            regarding the study of German history and political and
            economic conditions.

383. NATIONAL JAPANESE AMERICAN STUDENT RELOCATION COUNCIL, 1942-1946.
        Records, 1942-1946.   20 cubic foot boxes.
        Private American organization for aid to relocated Japanese
            American students.
        Correspondence, questionnaires, student education records, and
            miscellanea, relating to efforts to place relocated
            Japanese American students in colleges in the U.S. during
            World War II.
        Preliminary inventory.
        Individual students may not be identified.
        Gift, National Japanese American Student Relocation Council,
            1947.

384. NATIONAL REPUBLIC, 1905-1960.
          Records, 1920-1960. 826 ms. boxes.
          Anticommunist American magazine. Clippings, printed matter,
              pamphlets, reports, indices, notes, bulletins, lettergrams,
              weekly letters, and photographs, relating to pacifist,
              communist, fascist, and other radical movements and to
              political developments in the United States and the Soviet
              Union.
          Register.
          Purchase, National Republic Publishing Company, 1960.

          Boxes 3, 5, 65, 70, 119, 156, 177,222-224, 245, 246, 285, and
              580 -- Newspaper clippings, leaflets, pamphlets, news
              releases, newsletters, notes, booklets, correspondence, and
              articles relating to various educational organizations.
          Boxes 17, 109-112, 242, 256, 392-397, 412, 413, 420, 467, 604,
              626, 712-714 -- Notes, leaflets, correspondence, newspaper
              clippings, lettergrams, yearbooks, articles, reports,
              booklets, pamphlets, and newsletters on young Americans:
              black youth, youth organizations, communist youth, and
              youth pioneers.
          Boxes 53 and 580 -- Newspaper clippings, reports, and articles
              on Boy Scouts and Girl Scouts.
          Boxes 59-60 -- Reports, pamphlets, and newspaper clippings on
              child care, child welfare, and child health in U.S.
          Boxes 106, 238, 258, 282, and 419 -- Newspaper clippings,
              notes, reports, pamphlets, and reports on propaganda.
          Boxes 107-108 -- Notes, reports, leaflets, newspaper
              clippings, and pamphlets on communist schools.
          Boxes 116, 133, 134, 244, 297, 298, 351, 352, 354, 355, 528,
              564, and 645 -- Reports, notes, newspaper clippings,
              articles, correspondence, pamphlets, and journals on
              various aspects of education.
          Box 264 -- Newspaper clippings, pamphlets, and articles on
              PTA.
          Boxes 295, 296, 300-310 -- Notes, correspondence, newspaper
              clippings, reports, newsletters, articles, leaflets,
              pamphlets, and booklets on schools, colleges, and
              universities in the U.S.
          Box 440 -- Notes and posters relating to Committee for
              International Student Cooperation.

385. NAYLOR, ROBERT.
          Correspondence, 1975. 1 folder.
          Typescript (photocopy).
          Chief of Operations, Vietnamese "Orphans' Airlift," San
              Francisco. Relates to the airlift of Vietnamese children
              from Vietnam to California. Includes extract of draft and

outline for a projected book by James Kolbe on the airlift.
Gift, R. Naylor, 1975.

386. NEW LEFT COLLECTION, 1964-1974.
        67 ms. boxes, 31 posters, 3 phonorecords, 1 microfilm reel.
        Booklets, leaflets, reports, and clippings, relating to the
            purposes, tactics, and activities of various New Left and
            right-wing groups, draft resistance, student disorders, and
            the anti-Vietnam War movement.
        Collected by Edward J. Bacciocco.
        Preliminary inventory.

        Most of the contents are related to campus unrest, youth, and
            black student unions.

387. NEWS RESEARCH SERVICE, LOS ANGELES.
        Report, n.d. "Summary Report on Activities of Nazi Groups and
            Their Allies in Southern California, 1936-1940."
            3 ms. boxes.
        Typescript.
        Private anti-Nazi organization.
        Relates to the German-American Bund and similar groups.
        Gift, Edward N. Barnhart, 1974.

        Box 1, Volume 1 -- Sections on propaganda, churches, schools,
            and radios.

388. NEW YORK (CITY) DEPARTMENT OF INVESTIGATION.
        Report, 1944. 1 folder.
        Typescript (mimeographed).
        Relates to causes of, and recommended measures to prevent,
            anti-Semitic vandalism and violence in New York City.

        Contains chart describing the educational backgrounds of
            vandals.

389. NIEDERPRUEM, WILLIAM J., COLLECTOR.
        Collection, 1917-1951. 5-1/2 ms. boxes.
        Military orders and reports, maps, pamphlets, clippings, and
            newspaper and periodical issues, relating to activities of
            the American Expeditionary Forces, particularly of the 32nd
            Division, in France during World War I; military operations

129

during World War II; and the postwar occupation of Japan.
Gift, W. J. Niederpruem, 1966.

Box 3 -- Issue of Facts in Review, July 1, 1940, with article
on Friedrich Froebel and his kindergarten.

390. NIEMOELLER, MARTIN, 1892- .
Memorandum (in German and English), 1945. "Die
Staatsrechtlichen Grundlagen zum Aufbau der
Bekenntnisschule" (Legal Foundations for the Construction
of Parochial Schools). 1 folder.
Typescript.
Anti-Nazi German clergyman. Includes a U.S. Army report
(printed), 1947, relating to the activities of
M. Niemoeller.

391. NORTON, ROBERT, 1896-1974.
Papers, 1935-1948. 3-1/2 ms. boxes.
American lawyer and journalist; editor, China Today.
Correspondence, speeches and writings, clippings, printed
matter, photographs, and other materials, relating to U.S.
relations with China and Japan, India's independence from
Great Britain, Japanese military incursions into China, and
United Nations assistance to China.
Gift, Irene Norton, 1977.

Box 2 -- Notes on education and United Nations.
Box 3 -- Notes relating to Corpus Christi School and its
curriculum; newsletters and leaflets relating to Spring-
field College and its courses for part-time students, 1943.

392. NOSSAL, FREDERICK.
Papers, 1944-1979. 79 ms. boxes, 2 oversize boxes,
2 scrapbooks.
Canadian journalist; Far East correspondent, 1959-1971,
stationed in Peking, 1959-1960; information officer, World
Bank, 1971-1979.
Drafts of writings, dispatches, clippings, serial issues,
photographs, slides, and other printed matter, relating to
political and other conditions in China, the Vietnam War,
political conditions elsewhere in Asia, and activities of
the World Bank.

Box 10 -- Book on Canada with section on education in that
country, 1959.
Box 11 -- Handbook on Japan with sections on education and
culture in that country, 1970.

Box 25 -- Newspaper clippings and notes on education in China
and control of education by Chinese government.
Box 26 -- Newspaper clippings on Chinese youth.
Box 47 -- Pamphlets and booklets on education and social
conditions in Malaysia, Taiwan, China, and East Pakistan
(Bangladesh).

393. OIDERMAN, M.
History, n.d. "Estonian Independence." 1/2 ms. box.
Typescript.
Relates to the history of Estonia during the Russian
Revolution and to the establishment of an independent
Estonian state. Prepared under the auspices of the
Estonian Foreign Office.

Sections on peace and propaganda.

394. OLDS, CHARLES BURNELL, 1872-1971.
Papers, 1895-1964. 1/2 ms. box.
American missionary in Japan, 1903-1939.
Letters, writings, and pamphlets, relating to Christianity in
Japan.
Gift, Leavitt Olds Wright, 1971.

Sections on religious education.

395. ORATA, PEDRO T.
Writings, 1978-1980. 1 folder.
President, Urdaneta Community College, Philippines. Relates
to education in the Philippines.
Gift, P. T. Orata, 1980.

Article on goal of democratizing Philippines education.
Bulletins of Barangory preschool, high school, and
community college. Articles and essays on Orata's
contributions to education in the Philippines.

396. ORION, WALTER HAROLD, 1894- .
Papers, 1947-1950. 1/2 ms. box, 1 envelope, 1 poster.
Captain, U.S. Navy; Acting Director, U.S. Education Mission to
Korea, 1948.
Reports, orders, printed matter, photographs, and a poster,
relating to American assistance in teacher-training
programs in South Korea.
Gift, W. H. Orion, 1979.

Book on Korea, 1948, with sections on social conditions and
refugee children. Report by staff of the Teacher Training
Center, Seoul National University, Korea, 1948.

397. OSUSKY, STEFAN, 1889-1973.
Papers (in English, French, Czech, and Slovak), 1910-1965.
95 ms. boxes, 2 card file boxes (1/3 linear foot), 1 album,
4 envelopes.
Czechoslovakian diplomat; Ambassador to Great Britain,
1918-1920; Ambassador to France, 1920-1940; Minister of
State, Czechoslovakian Government-in-Exile, 1940-1943.
Correspondence, memoranda, reports, clippings, printed matter,
memorabilia, and photographs, relating to Czechoslovakian
politics and diplomacy and European diplomatic relations
between the two world wars.
Register.
Gift, Pavla Osusky, 1974.

Box 12 -- Correspondence and notes relating to Workers'
Educational Association, 1940.
Box 13 -- Reports and memoranda relating to Association of
Allied Professors and Lecturers in Great Britain,
1942-1943.
Box 21 -- Notes and an issue of Oxford University Gazette,
March 21, 1941, relating to Oxford University's activities.
Box 23 -- Proposals and notes for organization of propaganda
service and creation of radiophonic center of social and
international education based upon Christian ideals.
Box 24 -- Notes on childhood and maturity.
Box 26 -- Note on industrialization and education.
Box 71 -- Report on development in nine captive countries,
with sections on education, October 1957-March 1958.

398. PADEREWSKI, IGNACY JAN, 1860-1941.
Papers (in Polish, English, and French), 1894-1941.
6-1/2 ms. boxes, 1 envelope, 1 album.
Polish statesman and musician; Premier, 1919.
Correspondence, speeches and writings, clippings, printed
matter, and photographs, relating primarily to the
establishment of an independent Polish State, the Paris
Peace Conference, Polish politics in the interwar period,
the occupation of Poland during World War II, and the
musical career of I. J. Paderewski.
Preliminary inventory.
Personal financial materials in four folders closed until
January 1, 1992. No handwritten material may be
reproduced.
Gift, Helena Liibke, 1975. Gift, Anne Appleton, 1976.

Box 6 -- Memorandum by Polish Committee for the Defense and
Peace concerning revisionist propaganda. Issue of Polish
Affairs, with article on struggle for scouting.

399. PADEREWSKI TESTIMONIAL FUND, 1941-1959.
Records, 1939-1959. 72 ms. boxes, 2 cubic foot boxes.
Organization for the relief of Polish refugees during and
after World War II.
Reports, correspondence, press releases, financial records,
printed matter, and photographs, relating to relief
activities carried on by the Fund and by the Paderewski
Hospital in Edinburgh, Scotland.
Preliminary inventory.
Gift, Paderewski Testimonial Fund, 1959.

Box 4 -- Issue of The Polish Review, with article on
universities of the Polish-Lithuanian Commonwealth.
Box 9 -- Correspondence relating to Catholic Youth Federation
of Connecticut, 1941.
Box 45 -- Handbooks on Puerto Rico, with sections on
education.

400. "PALESTINE RESISTANCE MOVEMENT THROUGH 30 JUNE 1970."
Study, 1970. 1/2 ms. box.
Typescript (photocopy).
Relates to the organization and activities of Palestine
liberation and resistance movements in the Middle East,
1947-1970.

Chapter III -- Sections on training of Palestinian boys,
girls, and women, and on social services.

401. PAN-AFRICAN CONGRESS, 6th, DAR ES SALAAM, TANZANIA, 1974,
Miscellaneous records, 1974. 1/2 ms. box.
Photocopy.
Reports, declarations, resolutions, speeches, and leaflets,
relating to the Pan-African movement, colonialism, and
worldwide problems of black people. Includes printed
matter about the Congress, collected by Alma Robinson and
Charles Ogletree.
Gift, A. Robinson and C. Ogletree, 1975.

Folder 1 -- Reports on technology, education, and the future
of Pan-African culture.
Folders 2 and 3 -- Reports on women's contributions to
Pan-African struggle and liberation of Africa, with
sections on education.

402. PANUNZIO, CONSTANTINE MARIA, 1884-1964.
       Papers (in Italian and English), 1921-1945. 17 ms. boxes.
       Italian-American sociologist.
       Writings, letters, clippings, bibliographies, and book lists,
           relating to Italian politics, fascism, church and state
           relations, anti-Semitism and racism, and to Benito
           Mussolini.
       Preliminary inventory.

       Box 4 -- Pamphlets and leaflets on foreign students in Italy.
       Box 5 -- Reports, articles, and newspaper clippings on
           education in Italy during fascist regime.
       Box 6 -- Newspaper clippings and articles relating to
           university and youth movement in Italy.

403. PARIS. PEACE CONFERENCE, 1919. U.S. DIVISION OF TERRITORIAL,
           ECONOMIC AND POLITICAL INTELLIGENCE.
       Miscellaneous records, 1917-1918. 7 ms. boxes, 3 card file
           boxes (1/2 linear foot).
       Organization created to prepare background information for the
           U.S. delegation to the Paris Peace Conference; known as the
           Inquiry.
       Memoranda, notes, and reports, relating to political and
           economic conditions in the Ottoman Empire and Latin
           America, proposals for new boundaries in Asia Minor,
           creation of an independent Armenia, and boundary disputes
           in South America.

       Box 2 -- Three volumes on Brazil, Boliva, Chile, Colombia,
           Ecuador, Paraguay, Peru, Uruguay, and Venezuela, with
           sections on education.
       Box 4 -- Reports relating to protection of American educa-
           tional and scientific enterprises in the Ottoman Empire.
       Box 5 -- Summary of reports on education in Turkey by Paul
           Monroe and McKenzie.

404. PARK, ALICE, 1861-1961.
       Papers, 1883-1957. 30 ms. boxes, 3 envelopes.
       American pacifist, feminist, and socialist; member, Henry Ford
           Peace Ship Expedition, 1915.
       Diaries, correspondence, pamphlets, clippings, and leaflets,
           relating to pacifism and the peace movement, the Ford Peace
           Ship Expedition, feminism, socialism, the labor movement,
           prison reform, child labor legislation, civil liberties,
           and a variety of other reform movements in the U.S.
       Register.
       Gift, A. Park, 1930. Subsequent increments.

Box 5 -- Newspaper clippings, journals, and notes relating to education and teachers.
Box 14 -- Newspaper clippings, articles, leaflets, and pamphlets on peace and youth.
Box 18 -- Pamphlets, articles, newspaper clippings, and leaflets on sex education.

405. PARKYN, GEORGE WILLIAM.
Writings, 1964-1977. 1 folder.
Printed.
Director, New Zealand Council for Educational Research, 1954-1968; Educational Consultant, United Nations Educational Scientific and Cultural Organization, 1968-1969. Relates to education, especially in international aspects.

"The Mental Health of the Gifted Child," 1964. "New Zealand Educational Studies," 1968. "Adapting the Curriculum and the Teaching-Learning Process to the Changing World," 1969. "Towards a Conceptual Model of Life-Long Education." 1973. "Comparative Education Research and Development Education," 1977.

406. PARMELEE, RUTH A., 1855-1973.
Papers, 1922-1945. 5 ms. boxes.
American physician and relief worker in Turkey, 1914-1917 and 1919-1922, Greece, 1922-1941 and 1945-1947, and Palestine, 1943-1945.
Diaries, notes, correspondence, reports, clippings, printed matter, and photographs, relating to refugee relief work and medical service in the Near East.
Gift, Mrs. W. H. Walker, 1974.

Box 4 -- Pamphlet on child care and child education.

407. PASTUHOV, VLADIMIR D., 1898-1967.
Papers (in English, French, Russian, and Chinese), 1927-1938. 58 ms. boxes, 13 albums, 1 envelope, 3 oversize packages (2 linear feet).
Secretary, League of Nations Commission of Enquiry in Manchuria, 1931-1934.
Correspondence, memoranda, reports, interviews, maps, photographs, and printed matter, relating to the investigation of the Manchurian incident of 1931.

Gift, Alexis Pastuhov, 1967. Gift, Serge D. Pastuhov, 1977.

Box 6 -- Report relating to League of Nations, with sections
    on education.
Boxes 32, 33, and 38 -- Pamphlet and books on antiforeign
    education in China.
Boxes 34, 35, and 54 -- Booklet, book, and reports on
    Manchuria, with sections on education.

408. PATRICK, MARY MILLS, 1850-1940.
    Papers, 1875-1924. 1 ms. box.
    President, Constantinople Woman's College, 1890-1924.
    Memoirs, entitled "Transformations," and letters, relating to
        the history of Constantinople Woman's College during World
        War I, conditions in Turkey during the war, Turkish
        society, and the Turkish educational system.

    Chapter 6 of memoirs is related to Turkish university system.

409. PECK, WILLYS RUGGLES, 1882-1952.
    Papers, 1911-1952. 3 ms. boxes, 1 oversize box, 1 envelope.
    American diplomatic and consular official in China, 1906-1926
        and 1931-1940; Minister to Thailand, 1941-1942.
    Diary, correspondence, memoranda, biography, and clippings,
        relating to Chinese foreign relations, domestic politics in
        China, and the Japanese occupation of Bangkok, Thailand,
        during World War II.
    Preliminary inventory.
    Gift, Mrs. L. C. Reynolds, 1953. Incremental gift, 1978.
        Gift, Celia Harris, 1970.

    Box 1 -- Typescript biography of Willys Peck in which his
        school days and his college life are described.

410. PENNINGTON, LEVI T.
    Correspondence, 1928-1962, with Herbert Hoover. 1 folder.
    Photocopy.
    President, Pacific College, Newberg, Oregon. Relates to
        Pacific college, disarmament, the National Committee on
        Food for the Small Democracies, and the Boys' Clubs of
        America.
    Purchase, University of Oregon, 1968.

411. PERRY, W. L., COLLECTOR.
    Miscellany, 1943. 1 folder.
    Pamphlets, leaflets, handbooks and miscellanea, issued as

guides to American soldiers in North Africa and Italy
during World War II.

Typewritten illustrated guide of Naples describing social
conditions, churches, and the University of Naples.

412. PETERKIN, WILBUR J., 1904-   .
    Papers, 1944-1945. 1-1/2 ms. boxes, 4 motion picture reels,
        1 envelope, memorabilia (1 linear foot).
    Colonel, U.S. Army; Executive Officer and Commanding Officer,
        Observer Mission to the Chinese Communists, 1944-1945.
    Diary transcripts, reports, maps, 16 mm films, and
        memorabilia, relating to Chinese communist forces and the
        Japanese occupation of China during World War II. Includes
        a rifle, a bayonet, a pistol, and a hand grenade used by
        the Chinese Communists during the Sino-Japanese Conflict.
    Gift, W. J. Peterkin, 1976. Subsequent increments.

    Box 1 -- Issue of China Pictorial, 1978, with section on
        Peking University.

413. PHILLIPS, ETHEL G., COLLECTOR.
    Collection on the New Deal, 1933-1941. 32 ms. boxes.
    Clippings from U.S. newspapers, relating to U.S. foreign and
        domestic policy during the New Deal and reflecting
        conservative criticism of that policy. Includes pamphlets
        issued by the American Liberty League, 1935-1936, and texts
        of radio broadcasts on the Ford Sunday Evening Hour,
        1936-1940.
    Gift, E. G. Phillips, 1939. Subsequent increments.

    Box 5, Bundle 15 -- School crisis, February 26, 1935.
    Box 9, Bundle 26 -- Schools and dollar tinkers.
    Box 11, Bundle 32 -- Youth, August 15, 1935.
    Box 14, Bundle 55 -- Student Union, December 30, 1939.
    Box 15, Bundle 58 -- Hamilton telling Youth Congress to purge
        Communists, February 5, 1940.
    Box 30, Bundle 4 -- Call for removal of teachers preaching
        alien social system, September 2, 1936.

414. PLATONOV, VALERIAN PLATONOVICH, 1809-   .
    Papers (in Russian, French, and Polish), 1815-1884.
        3-1/2 ms. boxes.
    Russian State Secretary for Polish Affairs, 1864-1866.

Correspondence, reports, and printed matter, relating to
   Russian governmental administration in Poland, political,
   economic, and religious conditions in Poland, and the
   Polish revolution of 1863-1864.
Gift, Ksenia Denikin, 1936.

Box 2 -- Pamphlet on history of Moscow University.
Box 4 -- Printed instructions by Russians on education in
   Poland.

415. PLATT, PHILLIP SKINNER, 1889- .
   Papers, 1916-1976. 1 folder, 1 envelope.
   American public health official; member of the Commission for
      Relief in Belgium, American Relief Administration, American
      Red Cross, and U.S. Army Sanitary Corps in Europe, 1916-
      1919. Memoirs (printed), 1976, and photographs, 1916,
      relating to relief work in Europe during World War I.
   Gift, P. S. Platt, 1957. Incremental gift, 1976.

   Memoirs include sections on Phillip Platt's school days, his
      postgraduate days, and Child Health Association.

416. PLATT, WILLIAM JAMES, 1916- .
   Papers, 1946-1978. 11-1/2 ms. boxes.
   Deputy Assistant Director General for Education, United
      Nations Educational, Scientific and Cultural Organization
      (UNESCO), 1970-1975.
   Speeches and writings, reports, memoranda, bulletins, serial
      issues, and other printed matter, relating to international
      educational developments, especially educational activities
      of UNESCO.
   Preliminary inventory.
   Gift, W. J. Platt, 1980.

   Box 2 -- Reports, articles, and notes on education in the
      developing countries, educational television, and
      mathematics education.
   Boxes 3 and 4 -- Memoranda, notes, and reports relating to
      UNESCO and educational reform, 1970-1977.
   Box 5 -- Reports on teacher education in Tanzania and on
      satellite-distributed educational television for developing
      countries.
   Boxes 8 and 9 -- UNESCO reports on education in various
      countries.
   Boxes 10 and 12 -- Various published and unpublished reports
      on education in different countries.

417. PLOTNICOV, LEONARD.
        Keypunch cards, n.d.   2 cubic foot boxes.
        Anthropologist.
        Relates to court cases, tax rolls, welfare, and education in
            Africa, 1951-1965.
        Gift, L. Plotnicov, 1974.

        Most of the contents are related to education in Nigeria.
        Box 1 -- Leonard Plotnicov's correspondence with the
            University of California, Berkeley.

418. POLAND. AMBASADA (Russia).
        Records (in Polish), 1941-1944. 54 ms. boxes.
        Polish Embassy in the Soviet Union.
        Reports, correspondence, accounts, lists, testimonies,
            questionnaires, certificates, petitions, card files, maps,
            circulars, graphs, protocols, and clippings, relating to
            World War II, the Soviet occupation of Poland, the Polish-
            Soviet military and diplomatic agreements of 1941, the
            re-establishment of the Polish Embassy in Moscow, Polish
            prisoners of war in the Soviet Union, deportations of
            Polish citizens to the Soviet Union, labor camps and
            settlements, relief work by the Polish Social Welfare
            Department delegations among the deportees, the Polish
            Armed Forces formed in the Soviet Union, evacuation of the
            Polish Embassy to Kuibyshev, evaucation of Polish citizens
            to the Middle East, the Katyn massacre of Polish officers,
            and the breakdown of Polish-Soviet relations in April 1943.
            Includes material on the Communist Party of the Soviet
            Union and the Soviet Government, 1928-1929.
        Register.
        Deposit, Jan Ciechanowski, 1945.

        Box 24 -- Reports on children, culture, and education.
        Boxes 41 and 49 -- Reports and correspondence on children and
            orphans.

419. POLAND. KONSULAT GENERALNY, NEW YORK.
        Records (in Polish), 1940-1948. 7 ms. boxes.
        Polish Consulate General in New York City.
        Correspondence, telegrams, memoranda, reports, agreements,
            minutes, histories, financial records, lists, press
            summaries, photographs, and printed matter, relating to the
            German and Soviet occupation of Poland during World War II,
            activities of the Polish Government-in-Exile (London), and
            displaced Polish citizens after World War II.
        Gift, Anne Appleton, 1976.

Box 4 -- Report on relief accorded to Polish citizens by
        Polish Embassy in the USSR, with section on schools.

420. POLAND. KONSULAT GENERALNY, PRETORIA.
        Records (in Polish), 1930-1957. 3 ms. boxes.
        Polish Consulate General in Pretoria.
        Correspondence, telegrams, circulars, notes, speeches,
            clippings, minutes, protocols, and seals, relating to
            Polish foreign relations with South Africa and Polish
            emigre organizations, fund raising for war relief, and
            consular activity in South Africa.
        Register.
        Gift, Tadeusz Kawalec, 1975.

        Box 1 -- Correspondence and notes on aid to Polish children in
            Russia and on social welfare.
        Box 2 -- Notes and correspondence relating to Ministry of
            Religion and Public Education, YMCA, youth, and students.

421. POLAND. MINISTERSTWO PRAC KONGRESOWYCH.
        Miscellaneous records (mainly in Polish), 1940-1944. 11-1/2
            ms. boxes.
        Ministry of Preparatory Work concerning the Peace Conference,
            Polish Government-in-Exile (London).
        Essays, bulletins, reports, and studies, relating to Poland's
            boundary disputes following World Wars I and II, events and
            conditions in Poland under German and Soviet occupation
            during World War II, Polish-Soviet relations, communism in
            Poland, and twentieth-century Polish agriculture, economy,
            foreign relations, history, politics, and government.
        Preliminary inventory.
        Deposit, Otton Laskowski, 1946. Deposit, Polish Research
            Centre, 1947.

        Box 7 -- Article on eastern frontier of Poland, with section
            on minorities' school.

422. POLAND. MINISTERSTWO SPRAW WEWNETRZNYCH.
        Issuances (in Polish), 1942-1944. 16 ms. boxes.
        Typescript (mimeographed).
        Ministry of the Interior of the Polish Government-in-Exile
            (London).
        Reports and bulletins, relating to Polish politics and govern-
            ment, social conditions in Poland, the German and Soviet
            occupations of Poland, and the Polish underground movement
            during World War II. Includes reports and studies prepared
            by the Ministries of National Defense and Military Affairs.

140

Preliminary inventory.
Deposit, Otton Laskowski, 1946. Deposit, Jozef Kisielewski, 1947.

Box 16 -- Polish news bulletin, with section on education for Polish children. Issue of Polish Fortnightly Review, with section on Polish universities and anniversary of martyrdom of Polish professors, 1940.

423. POLISH GREY SAMARITANS.
Records, 1918-1965. 3 ms. boxes.
Organization of Polish-American women relief workers.
Memoirs, reports, correspondence, printed matter, photographs, and memorabilia, relating to relief activities carried on in Poland at the end of World War I and to conditions in Poland at that time. Includes memoirs by Martha Gedgowd and Amy Pryor Tapping, members of Polish Grey Samaritans.
Gift, Martha Gedgowd and Amy Pryor Tapping, 1957. Subsequent increments.

Box 2 -- Pamphlet on problems of Cieszyn Silesia, with section on education.

424. POLISH INFORMATION SERVICE, NEW YORK.
Memorandum, n.d. 1 folder.
Typescript.
Polish Government agency.
Relates to the controversy between Germany and Poland between the two world wars regarding the decision of the Polish Government to destroy the bridge at Opalenica, Poznan Province, that has been constructed by the German Government in 1909.

Box 3 -- Notes and clippings relating to youth organizations.

425. POLISH RESEARCH CENTRE, LONDON.
Collection, 1939-1948. 1 ms. box, 34 reels of microfilm.
Reports, studies, bulletins, and printed matter, issued by the Polish Research Centre, the Polish Ministries of Foreign Affairs and Information and Documentation, and other agencies of the Polish Government-in-Exile (London), relating to Polish-Soviet relations, conditions in occupied Poland, Polish underground movements, and Polish refugees in Great Britain, during and after World War II.
Gift, Jozef Garlinsky, 1947.

Leaflets and posters used as propaganda by Polish people in
England. Pamphlet related to Polish students.

426. POOL, ITHIEL DE SOLA, 1917-   , <u>COLLECTOR.</u>
      Collection on American Trotskyism, 1905-1948. 1/2 ms. box.
      Mimeographed letters and circulars, pamphlets, and leaflets,
         relating to American Trotskyism, especially to factional
         disputes within the U.S. Socialist Workers Party, 1938-
         1940, and to Trotskyist activities in the antifascist,
         antiwar labor movements. Includes some radical non-
         Trotskyist material.
      Gift, I. de Sola Pool, 1950.

      Information bulletins by National Appeal Youth Association.
         Leaflet by Court of Students of the University of Chicago.
         Leaflets by American Student Union on Peace.

427. PORTUGUESE REVOLUTION COLLECTION.
      (In Portuguese), 1974. 1 folder.
      Poster and ephemera, relating to the revolution in Portugal in
         April 1974, issued by various political groups.
      Preliminary inventory.
      Purchase, Cornelius Drijver, 1975.

      Some of the contents are in English.
      Posters and leaflets by the International Union of Students
         against NATO.

428. POSSONY, STEFAN THOMAS, 1913- .
      Papers (in English and French), 1940-1977. 27 ms. boxes.
      American political scientist; Senior Fellow (Emeritus), Hoover
         Institution on War, Revolution and Peace.
      Correspondence, writings, reports, research notes,
         bibliographic card files, term papers, examination papers,
         periodical articles, and newspaper clippings, relating to
         military science, technology, national defense, inter-
         national relations, Soviet foreign policy, revolution in
         the twentieth century, and communism.
      Gift, S. T. Possony, 1978.

      Boxes 9, 13, 15, and 20 -- Term paper on communist propaganda.
      Box 13 -- Term paper on youth in Soviet Russia.
      Box 17 -- Paper by student at Army War College entitled "A
         World Alliance of Free Men," with section on peaceful
         coexistence.

429. POTULICKI, MICHAL, 1897- .
        Papers (in Polish), 1933-1945. 2-1/2 ms. boxes.
        Polish law professor; Principal Legal Adviser, Foreign
           Ministry, Polish Government-in-Exile (London), 1941-1945;
           Secretary General, Inter-Allied Research Committee
           (London).
        Bulletins, reports, studies, correspondence, notes, and
           clippings, relating to Polish politics and government,
           German war crimes, Germany during World War II, prisoners
           of war in Germany, the German invasion of Poland, and
           Polish relations with Britain, France, and the Soviet
           Union. Includes bulletins, reports, and studies of the
           Inter-Allied Research Committee (London), relating to
           German propaganda during World War II, the German
           mentality, and nazism.
        Preliminary inventory.
        Deposit, M. Potulicki, 1946.

        Some of the contents are in English and German.
        Box 2 -- Report entitled "Some Aspects of the Organization of
           German Thinking," October 1944, with sections on German
           education and German youth organizations.

430. POWERS, JOSHUA B., 1892- , COLLECTOR.
        Collection on Homer Lea, 1876-1962. 6 ms. boxes, 1 album,
           5 envelopes.
        Correspondence, telegrams, biographies, articles, pamphlets,
           clippings, writings, photographs, maps, scrapbooks, and
           memorabilia, relating to Homer Lea, military adviser to Sun
           Yat-sen and author of The Valor of Ignorance, and to the
           revolutionary movement in China, ca. 1900-1920. Includes
           writings and correspondence of H. Lea, Ethel Lea, and
           J. B. Powers.
        Register.
        Gift, J. B. Powers, 1968.

        Box 3 -- Copy of document by Circuit Court of the City of
           St. Louis, State of Missouri, relating to Chinese-American
           Educational Association.

431. PRESIDENT'S RESEARCH COMMITTEE ON SOCIAL TRENDS, 1929-1932.
        Reports, 1932. 10 ms. boxes.
        Typescript.
        Committee established by President Herbert Hoover to study
           social conditions in the United States.
        Relates to demographic, educational, racial, recreational,
           cultural, religious, medical, legal, and governmental
           aspects of society; urban and rural trends; and the role of

the family. Reports published under the title <u>Recent Social Trends in the United States</u> (New York: McGraw-Hill, 1935).
Gift, Ray Lyman Wilbur, 1933.

Box 1 -- Reports with sections on education and educational institutions.
Box 3 -- Reports on education.
Box 8 -- Pamphlet on social changes in the United States, with sections on education, June, 1932.

432. PRESTON, ARCHIBALD E.
Papers, 1917-1918. 1/2 ms. box.
Captain, U.S. Army Corps of Engineers. Correspondence, orders, training manuals, and maps, relating to U.S. military engineering activities in the U.S. and France during World War I.

Textbooks on construction of dugouts and program of instruction relating to Engineer Officers' Training School, 1917.

433. PRICE, RAYMOND KISSAM, JR., 1930- .
Papers, 1953-1977. 141 ms. boxes.
Special Consultant to President Richard M. Nixon, 1969-1974.
Speeches and writings, correspondence, memoranda, reports, notes, press summaries, clippings, and other printed matter, relating to U.S. foreign and domestic policy during the administration of President Richard M. Nixon and to the presidential elections of 1968 and 1972.
Closed until the death of R. K. Price, Jr.
Gift, R. K. Price, Jr., 1980.

Box 7 -- Article on career education, May 1973.
Boxes 52, 98, and 110 -- Notes, newspaper clippings, reports, and articles on education.
Box 96 -- Newspaper clippings on vocational education.
Boxes 102 and 111 -- Newspaper clippings, notes, articles, reports, and memoranda on campus unrest and student revolt.
Boxes 104, 105, 107-109, 120-122 -- Notes, reports, memoranda, articles, and correspondence on schools and desegregation.
Boxes 127, 130, and 140 -- Correspondence, memoranda, notes, and reports on children and youth.
Box 129 -- Memoranda and reports on education.

434. PRONIN, DIMITRI, 1900- .
History, n.d. "Europe in Flames." 1/2 ms. box.
Typescript (photocopy).

Relates to the Soviet and German occupation of Poland, 1939-1945.
Gift, D. Pronin, 1971.

Chapter 6 -- Pronin's children and their education in Russian school in Poland.

435. PROPAGANDA, COMMUNIST -- RUSSIA.
Collection (in Russian), 1929-1931. 1 folder.
Printed.
Leaflets and posters, propagating atheism and communism. Issued in the Soviet Union.

Leaflets and posters are illustrated with cartoons.

436. PROPAGANDA IN SOUTH KOREA.
(In Korean and English), 1948. 1 folder.
Propaganda material, including posters, bulletins, and leaflets, issued by the South Korean Government, U.S. occupation authorities, and South Korean Communists, for distribution in South Korea.

437. PROPAGANDA, RUSSIAN.
(In Russian), ca. 1914-1917. 1 ms. box.
Printed.
Postcards and miscellanea, issued as Russian Imperial propaganda during World War I.

438. PROTESTANT EPISCOPAL CHURCH IN THE U.S.A.
Collection, 1974-1978. 1 folder.
Clippings and other printed matter, relating to alleged Marxist influence in the Protestant Episcopal Church in the U.S.A. and in the World Council of Churches. Includes an Episcopalian study guide entitled Struggling with the System: Probing Alternatives (1976).
Gift, anonymous, 1978.

Sections on Christianity and religious education.

439. PROTESTING COMMITTEE AGAINST THE U.S. MARINES' VIOLENCE.
Propaganda (in Chinese), 1947. 1 folder.
Anti-American propaganda distributed at the National University of Taiwan in Taipei.

440. PRUITT, IDA, 1888- .
      Miscellaneous papers, 1911-1948. 1 folder.
      American missionary in China; member, American Committee in
          Aid of the Chinese Industrial Cooperatives, 1940-1951.
      Letters, reports, and printed matter, relating to missionary
          and social work in China, the Sino-Japanese conflict, and
          Chinese industrial cooperatives.
      Gift, Henry P. Sheng, 1974.

      Newsletter on colleges in China and several reports on social
          conditions and education in that country.

441. PUERTO RICO CHILD HEALTH COMMITTEE.
      Disbursement vouchers, 1930-1934. 34 ms. boxes.
      Commission for promotion of child welfare in Puerto Rico.
          Vouchers drawn on accounts of the U.S. Department of
          Education and the American Relief Administration Children's
          Fund.
      Preliminary inventory.
      Gift, Ray Lyman Wilbur.

442. PUSTA, KAAREL ROBERT, 1883-1964.
      Papers (in Estonian, French, and English), 1918-1964.
          20 ms. boxes.
      Estonian diplomat; Foreign Minister of Estonia, 1924-1925.
      Correspondence, speeches and writings, memoranda, reports,
          printed matter, and photographs, relating to Estonian
          politics and diplomacy, Soviet-Baltic State relations, the
          League of Nations, international law, and Estonian emigre
          politics.
      Preliminary inventory.
      Gift, Mrs. K. R. Pusta, 1964.

      Box 19 -- Report on Latvia and its Baltic neighbors, 1942,
          with section on education.

443. QUINN, FREDERICK.
      Papers (in French, English, and German), 1822-1974.
          16 ms. boxes, 3 microfilm reels, 4 phonotapes,
          2 envelopes.
      American anthropologist.
      Research notes and drafts, lists, writings, interviews, copies
          of government documents, printed matter, tapes of tribal
          chants, and photographs, relating to the Beti society of
          the Cameroon. Used by F. Quinn as research material for
          his dissertation, "Changes in Beti Society, 1887-1960"
          (University of California, Los Angeles, 1970).

146

Register.
Purchase, F. Quinn, 1972. Incremental gift, 1975.

Box 12 -- Writings and notes on influence of women in social
    structure of Beti society, with sections on education.
Box 15 -- Notes and writings on twenty-five years of
    missionary work of Pallotime Fathers in Cameroon, with
    sections on education.

444. RADICALISM -- LOS ANGELES.
    Reports, 1924. 1 folder.
    Typescript (mimeographed).
    Relates to activities of the Workers' (Communist) Party, the
        Industrial Workers of the World, and other leftist
        organizations in Los Angeles during this period.

    Reports on Educational League and educational propaganda.

445. RADIO FREE EUROPE/RADIO LIBERTY.
    Questionnaires (in English and German), 1969-1972.
        5 ms. boxes.
    Interviews of Soviet citizens, relating to their radio-
        listening habits and opinions of Western radio stations
        broadcasting into the Soviet Union.
    Closed during the lifetime of Max Ralis.
    Gift, M. Ralis, 1980.

446. RAEMAEKERS, LOUIS, 1869-1956.
    Papers (in English, French, and Dutch), 1903-1939. 12 ms.
        boxes, 9 drawers (18 linear feet), 2 albums, 3 envelopes.
    Dutch cartoonist.
    Correspondence, clippings, newspaper issues, photographs,
        cartoons, sketches, and paintings, relating to art work of
        L. Raemaekers, especially anti-German cartoons drawn by
        L. Raemaekers during World War I.
    Preliminary inventory.
    Gift, L. Raemaekers, 1944.

    Boxes 5-9 and 11 -- Newspaper clippings with cartoons by Louis
        Raemaekers.
    Box 12 -- Postcards with cartoons by Raemaekers and others.
        Cartoons deal with various topics, including education.

447. RAND CORPORATION.
    Reports, 1965-1972. 3 ms. boxes.
    Printed.

Relates to the organization, operations, motivation, and
morale of Viet Cong and North Vietnamese troops, 1964-1968,
based on 2,400 interviews with Vietnamese.
Preliminary inventory.
Gift, Rand Corporation, 1976.

Box 1 -- Report on Viet Cong and North Vietnamese troops, with
section on younger Viet Cong generation, and Vietnamese
youth.

448. RAYMOND, EDWARD A.
"Foreign Students, the Soviet Educational Weapon," 1973.
1 microfilm reel.

449. REAGAN, RONALD, 1911- .
Papers, 1966-1981. 2,700 linear feet.
Governor of California, 1967-1975.
Correspondence, cabinet proceedings, speeches, notes,
legislation, campaign material, press releases, printed
matter, video tapes, film, and phonotapes, relating to
California politics and government, to the candidacy of
Ronald Reagan for the 1976 and 1980 Republican presidential
nomination, and to the presidential election of 1980.
Preliminary inventory.
May be used with permission of Ronald Reagan or one of the
trustees of the collection. Material already released
publicly is open without restriction.
Gift, Ronald Reagan, 1975. Subsequent increments.

Collection contains approximately 16 linear feet of material
relating to education in California during his two terms as
governor, 1967-1975. Materials relate to primary and
secondary education as well as to higher education in the
state.

450. REDLICH, FRITZ, 1892- .
Correspondence (in German and English), 1928-1958.
1/2 ms. box, 1 envelope.
German-American economist and historian.
Correspondence, primarily with Wilhelm Gehlhoff, German
economist, concerning conditions in German universities
after World Wars I and II. Includes personal letters
received by Annemarie Labes, sister of F. Redlich,
1947-1957.
Gift, F. Redlich.

451. REED, ALICE C., 1890- .
Excerpts from letters, 1916-1948. 1 folder.
American missionary in China, 1916-1948. Relates to social
conditions and Christian missionary work in China.
May not be quoted without permission of A. C. Reed.
Gift, A. C. Reed, 1967.

Letters describe missionary schools and colleges.

452. "DIE REVOLUTION IN DER DEUTSCHEN ERZIEHUNG" (THE REVOLUTION IN
GERMAN EDUCATION).
Memorandum (in German), n.d. 1 folder.
Typescript.
Relates to education in Germany under national socialism
during World War II.

453. RHODES, CECIL JOHN, 1853-1902.
Miscellany, 1886-1930. 1/2 ms. box, 1 envelope.
British financier and politician. Copies of letters,
clippings, and miscellanea, relating to C. Rhodes, to the
Rhodes scholarships, and to the Rhodes Scholar reunion at
Oxford University in 1929. Includes a copy of the will of
C. Rhodes.

Some of the contents are in German.
Booklet relating to proceedings at unveiling of the Rhodes
Memorial Tablet.

454. RICARDO-CAMPBELL, RITA, 1920- .
Papers, 1964-1976. 38 ms. boxes.
American economist and educator; Chairman, Western Interstate
Commission for Higher Education, 1970-1971.
Correspondence, memoranda, reports, and printed matter,
relating to the administration and financing of higher
education, the Western Interstate Commission for Higher
Education, the Mountain States Regional Medical Program,
and the National Center for Higher Education Management
Systems.
Preliminary inventory.
Gift, R. Ricardo-Campbell, 1978.

Boxes 1, 10, 13-19, 32, and 33 -- Reports, pamphlets,
newsletters, and memoranda on higher education.
Box 3 -- Report entitled "The Compact for Education."
Box 8 -- Correspondence, newspaper clipping, and pamphlet on
minority students' programs.
Box 9 -- Data dictionary with section on students.
Box 11 -- Correspondence, memoranda, and newspaper clippings
on special education and rehabilitation program.

149

Boxes 12 and 20 -- Reports and memoranda on student unrest on
   university campuses.
Boxes 21, 24, and 34 -- Reports, issues of Educational Record
   and other printed matter on education.
Box 36 -- Annotated bibliography on graduate education.

455. RICHARDSON, GRACE, COLLECTOR.
      Miscellany, 1919. 1 folder.
      Printed matter, clippings, and badges, relating to the League
         to Enforce Peace, the American Red Cross, a 1919 reception
         for President Woodrow Wilson in Omaha, Nebraska, and
         women's suffrage in Nebraska.
      Preliminary inventory.
      Gift, G. Richardson, 1949.

      Issue of The Woman Citizen, with articles on famous women and
         their contributions.

456. RICHTER, HARALD, COLLECTOR.
      Collection (in German), 1968-1970. 2 ms. boxes.
      Bulletins, leaflets, clippings, and ephemeral printed and
         mimeographed material, primarily issued at the Universitaet
         Hamburg by student protest groups, relating to the
         university and to German and world politics. Includes some
         material relating to West German student radicalism.

457. RIEFFEL, ARISTIDE, 1859-1941.
      Papers (in French and English), 1890-1941. 20 linear feet.
      French journalist and pacifist.
      Correspondence, writings, pamphlets, clippings, and
         photographs, relating primarily to the temperance movement
         in France and the U.S., pacifism, international arbi-
         tration, the Society for Arbitration between Nations,
         Alfred Nobel, and the Nobel Peace Prize.
      Gift, Mireille Rieffel Gale, 1976.

      Box 5 -- Handwritten notes relating to colleges and education
         in America, 1929.
      Box 6 -- Handwritten notes on social, moral, religious, and
         educational issues.

458. RIETVELD, HARRIET.
      Papers, 1925-1941. 1/2 ms. box.
      Missionary.
      Notes, educational material, and printed matter, relating to
         missionary work of the Young Women's Christian Association

in Chefoo, China; to 1931 flood relief in China; and to
other missionary activities in China.
Gift, H. Rietveld, 1973.

Most of the contents are in Chinese.

459. RIXFORD, MARY C., <u>COLLECTOR.</u>
Pamphlets (printed), 1914-1922. 2 ms. boxes.
Related to Allied propaganda, primarily British, during World
War I and to medical aspects of the war, especially
activities of the American Red Cross.

Pamphlet on regulations of Hotchkiss School, 1915.

460. ROBB, FELIX C.
Papers, 1955-1965. 1/2 ms. box.
American educator; Director, Southern Association of Colleges
and Schools; member, Korean Project, George Peabody College
for Teachers, 1956-1962.
Correspondence, writings, photocopies of contracts, and
printed matter, relating to a project of the George Peabody
College for Teachers to provide technical assistance for
the improvement of education in South Korea.
Gift, F. C. Robb, 1978.

Includes book on teacher education in Korea.

461. ROBINSON, JACOB, <u>EDITOR.</u>
Bibliography, 1958. <u>Guide to Research in Jewish History,
1933-1945: Its Background and Aftermath.</u> 1 volume.
Typescript (mimeographed).
Published (New York, 1958). Edited by J. Robinson and Philip
Friedman.

Section on propaganda and list of depositories of Jewish
documents in the United States and the world.

462. ROBNETT, GEORGE WASHINGTON, 1890-1970.
Papers, 1932-1963. 1/2 ms. box.
American author and lecturer; Executive Director, Church
League of America, and National Laymen's Council,
1937-1956.
Reports, speeches, and writings, relating to federal control
of education and to socialist and communist movements in
America.
Preliminary inventory.

Gift, Mrs. G. W. Robnett, 1974.

Article on unionists' drive to capture the minds of youth and newspaper clippings on education.

463. ROMANIAN NATIONAL COMMITTEE, WASHINGTON, D.C.
       Records (in Romanian and English), 1946-1975.
          19-1/2 ms. boxes.
       Anticommunist Romanian emigre organization.
       Correspondence, memoranda, minutes of meetings, reports,
          financial records, printed matter, press releases,
          speeches, and writings, relating to communism in Romania,
          anticommunist emigre activities, the Assembly of Captive
          European Nations, the National Committee for a Free Europe,
          and the Free Europe Committee.
       Closed until January 1, 1987.
       Gift, Constantin Visoianu, 1976. Incremental gift, 1977.

       Boxes 17 and 18 -- Information bulletins with sections on
          education in Romania, 1950.
       Box 19 -- Reports, correspondence, and minutes of meetings
          related to Carol I University.

464. "ROMANIA'S INTERNAL POLICY SINCE WORLD WAR I."
       Memorandum, n.d. 1 folder.
       Typescript.
       Relates to political conditions and rural social structure in
          Romania between the two world wars.

       Essay on Romania's internal policy, with section on village
          teachers in that country.

465. ROSTOVTSEFF, FEDOR.
       Papers (in Russian), n.d. 2 ms. boxes.
       Russian emigre teacher in France.
       Writings, reports, notes and outlines for lectures, clippings,
          memorabilia, and syllabi for courses in Russian high
          schools in Paris, relating to Russian history from 1850 to
          1940, French history, and logic.
       Gift, F. Rostovtseff.

466. ROUCEK, JOSEPH SLABEY, 1902- .
       Papers, 1920-1949. 38 ms. boxes, 2 envelopes.
       American sociologist and political scientist.
       Correspondence, writings, clippings, photographs, slides, and
          miscellanea, relating to Slavs in the U.S. and politics,

social conditions, and education in Eastern Europe,
especially the Balkan countries.
Register.
Gift, J. S. Roucek, 1949.

Box 1 -- Writings on different aspects of education in
Czechoslovakia, Albania, Yugoslavia, Latvia, Bulgaria,
Romania, and Greece.

467. ROWE, DAVID NELSON, 1905- .
Papers (in English and Chinese), 1931-1974. 136 ms. boxes,
1 oversize box.
American political scientist; Special Assistant to the U.S.
Ambassador to China, 1941-1942.
Correspondence, speeches and writings, notes, reports, printed
matter, photographs, slides, phonotapes, microfilm, maps,
posters, postcards, and memorabilia, relating to Chinese
history and foreign relations, Asian area studies, Japanese
World War II propaganda, application of the People's
Republic of China for admission to the United Nations, and
communism in Asia.
May not be used without written permission of D. N. Rowe.
Deposit, D. N. Rowe, 1978.

Box 14 -- Proposals for improvement of teaching in smaller
colleges of the United States in field of international
relations; correspondence, reports, and booklet on visual
education.
Boxes 50 and 118 -- Correspondence, memoranda, reports, notes,
and articles on world youth and World Youth Crusade for
Freedom.
Box 58 -- Issues of Afro-Asia by American Afro-Asian
Educational Exchange, Inc.
Box 66 -- Reports of Senate hearings entitled "Subversive
Influence in the Educational Process," 1952-1955.
Box 104 -- Correspondence, reports, pamphlet, and leaflet
relating to American Association of Teachers of Chinese
Language and Culture.
Box 110 -- Pamphlet entitled "Toward a Better Understanding of
Yale."
Box 114 -- Chart on brain drain relating to annual inflow and
outflow of Chinese students.

468. RUARK, ARTHUR EDWARD, 1899-1979.
Papers, 1885-1979. 61 ms. boxes.
American physicist; Assistant and Senior Associate Director of

Research, Atomic Energy Commission, 1961-1969.
Writings, technical reports, reprints, lectures, corres-
    pondence, notes, and printed matter, relating to physics.
Gift, Mary Lee Fennel, 1980.

Box 1 -- Newspaper clipping relating to one of France's most
    prestigious schools, Ecole Nationale d'Administration, and
    its academic program.

469. RUHL, ARTHUR.
    Series of articles, 1925. "Russia Revisted." 1 folder.
    Typescript.
    American visitor to Russia.
    Relates to social conditions and the situation of industry,
        education, and religion in Russia.

    Article No. 3 -- "Education and the Young Generation."

470. RUSSELL, MRS. HENRY POTTER.
    Papers, 1946-1958. 25 ms. boxes.
    Member, U.S. National Committee for UNESCO.
    Correspondence, reports, memoranda, position papers,
        resolutions, and minutes, relating to the activities of the
        United Nations Educational, Scientific and Cultural
        Organization and the U.S. National Commission for UNESCO.
    Gift, Mrs. H. P. Russell, 1954. Incremental gift, 1960.

    Some of the contents are in French.
    Box 2 -- Reprinted article by the San Francisco Chronicle
        entitled "UNESCO Beats the Sextuplicates," January 12,
        1951.
    Box 13 -- UNESCO report on education.
    Box 15 -- UNESCO's problems and participation of nations.

471. RUSSIA. DEPARTAMENT POLITSII. ZAGRANICHNAIA AGENTURA, PARIS.
    Records (mainly in Russian), 1883-1917. 203 ms. boxes.,
        10 volumess of clippings, 163,802 biographical and
        reference cards, 8 linear feet of photographs.
    Russian Imperial Secret Police (Okhrana), Paris office.
    Intelligence reports from agents in the field and the Paris
        office, dispatches, circulars, headquarters' studies,
        correspondence of revolutionaries, and photographs,
        relating to activities of Russian revolutionists abroad.
    Preliminary inventory.
    Deposit, Vasilii Maklakov, 1926. One item purchased from
        Jacob Rubin, 1976.

Boxes 194 and 195 -- Notes, card-notes, correspondence,
leaflets, writings, reports, and newspaper clippings
relating to student and other emigre groups.
Box 225 -- Books on learning French and Italian and pamphlet
used as guide for students of Russian language.

472. RUSSIA. POSOL'STVO (France).
Records (in Russian and French), 1917-1924. 36-1/2 ms. boxes.
Russian Embassy in France.
Correspondence, reports, memoranda, and notes, relating to
relations between France and the Russian Provisional
Government, the Russian Revolution, counterrevolutionary
movements, the Paris Peace Conference, and Russian emigres
after the revolution.
Register.
Gift, Vasilii Maklakov, 1926. Incremental gift,
G. de Lastours, 1961.

Box 28 -- Reports, notes, and memoranda on propaganda.

473. RYAN, JOHN W., COLLECTOR.
Collection on literacy in Iran (in English and Persian),
1976-1978. 1 folder.
Pamphlets and bibliographies, published by the National
Committee for World Literacy Programme and the
International Institute for Adult Literacy Methods,
relating to literacy in Iran.
Gift, J. W. Ryan, 1978.

474. RYAN, PAUL B., 1913- .
Papers, 1968-1976. 33 ms. boxes.
Captain, U.S. Navy; Research Associate, Hoover Institution on
War, Revolution and Peace. Reports and research notes,
relating to the Panama Canal. Used as research material
for the book by P. B. Ryan, The Panama Canal Controversy:
U.S. Diplomacy and Defense Interests (Stanford: Hoover
Institution Press, 1977).
Gift, P. B. Ryan, 1978.

Box 1 -- Research papers of Naval and Army War Colleges on the
Panama Canal.
Box 8 -- Articles and newspaper clippings relating to U.S.
campuses and Panama Canal, 1967-1977.

475. SALISBURY, LAURENCE E., 1891-1976.
Papers, 1916-1973. 4 ms. boxes.

American diplomat; Deputy Assistant Chief, Division of Far
Eastern Affairs, U.S. Department of State, 1941-1944;
editor, Far Eastern Survey, 1944-1948.
Correspondence, writings, reports, and memoranda, relating to
American foreign relations with China, Japan, and the
Philippines and to political developments in the U.S.
Register.
Purchase, estate of L. E. Salisbury, 1977.

Box 2 -- Reports and newspaper clippings on religious life of
university students in Japan.
Box 4 -- Articles on Japanese education.

476. SALNAIS, VOLDEMARS, 1886-1948.
Papers (mainly in Latvian), 1918-1945. 1-1/2 ms. boxes,
2 envelopes.
Latvian diplomat; delegate to the League of Nations,
1921-1934; Minister to Sweden, Norway, and Denmark,
1937-1940.
Correspondence, reports, clippings, printed matter, and
photographs, relating to Latvian independence movements,
foreign relations, and women's organizations, Latvians in
Siberia, the Latvian National Council in Siberia
(Vladivostok), and the Office of the Latvian Representative
in the Far East and Siberia. Includes materials collected
by Milda Salnais.
Register.
Gift, Lilija Salnais, 1975.

Box 1 -- Reports, notes, and newspaper clippings on services
of Latvian YMCA and Latvian National League of Women for
the promotion of peace and education.

477. SAMS, CRAWFORD F.
Papers, 1923-1979. 15 ms. boxes, 1 oversize box,
12 envelopes.
Brigadier General, U.S. Army Medical Corps; Chief Surgeon,
U.S. Army Forces in the Middle East, 1942-1943; Chief,
Public Health and Welfare Section, General Headquarters;
Supreme Commander for the Allied Powers, 1945-1951.
Correspondence, orders, speeches and writings, research data,
printed matter, certificates, and photographs, relating to
U.S. military medical activities in the Middle East during
World War II and in the Korean War, to Allied public health
activities in occupied Japan, and to scientific research on
effects of radiation.

Box 1 -- Report on assignment of medical doctors to different

areas of the world; sections on medical service schools;
the Infantry School; and social conditions in various
countries.
Box 8 -- Reports on public health and welfare in Japan, with
sections on education and child care.

478. SAMSONOW, MICHAEL S., 1900-1973.
Papers (in English and French), 1919-1967. 1/2 ms. box,
1 envelope.
Hungarian-American historian.
Memoirs, writings, and a photograph, relating to Tsar
Alexander III of Russia, Russian emigres in Hungary after
the Russian Revolution, and the provisions for a veto in
the United Nations Charter.
Gift, M. S. Samsonow, 1970. Subsequent increments.

Writings on peace and peacemaking attitude of Tsar Alexander
III of Russia. Essay entitled "Pages of Diplomatic History
from a Hungarian Diary," with section on Hungarian
universities and their high scholastic and academic
standards.

479. "SANTO TOMAS INTERNMENT CAMP, JANUARY 4, 1942 TO SEPTEMBER 27,
1943."
Report, 1943. 1 volume.
Typescript.
Relates to living conditions in the Japanese prison camp for
American and other civilian internees at Santo Tomas,
Philippines. Prepared by released prisoners.

Section relating to educational program of the camp.

480. SATORN, PINYO, COLLECTOR.
Printed matter (in Thai), 1976-1977. 4 ms. boxes.
Minister of Education, Thailand, 1976-1977.
Relates to education in Thailand. Published by Thai Ministry
of Education.
Preliminary inventory.
Gift, P. Satorn, 1978.

Box 1 -- Booklet in English entitled "Thailand National
Educational Scheme 1977."

481. SCAPINI, GEORGES, 1893- .
Papers (in French), 1928-1963. 15-1/2 ms. boxes,
3 oversize boxes.

French diplomat and politician; Deputy, National Assembly,
    1928-1940; Ambassador to Germany and Chief of the
    Diplomatic Service for Prisoners of War, 1940-1944.
Correspondence, memoranda, reports, writings, legal documents,
    printed matter, and photographs, relating to French
    politics, French prisoners of war in Germany during World
    War II, and the trial of Georges Scapini as a Nazi
    collaborator, 1952.
Preliminary inventory.
May not be used until March 1, 1998, without written
    permission of Lucie Marie Scapini, Jean-Marie Scapini,
    Francois-Marie Scapini, Pierre Arnal, or J. Chaperon.
Gift, Lucie Marie Scapini, 1978.

Boxes 8 and 9 -- Reports, memoranda, correspondence, notes,
    bulletins, pamphlets, and leaflets relating to education of
    French prisoners of war, 1940-1944.

482. SCHENCK, HUBERT GREGORY, 1897-1960.
    Papers, 1943-1959. 21 ms. boxes, 34 envelopes.
    Colonel, U.S. Army; Chief, Natural Resources Section, General
        Headquarters, Supreme Commander of the Allied Powers,
        Japan, 1945-1951; Chief, Mutual Security Mission to Taiwan,
        1951-1954; Consultant, U.S. Foreign Operations Adminis-
        tration, 1954-1955.
    Correspondence, diary, mimeographed reports, and newspaper and
        magazine clippings and photographs, relating to the Allied
        occupation of Japan, relations between Taiwan and the U.S.,
        and ecomonic affairs in Japan and Taiwan.
    Preliminary inventory.
    Gift, H. G. Schenck, 1950. Subsequent increments.

    Box 10 -- UNESCO reports relating to Asia and the U.S.
    Box 11 -- Reports by Phi Beta Kappa Association on education
        in Japan, 1948-1949, and pamphlet on Tsuda College for
        Japanese women.
    Box 16 -- Reports on education in Taiwan.

483. SCHNEIDER, ELIZABETH.
    Letters, 1977. 1 folder.
    Typescript.
    American visitor to South Africa.
    Relates to political and racial unrest at the University of
        Witwatersrand, Johannesburg, South Africa. One letter is
        written on the obverse side of a leaflet, possession of
        which was illegal.
    Gift, Jack Schneider, 1977.

Several university students were arrested for distribution of
leaflets under Rioters Assemblies Act in South Africa.

484. SCHOLLY, NORA.
    Textbook (in German), 1945. "Lustiges Lesen" (Merry Reading).
        1 volume.
    Printed.
    Austrian elementary school textbook published under
        supervision of Allied occupation authorities.

    Textbook is illustrated.

485. SCHWIMMER, ROSIKA, 1877-1948.
    Papers, 1914-1937. 2 ms. boxes, 1 envelope.
    Hungarian feminist and pacifist.
    Correspondence, petitions, clippings, printed matter, and
        photographs, relating to the pacifist movement during World
        War I, the Henry Ford Peace Expedition, the International
        Congress of Women, and the presentation of the World Peace
        Prize to R. Schwimmer in 1937.
    Preliminary inventory.
    Purchase, R. Schwimmer, 1937.

    Some of the contents are in German and French.
    Box 1 -- Newspaper clippings and articles on great women and
        their efforts for world peace; newspaper clippings on
        youth.
    Box 2 -- Newspaper clipping on the problem child and its
        treatment; article relating to case of a married woman
        teacher.

486. SCIPIO, LYNN A., 1876-   , COLLECTOR.
    Photographs, 1920-1922. 1 album.
    Depicts educational and relief work of the Young Men's
        Christian Association among Russian, Armenian, and other
        refugees in Constantinople, Turkey.

    Album was presented to Dean Lynn Scipio of Robert College in
        recognition of his services as a member of YMCA.
    Description under each photo.

487. SCOTT, RODERICK.
    Papers, 1916-1958. 2 ms. boxes.
    American missionary in China; official, Fukien Christian
        University, Foochow, China, 1917-1949.
    Correspondence, reports, newsletters, photographs, writings,

159

and textbooks, relating to missionary activity and social
conditions in China and to Fukien Christian University.
Gift, Mrs. R. Scott, 1971.

Some of the materials are in Chinese.
Box 2 -- Historical sketch and illustrated brochure of Fukien
Christian University.

488. SEABURY, PAUL.
Papers (in German), 1975-1977. 1-1/2 ms. boxes.
American political scientist.
Writings, leaflets, correspondence, notes, clippings, reports,
books, and other printed matter, relating to West German
university reform, higher education in West Germany,
government regulation of West German universities, and the
International Council on the Future of the University.
Gift, P. Seabury, 1977.

Some of the writings are in English.
Box 1 -- Book on reviews of national policies for education in
Germany, 1972, and writings on governmental regulations of
universities in that country.

489. SEREBRENNIKOV, IVAN INNOKENTIEVICH, 1882- .
Papers (in Russian), 1906-1948. 25 ms. boxes, 29 albums,
11 envelopes.
Russian journalist; official, Siberian Government, Omsk,
1917-1918.
Diaries, correspondence, writings, photographs, clippings, and
notebooks, relating to the Russian Civil War in Siberia,
Russian emigres in the Far East, and Chinese history and
culture.
Register.
Consult archivist for access.
Purchase, I. I. Serebrennikov, 1951.

Box 9 -- Articles on Asia as cradle of the first civilization;
children and creation of words by children.
Box 11 -- Articles on high school education.

490. SEYMOUR, J. MATT, COLLECTOR.
Collection (in English and Malayan), 1960-1970.
1/2 ms. box.
Directives, syllabi, textbooks, and other instructional
materials relating to education in Malaysia.

Math and social studies textbooks, curricula of primary and

junior secondary schools, and guide booklets for primary
school teachers.

491. SHARP, WALTER RICE, 1896- .
       Papers, 1922-1968. 1 ms. box.
       American political scientist; consultant to various United
           Nations organizations.
       Writings, correspondence, memoranda, minutes, loyalty board
           interrogatory, and printed matter, relating to adminis-
           tration of the United Nations and other international
           organizations.
       Gift, Doris B. Sharp, 1980.

       Text of address entitled "The Role of UNESCO: A Critical
           Evaluation."

492. SHEIMAN, BORIS.
       Translations, 1936-1939. 1/2 ms. box.
       Typescript.
       Soviet statutes and articles published in Soviet journals,
           1932-1938, relating to the Soviet judicial and penal
           systems, labor, social and welfare legislation, and the
           legal position of the family in Soviet society.
       Preliminary inventory.
       Gift, University of California Law School.

       Report on problem children: juvenile delinquents and their
           care in children's institutions in USSR.

493. SHISHMANIAN, JOHN AMAR, 1882-1945.
       Papers (in English, French, and Armenian), 1903-1945.
           1 ms. box.
       Captain, French Foreign Legion, during World War I.
       Correspondence, printed matter, photographs, and memorabilia,
           relating to the Armenian-Turkish conflict at the end of
           World War I and to the Armenian question at the Paris Peace
           Conference.
       Preliminary inventory.
       Gift, Georgia Cutler, 1941. Subsequent increments.

       Article on Michigan students' art exchange, November 1934.
       Issue of USSR in Construction, with section on education.

494. SHOCKLEY, WILLIAM BRADFORD, 1910- .
       Miscellaneous papers, 1980. 1 folder.
       Photocopy.

American physicist; Nobel laureate.
Correspondence, press release, and circulars, relating to
    international protest of Soviet reprisals against the
    dissident physicist Andrei Sakharov.
Gift, W. B. Shockley, 1980.

Related to International Sakharov Tribunal with signatures of
    some Nobel Prize winners concerning Sakharov's freedom.
    Notes on Sakharov's philosophy on progress, peaceful
    coexistence, intellectual freedom, freedom of
    communication, and welfare of humanity for the promotion of
    education.

495. SHOUP, DAVID MONROE, 1904- .
        Papers, 1927-1971. 27-1/2 ms. boxes, 2 cubic foot boxes,
            5 oversize boxes (5 linear feet).
        General, U.S. Marine Corps; Commander of Marine forces at
            Tarawa, 1943; Chief of Staff, 2d Marine Division, 1944;
            Commandant of the Marine Corps, 1960-1963.
        Correspondence, memoranda, writings, printed matter,
            photographs, films, and sound recordings, relating to the
            Tarawa campaign, other World War II campaigns in the
            Pacific Theater, postwar activities of the Marine Corps,
            and the Vietnam War.
        Gift, D. M. Shoup, 1976. Incremental gift, 1977.

        Box 26 -- Texts of speeches on youth of America.

496. SHRIVER, HARRY C., <u>COLLECTOR.</u>
        Printed matter, 1941-1945. 4 ms. boxes.
        Relates to U.S. propaganda efforts in World War II. Issued by
            the U.S. Office of War Information.
        Gift, H. C. Shriver, 1978.

        Box 2 -- Notes and newspaper clippings on free speech and
            constitutional rights in the U.S.

497. SHULTZ, GEORGE PRATT, 1920- .
        Papers, 1969-1974. 263 ms. boxes.
        U.S. Secretary of Labor, 1969-1970; Director, Office of
            Management and Budget, 1970-1972; Secretary of the
            Treasury, 1972-1974.
        Correspondence, memoranda, reports, speeches, press releases,
            notes, and printed matter, relating primarily to economic
            policies of Richard M. Nixon's presidency.
        Preliminary inventory.
        Closed until processed by archives staff.

Deposit, G. P. Shultz, 1977.

Box 4 -- Correspondence, notes, and articles relating to U.S. Naval Academy.
Boxes 15, 121, 123, 192, and 211 -- Correspondence, memoranda, reports, and pamphlets on school desegregation.
Boxes 101, 105, and 107 -- Memoranda, reports, notes, and correspondence on aid to education.
Box 146 -- Notes, memoranda, and correspondence on student unrest.
Box 210 -- Correspondence and memoranda on health, education, and welfare.

498. SIMMONS, ROBERT GLENMORE, 1891-1969.
Papers, 1929-1962. 1 ms. box.
Photocopy of original papers located at the Herbert Hoover Presidential Library.
U.S. Representative from Nebraska, 1923-1933; Chief Justice, Nebraska Supreme Court, 1938-1962.
Memoirs, correspondence, and memoranda, relating to U.S. politics and to the relationship between R. G. Simmons and Herbert Hoover.
Exchange, Herbert Hoover Presidential Library, 1971.

Autobiography of Judge Robert Simmons in which he describes his school years and schooling.

499. SLAVIK, JURAJ, 1880-1969.
Papers (in Czech, Slovak, and English), 1934-1966.
44 ms. boxes.
Czechoslovakian diplomat and statesman; Ambassador to Poland, 1936-1939; Minister of the Interior, 1940-1945; Minister of Foreign Affairs, 1945-1946; Ambassador to the U.S., 1946-1948.
Correspondence, speeches and writings, reports, dispatches, memoranda, telegrams, and clippings, relating to Czechoslovakian relations with Poland and the U.S., political developments in Czechoslovakia, Czechoslovakian emigration and emigres, and anticommunist movements in the U.S.
Gift, Gita Slavik, 1976.

Box 1 -- Report on Czechoslovak State School in Great Britain.
Box 14 -- Text of speech on Czechoslovakia's democratic system of education.
Box 28 -- Pamphlet by Council of Free Czechoslovakia, with sections on oppression in education, obligatory schools, and terror at colleges and universities.

500. SLJIVAR, VOJISLAV, 1925- .
        Papers (in Serbo-Croatian), 1960-1977. 1 ms. box.
        Serbian emigre in the U.S.
        Correspondence, reports, pamphlets, clippings, printed matter,
            and photographs, relating to his education in Germany and
            the U.S., the Serbian monarchy, Serbs in the U.S., the
            Serbian Orthodox Church in the U.S., and Yugoslav history
            after World War II.
        Closed until December 1992.
        Deposit, V. Sljivar, 1977. Incremental deposit, 1978.

        Some of the contents are in English.
        Booklet entitled: "Ruprecht-Karl-Universitat Heidelberg,"
            June 1965, guide for non-German students at the University
            of Heidelberg.

501. SMITH, EDDIE.
        Diary extracts, 1963-1964. 1-1/2 ms. boxes.
        Typescript.
        Peace Corps worker in Ghana, 1963-1964. Relates to the Peace
            Corps and social conditions in Ghana. Edited by George
            Jenkins. Revised version published under the title, Where
            Now Black Man?
        Gift, G. Jenkins, 1972.

        Sections on education and youth in Ghana.

502. SMITH, RALPH C., 1893- .
        Papers, 1917-1966. 26 ms. boxes, 2 oversize boxes
            (1 linear foot).
        Major General, U.S. Army; Commanding General, 27th Division,
            1942-1944; Military Attache to France, 1945-1946.
        Correspondence, reports, writings, and printed matter,
            relating to the American Expeditionary Forces in France
            during World War I, activities of the Command and General
            Staff School and Army War College in the interwar period,
            and American military operations in the Pacific Theater
            during World War II.
        Gift, R. C. Smith, 1978.

        Some of the contents are in French.
        Box 14 -- Two French Ministry of Education textbooks on
            democracy, 1948-1949.
        Box 16 -- Report on propaganda used at the General Staff
            College.

503. SMITH, RALPH ELBERTSON, 1910- .
        Study, 1977. "Academic Grading: Basic Issues and
           Recommendations." 1 folder.
        Typescript (photocopy).
        American economist.
        Relates to grading systems in American colleges and
           universities.
        Gift, R. E. Smith, 1977.

        Project by R. Elberton, Smith Professor of Economics at
           California State Polytechnic University, San Luis Obispo,
           in which conflict in grading philosophies is mentioned and
           uniform grading system is recommended.

504. SOLOW, HERBERT, 1903-1964.
        Papers, 1924-1976. 12 ms. boxes.
        American journalist; editor, Fortune Magazine, 1945-1964.
        Correspondence, speeches and writings, memoranda, depositions,
           clippings, and other printed matter, relating to the
           communist movement in the U.S., the Non-Partisan Defense
           League, the Commission of Inquiry into the Charges Made
           Against Leon Trotsky in the Moscow Trials, Soviet espionage
           in the U.S., Whittaker Chambers and the Alger Hiss case,
           Zionism, the Nuremberg Trial of Major German War Criminals,
           1945-1946, and post-World War II international business
           enterprises. Includes some papers of Sylvia Salmi Solow,
           1964-1976.
        Gift, Cassandra Johnson, 1977.

        Box 3 -- Article and newspaper clipping on colleges and
           academic freedom.
        Box 4 -- Article on refugee scholars in U.S., 1942.
        Box 6 -- Notes, correspondence, and newspaper clippings on
           education.
        Box 8 -- Article on education in Russia, June 1958.

505. SOUTHERN AFRICA COLLECTION, 1969-1977.
        8 ms. boxes. 1 oversize box (1 linear foot).
        Leaflets, newsletters, pamphlets, photographs, and ephemera of
           various political action groups and other organizations,
           relating to political and economic developments in southern
           African countries, including Angola, Mozambique, Rhodesia
           (Zimbabwe), South Africa, and South West Africa (Namibia).
           Collected by African Curatorship, Hoover Institution on
           War, Revolution and Peace.
        Preliminary inventory.

Box 1 -- Report on Worker's Education Project.

Box 2 -- Reports of U.S.-South Africa Leadership Exchange
Program with information on education in South Africa.

Box 8 -- Issue of <u>Free South Africa</u>, May 1973, with article on
education in South Africa.

506. SPROUSE, PHILIP D., 1906-1977.
Papers, 1945-1964. 2 ms. boxes, 18 envelopes.
American diplomat; member of George C. Marshall and Albert C.
Wedemeyer Missions to China, 1945-1947; Ambassador to
Cambodia, 1962-1964.
Printed matter, clippings, maps, invitations, programs, diplo-
matic list, and photographs, relating to American relations
with China and Cambodia, the Marshall Mission of 1945-1946,
and cultural and political conditions in Cambodia.
Gift, P. D. Sprouse, 1974.

Box 2 -- Leaflets, pamphlets, and booklets on culture and
education of Indochina.

507. SQUIRES, DUANE.
Speech, 1933, "British Propaganda at Home and in the United
States, 1914-1917." 1 folder.
Typewritten transcript.
Speech, delivered at Urbana, Illinois, December 28, 1933.

508. STALEY, EUGENE, 1906- .
Study guide series, 1978. "World Studies' Project: Some
Preliminary Drafts." 1 folder.
American economist and educator.
Relates to world problems, such as peace, international
organization, population growth, food supply, the
environment, and human rights. Designed for secondary,
college, and adult education courses.
Gift, E. Staley, 1980.

Project is based on need for education on the world community
and its problems.

509. <u>STANFORD COMMUNIST.</u>
Newspaper issues, 1949. 1 folder.
Typescript (mimeographed).

Organ of the Stanford (University) Club of the Communist
    Party. Two genuine issues, January-February 1949; and one
    false issue, actually issued by anticommunists, February
    1949.

Leaflets relating to education and communism.

510. STANFORD LISTENING POST, 1940-1945.
    Records, 1940-1945. 29 ms. boxes, 1 envelope.
    Project of the Hoover Institution on War, Revolution and Peace
        to record and analyze trans-Pacific radio broadcasts.
    Correspondence, transcripts of radio broadcasts, study papers,
        notes, and card indexes, relating to radio broadcasts from
        East and Southeast Asia.
    Register.

    Boxes 22-29 -- Correspondence, drafts of study papers,
        outlines and plans, notes, and broadcast transcripts of
        project to study and compare propaganda methods of China
        and Japan as revealed in their radio broadcasts.

511. STANFORD NISEI ALUMNI NEWSLETTER.
    Newsletter issues, 1944-1945. 1 folder.
    Typescript (mimeographed).
    Newsletter of Japanese American alumni of Stanford University.
        Relates to Japanese American activities during World
        War II.

    Relates to return of Japanese Americans to California.

512. STANFORD UNIVERSITY. DRAFT COUNSELING OFFICE, 1967-1973,
        COLLECTOR.
    Printed matter, 1967-1973. 3 ms. boxes.
    Newsletters, handbooks, leaflets, and ephemeral publications
        of government agencies, legal organizations, and political
        action groups, relating to military conscription in the
        United States.
    Preliminary inventory.
    Gift, Stanford University, 1973.

    Box 1 -- Report of White House Conference on Youth; news-
        letters and reports on women's campaign for peace.
    Boxes 2 and 3 -- Reports, pamphlets, newsletters, leaflets,
        and articles on draft resistance by students and selective
        service system.

513. STANFORD UNIVERSITY. INSTITUTE OF HISPANIC AMERICAN AND
        LUSO-BRAZILIAN STUDIES, COLLECTOR.
        Printed matter (in English, Spanish, and Portuguese),
            1954-1965. 783 ms. boxes.
        Pamphlets, clippings, and serial issues, relating to
            political, social, and economic conditions in Latin
            America, Spain, and Portugal.
        Register.
        Gift, Institute of Hispanic American and Luso-Brazilian
            Studies, 1965.

        Clippings and pamphlets on education, youth, and social
            conditions in Latin America, Spain, and Portugal.

514. STARR, CLARENCE T.
        Papers, 1923-1941. 1 ms. box.
        American mining engineer in the Soviet Union, 1928-1931.
        Correspondence, writings, notes, transcripts of testimony and
            printed matter, relating to the Soviet coal-mining
            industry, forced labor in the Soviet Union, and efforts to
            secure an embargo on Soviet imports into the U.S.
        Gift, Mrs. Leon Howard, 1960.

        Pamphlet on communist propaganda among American youth, April
            1953.

515. STAVRIANOS, LEFTEN STAVROS, 1913- .
        Papers (in English and Greek), 1942-1963. 4 ms. boxes.
        American historian.
        Writings, press releases, press translations and digests,
            reports, memoranda, clippings, and pamphlets, relating to
            political and military developments in Greece and Cyprus,
            especially during the Greek civil war period, 1944-1949.
            Includes material collected by a member of the Allied
            Mission for Observing Greek Elections of March 31, 1946.
        Register.
        Gift, L. S. Stavrianos, 1973.

        Pamphlet and newspaper clippings on Greek children during and
            after the civil war. Reports to the United Nations Social
            and Economic Commission on Child Welfare in Greece.

516. STERLING, J. E. WALLACE, COLLECTOR.
        Collection on world affairs, 1937-1951. 5 ms. boxes.
        Communiques of the belligerent governments printed in the New
            York Times, 1942-1945, relating to military operations
            during World War II; and reports from diverse sources,

relating to Japanese foreign policy, 1937-1939, postwar
Japanese educational reform, postwar Soviet foreign policy,
and the Chinese Revolution of 1949.

Box 5 -- Text of address by Shigeru Nambara, President of the
University of Tokyo, on ideals of educational reforms in
Japan at First National Conference on the Occupied Areas,
sponsored by the American Council on Education,
December 10, 1949.

517. STEVENS, HARLEY C.
Papers, 1901-1961. 3 ms. boxes.
Vice-President, American Independent Oil Company.
Texts of treaties, concessions, and agreements between various
    oil companies and governments of the Middle East, relating
    to Middle Eastern oil concessions.
Preliminary inventory.

Box 3 -- Reports, letters, and newsletters concerning
    education in Arab countries.

518. STOCKTON, GILCHRIST BAKER, 1890-1973.
Papers, 1911-1959. 11 ms. boxes.
Commission for Relief in Belgium and American Relief
    Administration worker during World War II; U.S. Minister to
    Austria, 1930-1933.
Correspondence, dispatches, reports, clippings, and
    photographs, relating to activities of the Commission for
    Relief in Belgium, 1915-1916, and of the American Relief
    Administration in Austria, 1919-1920; to U.S. and Florida
    politics, 1924-1928; to U.S.-Austrian relations, 1930-1933;
    and to the establishment of the Jacksonville, Florida,
    Naval Air Base.
Register.
Gift, G. Stockton, Jr., 1975.

Box 11 -- Correspondence, reports, newspaper clippings, and
    pamphlets relating to Oxford University academic record;
    Rhodes Scholarships, Florida's Rhodes Scholars at Oxford,
    and Princeton University Alumni Association.

519. STORY, RUSSELL MC CULLOCH, 1883-1942.
Papers, 1917-1921. 1/2 ms. box, 1 envelope, 6 boxes of slides
    (2 linear feet).
War Work Secretary, Young Men's Christian Association in
    Russia, 1917-1918.
Letters, photographs, and glass slides, relating to relief

work in Russia, conditions in Moscow and elsewhere in
Russia during the Russian Revolution, and the Czech Legion
and depicting scenes in Japan, Russia, and western Europe.
Preliminary inventory.
Gift, Gertrude A. Story, 1957. Gift, Katherine S. French,
    1972.

Scenes of schools and students.

520. STRONG, SYDNEY.
    Newsletters, 1932-1933. 1 folder.
    Typescript (mimeographed).
    Observer at the Geneva Disarmament Conference.
    Relates to the conference and to the world disarmament
        movement.

    Reports, memoranda, and leaflets on peace and youth.

521. STRUVE, PETER B., 1870-1944.
    Papers (mainly in Russian), 1890-1976. 29 ms. boxes,
        1 envelope.
    Russian journalist, historian, and politician; Minister of
        Foreign Affairs in the Baron Petr Vrangel' Government,
        1919-1921.
    Correspondence, speeches and writings, reports, memoranda,
        essays, photographs, and printed matter, relating to
        Russia in World War I, the Russian Revolution and Civil
        War, anti-Bolshevik movements, the Russian economy and
        industry, Russians in foreign countries, and conditions in
        the Soviet Union after the Revolution.
    Register.
    Purchase, Gleb P. Struve, 1979.

    Boxes 1 and 13 -- Correspondence and notes relating to
        academic organizations and academic questions.
    Box 7 -- Correspondence relating to student organizations,
        1925-1927.
    Box 15 -- Notes on Sons of Russia.
    Box 16 -- Notes relating to propaganda; German Teachers'
        Delegation in USSR; and article on communist youth.
    Box 26 -- Notes on emigre youth.

522. STUDENTS FOR A DEMOCRATIC SOCIETY.
    Records, 1958-1970. 41 microfilm reels.

Microfilm copy of originals at the State Historical Society of
    Wisconsin.
U.S. student organization, relating to student movements and
    political activity among students.
Guide.

523. SULLIVAN, MARK, 1874-1952.
    Papers, 1883-1952. 62 ms. boxes, 10 scrapbooks, 3 envelopes.
    American journalist; editor, Collier's Weekly, 1912-1919;
        columnist, New York Herald-Tribune, 1923-1952.
    Correspondence, diaries, speeches and writing, memoranda, and
        printed matter, relating to journalism and social,
        political, and economic developments in the United States.
    Register.
    Gift, M. Sullivan, Jr., 1955. Gift, Mrs. L. Metcalfe Walling,
        1968, with subsequent increments.

    Box 22 -- Notes, timetables, and pamphlets relating to West
        Chester Normal School; newspaper clipping relating to
        Barnard College.
    Box 35 -- Newspaper clippings, pamphlets, leaflets, and
        articles on propaganda.

524. SUNG, TZU-WEN, 1894-1971.
    Papers (in English and Chinese), 1933-1960. 57 ms. boxes,
        1 oversize box, 2 envelopes, 2 microfilm reels, 1 mask,
        8 albums.
    Chinese Minister of Finance, 1925-1933, and Minister of
        Foreign Affairs, 1941-1945, including correspondence,
        speeches and writings, reports, and memoranda, 1933-1960,
        relating to Chinese economic and political conditions and
        foreign relations.
    Boxes 36-39 (Schedule A) and Boxes 6-18 (Schedule B) are
        restricted until 1995.
    Gift, Laurette Soong Feng, 1980.

    Box 35 -- Pamphlet on reconstruction in China, with section on
        education in that country.

525. SURVEY OF RACE RELATIONS, 1923-1925.
    Records, 1924-1927. 37 ms. boxes.
    Anthropolgical investigative project sponsored by various
        private organizations.
    Reports, correspondence, interview transcripts,
        questionnaires, and printed matter, relating to the social
        and economic status of Chinese, Japanese, other Oriental,
        Mexican, and other minority residents of the Pacific Coast

of the U.S. and Canada, and to race relations on the
Pacific Coast.
Preliminary inventory.

Incomplete investigation by a group of scholars in the early
1920s of economic, religious, educational, civic,
biological, and social conditions among Chinese, Japanese,
and other nonwhite residents of the Pacific Coast of the
United States and Canada.
Box 3 -- Reports on Japanese education, 1923-1924.

526. TALBOT, PHILLIPS, 1915- .
Letters, 1939-1950, to Walter S. Rogers. 1 folder.
Typescript (mimeographed).
Associate, Institute of Current World Affairs, 1938-1941 and
1946-1951.
Relates to political and social conditions in India and the
Indian independence movement.

Letters relating to Aligarh Muslim University in India, its
students, and their activities. Letters relating to
Mahatma Gandhi, Nehru, and other freedom fighters of India
and their contributions to education and social mobility in
that country.

527. TARR, CURTIS W., 1924- .
Papers, 1963-1981. 14 ms. boxes.
President, Lawrence University, 1963-1969; U.S. Assistant
Secretary of the Air Force for Manpower and Reserve
Affairs, 1969-1970; Director, Selective Service System,
1970-1972; Under Secretary of State for Security
Assistance, 1972-1973; Chairman, Defense Manpower
Commission, 1974-1976; Vice-President, Deere and Co.,
1973- .
Diaries, memoir, and printed matter, relating to his
experiences as a soldier in World War II, his public and
educational careers, American military and foreign policy
and military conscription during the administrations of
Presidents Richard M. Nixon and Gerald R. Ford, and the
operations of Deere and Company, a multinational
corporation.
Access requires the written permission of C. W. Tarr during
his lifetime and, after his death, of his wife.
Deposit, C. W. Tarr, 1974. Subsequent increments.

Boxes 1-4 -- Memoirs of Curtis Tarr's educational career,
particularly as President of Lawrence University.

528. TARSAIDZE, ALEXANDRE GEORGIEVICH, 1901-1978.
        Papers (in English, Russian, French, German, and Georgian),
            1648-1978. 33 ms. boxes, 9 oversize boxes, 16 reels of
            film, 1 box of film fragments.
        Georgian-American author and public relations executive.
        Correspondence, speeches and writings, research notes, printed
            matter, photographs, engravings, lithographs, and maps,
            relating to the history of Georgia (Transcaucasia), the
            Romanov family, Russian-American relations, and the
            Association of Russian Imperial Naval Officers in America.
            Includes photocopies of Romanov family letters, photographs
            of Russia during World War I by Donald C. Thompson, and a
            documentary film on Nicholas II.
        Preliminary inventory.
        Gift, A. G. Tarsaidze, 1978.

        Box 5 -- Russian-American semimonthly magazines with articles
            on education, culture, Sunday schools, and minorities in
            Russia.

529. TELESCO, LEE, COLLECTOR.
        Collection on the Philippines, 1942-1953. 1 ms. box.
        Reports, letters, proclamations, newsletters, and miscellanea,
            relating to Allied guerrilla and intelligence activities in
            the Philippines during World War II, especially to
            activities of the First MacArthur Division. Includes
            examples of Japanese propaganda and reports of Japanese
            atrocities in the Philippines.
        Preliminary inventory.
        Gift, L. Telesco, 1947. Subsequent increments.

        Text of address by General MacArthur to all Filipino patriots,
            October 26, 1941.

530. TERRAMARE OFFICE, BERLIN.
        Issuances (in English and German), 1934-1937. 1 ms. box.
        Berlin publishing house.
        Essays, serial issues, and press releases, distributed as
            propaganda in Great Britain and the U.S., relating to
            aspects of the Nazi regime, including foreign policy,
            economic policy, compulsory labor, social welfare,
            education, culture, racial policy, and the place of women
            in German society.
        Gift, Indiana University Library, 1965.

        Essay No. 5 -- Professional training of youth in the New
            Germany.
        Essay No. 16 -- National Socialist education of German women.

531. THELANDER, HULDA EVELYN, 1896- .
Papers, 1926-1927. 1 folder.
American pediatrician in China, 1926-1927. Diary and excerpts
from letters (typewritten), relating to public health in
China and to general description of conditions in China.
Gift, H. E. Thelander, 1970.

Brief description of educational institutions of China.

532. THOMAS, DONALD ROFF, 1924-1979.
Papers, 1958-1979. 16 ms. boxes.
American educator; Director, U.S. Office of Economic
Opportunity Training and Development Center, 1965-1967;
Dean, School of Education, American University, 1972-1976.
Writings, notes, correspondence, memoranda, reports, studies,
minutes, sound recordings, and printed matter, relating to
education in the U.S., especially of disadvantaged and
minority children.
Gift, Sarah H. Thomas, December 1980.

Boxes 1, 5, and 11 -- Reports, leaflets, minutes of meetings,
and printed matter on education.
Boxes 2 and 3 -- Reports, pamphlets, newspaper clippings,
articles, and typescripts of books on youth, adolescents,
and curricula in schools.
Boxes 4, 6, and 10 -- Journals, notes, photocopies of books,
reports, articles, and leaflets on teacher education and
education in different states.
Box 7 -- Reports and articles on multicultural education and
curriculum development projects.
Box 8 -- Pamphlets, leaflets, and articles relating to
audiovisual education.
Boxes 9, 12, 13, and 14 -- Reports and articles on
disadvantaged and minority education.

533. TOKYO DAIGAKU.
Statement, 1957. 1 folder.
Printed.
Relates to the dangers from radioactive fallout resulting from
nuclear weapon testing. Signed by members of the College
of General Education of Tokyo University.

Statement by members of College of General Education and
letter by Y. Danno, Professor of Social Science in the
College of General Education.

534. TORRES QUINTERO, M. GREGORIO.
> Commission, 1917. 1 folder.
> Typescript.
> Head, Yucatan Department of Public Education.
> Commission from the State of Yucatan, charging M. G. Torres
> Quintero with a study of the educational system of the
> United States.

535. TRAINOR, JOSEPH C.
> Papers, 1944-1952. 76 ms. boxes, 1 album, 2 envelopes.
> Deputy Chief, Education Division, Civil Information and
> Education Section, General Headquarters, Supreme Commander
> for the Allied Powers in Japan, 1945-1951.
> Writings, memoranda, reports, surveys, handbooks, maps,
> photographs, and printed matter, relating to educational
> reform in Japan during the Allied occupation.
> Register.
> Gift, J. C. Trainor, 1972.

> Boxes 1, 2, 4-9, 14, 19-23, 26, 27, 32, 33, 38, 46, 48, 49,
> 52, and 53 -- Reports, memoranda, and notes on elementary
> and secondary education, school system, and educational
> reform in Japan.
> Boxes 3, 34, and 35 -- Notes, reports, and memoranda on
> education in Japan and Korea.
> Boxes 10-13, 16, 17, 54, 56, and 73 -- Report, memoranda, and
> notes on Japanese higher education.
> Box 15 -- Reports on audiovisual education.
> Boxes 28, 50, and 51 -- Memoranda and reports on Japanese
> student movements and student organizations in Japan.
> Boxes 30, 31, 42-45, 47, 66-70, 72, and 74 -- Memoranda,
> notes, and reports related to the activities of various
> educational organizations in Japan.
> Boxes 55 and 75 -- Report on U.S. education mission to Japan.
> Boxes 63 and 64 -- Memoranda and reports on women's education
> and youth organizations in Japan.

536. TREAT, PAYSON J., 1879-1972.
> Papers, 1855-1973. 63 ms. boxes, 1 album, 7 envelopes,
> 12 maps, 4 scrolls.
> American historian.
> Correspondence, reports, interviews, copies of diplomatic
> records, speeches, writings, notes, maps, memorabilia, and
> printed matter relating to his research interests in the
> diplomatic history of Japan, China, and other countries of
> the Far East. A pamphlet collection on World War I.
> Register.
> Gift, P. J. Treat, 1960. Subsequent increments.

Box 35 -- Essay entitled "Toward Understanding of Stanford
University," February 1966, with section on undergraduate
education at Stanford University.
Box 44 -- Folder of correspondence relating to universities of
China, with report on conditions of education in China,
June 1909.

537. TSING HUA ALUMNI ASSOCIATION.
Circular, 1927. 1 folder.
Typescript (mimeographed).
Organization of alumni of Tsing Hua University, China.
Relates to activities of the organization.

Memorandum related to drafting of constitution of THAA.

538. TUCK, WILLIAM HALLAM, 1890-1966.
Papers, 1914-1957. 7 ms. boxes.
American relief worker in World Wars I and II.
Writings, correspondence, memoranda, reports, printed matter,
and photographs, relating to World War I relief activities
of the Commission for Relief in Belgium and American Relief
Administration; World War II relief activities of the
Commission for Relief in Belgium, Finnish Relief Fund, and
National Committee on Food for the Small Democracies; World
War II Allied military governments; and the world food
survey of the Famine Emergency Committee, 1946.
Gift, Mr. and Mrs. W. H. Tuck, 1962. Subsequent increments.

Box 4 -- Report of community service in the city of New York,
with section on youth and justice, 1940.

539. TULE LAKE WAR RELOCATION AUTHORITY CENTER (California)
COLLECTION, 1942-1943.
1 ms. box.
Correspondence and photographs, relating to conditions in the
Tule Lake War Relocation Authority Center, a U.S.
internment camp for Japanese Americans during World
War II.
Gift, John Douglas Cook, 1970.

Report relating to prevalent fear in the Tule Lake Community,
September 1942, with sections on education.

540. TURKISH WILSONIAN LEAGUE.
Letter, 1918, to Woodrow Wilson, 1 folder.
Typescript.

Organization of Turkish civic leaders.

Requests American assistance for the modernization of Turkish
governmental administration.

Related to popular movement by majority of newspapers and
leaders in all professions, including educators, appealing
to President Wilson to teach Turkish people how to elimi-
nate their racial, religious, and educational problems.

541. TURNER, ROBERT F., 1944- .
Papers, 1963-1972. 43 ms. boxes, 1 album, 17 envelopes,
1 phonotape.
Public affairs officer, U.S. Embassy in South Vietnam,
1970-1972.
Writings, reports, speeches, press releases, printed matter,
clippings, and photographs, relating to political, social,
and cultural conditions in Vietnam and to the Vietnam War.
Register.
Deposit, R. F. Turner, 1974. Incremental deposits, 1977-1978.

Boxes 9 and 10 -- Newspaper clippings, memoranda, and reports
on elementary, secondary, higher, and vocational education
in South Vietnam.
Box 24 -- Memoranda and a study related to People's
Revolutionary Youth Group in Vietnam.
Box 28 -- Report by military tribunal in Saigon on commitment
to martyrdom of a teacher and some high school students.
Box 31 -- Reports and pamphlets on Vietnamese Boy Scout
Association.
Box 32 -- Newspaper clippings on women and youth in South
Vietnam.

542. UNITED NATIONS ASSOCIATION OF THE UNITED STATES OF AMERICA. SAN
FRANCISCO CHAPTER.
Records, 1945-1970. 37 ms. boxes, 2 oversize boxes,
74 motion picture reels.
Private American organization for support of the United
Nations.
Correspondence, memoranda, reports, agreements, minutes,
histories, financial records, lists, press summaries,
pamphlets, posters, clippings, motion pictures, photo-
graphs, and printed matter, relating to the operations of
United Nations organizations, world politics, and inter-
national human rights.
Gift, Mrs. Robert Digiorgio, 1977.

Boxes 8, 13, 29, and 34 -- Notes, reports, and pamphlets on
UNESCO and world illiteracy.

Box 11 -- U.N. reports, with sections on education, 1950-1956.
Boxes 19, 20, and 26 -- Correspondence and notes relating to
    Education Committee.
Box 31 -- Report on problems of Hungary, with sections on
    education and students.
Box 32 -- Progress reports of several countries, with sections
    on education, 1963.
Box 33 -- Issues of Changing World, 1945-1949, with articles
    on youth.

543. UNITED NATIONS RELIEF AND REHABILITATION ADMINISTRATION
        COLLECTION, 1943-1948. 4 ms. boxes.
    Pamphlets, journals, and printed matter, relating to the
        relief and reconstruction activities of the United Nations
        Relief and Rehabilitation Administration, particularly in
        China.
    Gift, Mrs. Edward Arnold, 1959.

    Box 4 -- Report on social reforms and education in modern
        Turkey, August 1947.

544. UNITED NATIONS RELIEF AND REHABILITATION ADMINISTRATION. CHINA
        OFFICE.
    Records, 1943-1948. 38 ms. boxes.
    International organization for World War II relief and
        reconstruction. Reports, manuals, bulletins, corres-
        pondence, and administrative orders, relating to social and
        economic conditions in China and to United Nations relief
        activities in China.
    Register.
    Gift, Pardee Lowe, 1947.

    Box 16 -- Issue of Princeton Alumni Weekly, vol. XLVIII,
        November 21, 1947, with reports and articles on campus life
        and students' activities at Princeton University.

545. U.S. AMERICAN RELIEF ADMINISTRATION. RUSSIAN OPERATIONS,
        1921-1923.
    Records, 1919-1925. 336 ms. boxes.
    U.S. Government agency to provide relief after World War I
        (unofficial agency after June 28, 1919, incorporated
        May 27, 1921).
    Correspondence, telegrams, memoranda, reports, agreements,
        minutes, histories, financial records, lists, press

178

summaries, and photographs, relating to relief operations,
food and public health problems, agriculture, economic
conditions, transportation and communications, and
political and social developments in Soviet Russia.
Register.
Gift, American Relief Administration, 1923.

Box 6 -- Correspondence and reports on anti-American
propaganda and Russian Boy Scouts.
Boxes 10, 22, 23, and 26 -- Correspondence, reports, notes,
newspaper clippings, and memoranda on education in Russia.
Box 71 -- Articles on reviews of medical education in Russia.
Box 114 -- Correspondence, report, and articles on students in
Russia.

546. U.S. ARMY. FAR EAST COMMAND. PSYCHOLOGICAL WARFARE BRANCH.
Leaflets (in Chinese and Korean), 1950-1953. 4 ms. boxes.
Printed.
Propaganda aimed at North Korean and Chinese soldiers during
the Korean War. Includes translations (mimeographed) of
the leaflets.

Most leaflets are illustrated with cartoons.

547. U.S. ARMY INFANTRY SCHOOL, FORT BENNING, GA.
Exercises, 1927-1928. 1 folder.
Typescript (mimeographed).
Relates to military tactics to be used in suppressing domestic
rebellions.
Gift, C. F. Elwell, 1947.

Military charts.

548. U.S. ARMY. SCHOOL FOR MILITARY GOVERNMENT AND ADMINISTRATION, NEW
YORK, 2d SECTION. GROUP V.
History, 1943. "The United States Military Government in the
Dominican Republic, 1916-1922: A Case History."
1 volume.
Typescript.

Section on public instruction in the Dominican Republic and
activities of Military Government in promoting education
and reducing illiteracy in that country.

549. U.S. ARMY THIRD ARMY. GENERAL STAFF, G-2.
Miscellaneous records, 1918-1919. 2 ms. boxes.
Reports, 1918-1919, including an official history of the U.S.

Third Army in France and Germany, November 14, 1918, to
July 2, 1919, and summaries of Third Army intelligence
reports, November 17, 1918, to June 28, 1919.

Box 2 -- Envelope containing essay on the Third Army,
November 14, 1918, to July 2, 1919, with sections on
educational work, athletic training, schools, and
charitable institutions.

550. U.S. CIVIL AFFAIRS TRAINING SCHOOL, STANFORD UNIVERSITY.
ecords, 1942-1945. 51-1/2 ms. boxes, 1 card file box,
3 phonorecords.
School for training civil affairs officers for military
government administration during World War II.
Correspondence, memoranda, reports, financial and personnel
records, handbooks, syllabi, and instructional materials,
relating to the politics, governments, economies and
cultures of Japan, other areas in the Pacific, and various
countries in Europe, and intelligence assessments of the
war in the Pacific.

Box 2 -- Memorandum on Albania, August 1943, with section on
education.
Box 5 -- Report of relief and rehabilitation problems in
French Indochina, with section on education.
Box 9 -- Articles and reports on propaganda, Japanese youth,
and mobilization of students in Japan.
Box 10 -- Reports of programs of Japan in Korea, with sections
on mobilization of students.
Box 13 -- Bibliographical lists of different topics, including
education in British colonies and education of illiterates
in China.
Boxes 29, 30, 44, and 45 -- Syllabi, notes, and reports
relating to curricula of Civil Affairs Training school.

551. U.S. COMMISSION ON ORGANIZATION OF THE EXECUTIVE BRANCH OF THE
GOVERNMENT, 1947-1949 and 1953-1955.
Records, 1947-1955. 27 ms. boxes.
Correspondence, reports, minutes, press releases, and printed
matter, relating to rationalization of the organization of
the executive branch of the U.S. Government.
Preliminary inventory.
Deposit, Herbert Hoover, 1955; subsequently donated, 1962.

Box 10 -- Reports on public welfare and education.

552. U.S. DEPARTMENT OF STATE. OFFICE OF EXTERNAL RESEARCH.
      Report series, 1951-1960. "The Soviet Union as Reported by
          Former Soviet Citizens." 1/2 ms. box.
      Typescript (photocopy).
      Summaries of interviews of defectors from the Soviet Union and
          other Eastern European communist countries, relating to
          their life histories and to their observations of
          political, social, and economic conditions in their native
          countries. Later reports entitled "The Soviet Bloc as
          Reported by Former Nationals."

      Reports on propaganda, political education, social relations,
          social welfare, and culture in Soviet Union.

553. U.S. MISCELLANEA, 1930-1967. 1 ms. box.
      Serial issues, pamphlets, leaflets, bulletins, newsletters,
          reports, directories, manuals, and notes, relating to
          political, social, economic, and military conditions in the
          U.S.

      Directories of National War College, 1962-1963. Pamphlet
          containing list of international conferences and meetings,
          no. 30, April 1, 1950. Some are related to education.

554. U.S. NATIONAL EMERGENCY COUNCIL.
      Report, 1936. 1/2 ms. box.
      Typescript (mimeographed).
      Relates to an assessment of federal government programs to
          promote economic recovery in the U.S. in 1935.

      Chapter IX, Page 91 -- Information on educational aid.

555. U.S. NATIONAL RESOURCES PLANNING BOARD. YOUTH SECTION.
      Study, 1941. "Post-Defense Planning for Children and Youth."
          1 folder.
      Typescript (mimeographed).
      Relates to national planning goals for youth in the areas of
          employment, health, social services, education, and
          recreation.

      Study prepared by Paul T. David, Paul R. Hanna,
          D. L. Harley, and Floyd W. Reeves.

556. U.S. NATIONAL STUDENT ASSOCIATION. INTERNATIONAL COMMISSION.
Records, 1946-1967. 313 ms. boxes, 7 envelopes.
Confederation of student bodies at American colleges and
universities.
Correspondence, reports, memoranda, minutes of meetings,
bulletins, circulars, questionnaires, notes, lists,
financial records, printed matter, and photographs,
relating to the international activities of the
association, including delegation and scholarship exchanges
with other nations, American representation at annual
International Student Conferences, relations with analogous
student organizations abroad, and the effects of world
politics on education.
Register.
Gift, U.S. National Student Association, 1968.

Boxes 97-101 -- Newspaper clippings, reports, pamphlets,
leaflets, correspondence, and memoranda on higher education
and literacy.
Box 132 -- Article relating to the conditions of students in
the Middle East.
Box 222 -- Newspaper clippings, reports, newsletters, and
reports on students and education in Israel.
Box 282 -- Reports, newsletters, and newspaper clippings
relating to Iranian students, Israeli students, and
education in both countries.

557. U.S. NAVAL AIR COMBAT INTELLIGENCE SCHOOL, QUONSET
POINT, R.I.
Manual, 1945. "Long Range Ship Recognition Simplified."
1 folder.
Typescript (mimeographed).
Relates to American and British World War II warships.
Includes photographs.
Gift, Lansing van der Heyden Hammond.

Illustrated manual used as textbook during World War II.

558. U.S. NAVAL RESERVE COLLECTION, 1940-1942.
1 folder.
Syllabi and examination questions used to train U.S. Naval
Reserve officers at the U.S. Naval Academy, U.S. Naval
Reserve schools, and U.S. Naval Reserve Officers' Training
Corps programs at various universities.

Course outline and curriculum notes relating to naval science,
tactics, and navigation training.

559. U.S. OFFICE OF CIVILIAN DEFENSE.
        Issuances, 1941-1943. 1 ms. box.
        Typescript (mimeographed) and printed.
        Pamphlets, bulletins, and memoranda, relating to civil
            defense, particularly blackout regulations, during World
            War II.
        Gift, Leland H. Brown.

        Pamphlet on protection of children and school property and
            printed matter on standard school lectures relating to
            civilian protection.

560. U.S. OFFICE OF WAR INFORMATION.
        Miscellaneous records, 1944-1945. 3-1/2 ms. boxes.
        U.S. Government organization for dissemination of war
            information and propaganda during World War II.
        Reports, press releases, clippings, and photographs, relating
            to background information on many countries during World
            War II and to dissemination of U.S. propaganda. Includes a
            mimeographed "Chronology of Adolf Hitler's Life," 1944,
            prepared as a reference source for the Office of War
            Information staff.

        Folders relating to different countries of the world. Each
            deals with background of a particular country and its
            relations with the U.S. government.
        Box 3 -- Chronology of Adolf Hitler's life.

561. U.S. PROVOST-MARSHAL-GENERAL'S BUREAU. MILITARY GOVERNMENT
        DIVISION. TRAINING BRANCH.
        Memorandum, 1945. "Principles, Practices, and Plans for
            Military Government and Occupation of Japan." 1 folder.
        Typescript (mimeographed).

        Section on education and religion.

562. U.S. WAR DEPARTMENT. COMMITTEE ON EDUCATION AND SPECIAL
        TRAINING -- COLLECTION, 1918-1919.
        2 ms. boxes.
        Correspondence, memoranda, reports, and syllabi, relating to
            the War Issues Courses conducted at Stanford University and
            various other colleges in the western U.S. under the
            auspices of the Committee on Education and Special Training
            of the U.S. War Department during World War I.
        Gift, J. S. P. Tatlock and Minna Stillman.

Box 1 -- Copy of <u>Texas History Teacher's Bulletin</u>, May 15, 1918, and a message to college men and women.
Box 2 -- Notes relating to Committee on Education and Special Training.

563. UTLEY, FREDA, 1898-1978.
Papers, 1911-1977. 92 ms. boxes.
British-American author, lecturer, and journalist; Director, American-China Policy Association.
Correspondence, writings, and printed matter, relating to social and political conditions in Russia, Japan, and China in the interwar period; the Sino-Japanese conflict; World War II; U.S. relations with China; Germany in the post-World War II reconstruction period; social and political developments in the Middle East; and anticommunism in the U.S.
Preliminary inventory.
Gift, Jon B. Utley, 1978.

Box 8 -- Booklet and issues of <u>New Iraq</u>, with information on education, literacy, and culture in that country, 1958-1960.
Box 18 -- Pamphlet on United Nations, with sections on UNESCO and American schools, December 1952.
Box 19 -- Issues of <u>Trends and Development</u>, May and December 1949, with information on communist propaganda and Communism in education.
Box 23 -- Issue of <u>Singapore News Summary</u>, September 15, 1956, with information on educational problems in that country.

564. VAMBERY, RUSZTEM, 1872-1948.
Papers (in Hungarian and English), 1887-1948. 9 ms. boxes.
Hungarian criminologist, author, educator, lawyer, and politician; Ambassador to the U.S., 1946-1948.
Correspondence, speeches and writings, reports, and printed matter, relating to criminology, to Hungarian domestic and foreign affairs, to Hungarian-American relations, and to Hungarian emigres in the U.S.
Register.
May be used only with permission of the Archivist and the Associate Director for Library Operations, Hoover Institution on War, Revolution and Peace. Applications must include resume and two letters of reference.
Purchase, Robert R. Vambery, 1975.

Box 5 -- Article on peace sovereignty; notes on education and crime.
Box 6 -- Essay on prison education.

565. VATCHER, WILLIAM HENRY, JR., 1920- .
        Papers, 1939-1965. 18 ms. boxes, 4 envelopes.
        American political scientist; member, United Nations Armistice
           Negotiations Team in Korea, 1951.
        Correspondence, writings, pamphlets, leaflets, slides, and
           photographs, relating to South African political parties;
           Afrikaner and African nationalism; the Afrikaner
           Broederbond; U.S., Japanese, and North Korean propaganda
           and psychological warfare methods during World War II and
           the Korean War; and the Trans-Siberian Railroad.
        Register.
        Gift, W. H. Vatcher, Jr., 1953. Subsequent increments.

        Box 2 -- Booklets and pamphlets on South African Student Union
           and education in South Africa.
        Box 3 -- Annual reports of National Union of South African
           Students and articles relating to South African National
           Youth Organization.
        Boxes 8-11 -- Study guides, texts, and workbooks for learning
           Japanese language.

566. VERNON, MANFRED C., <u>COLLECTOR.</u>
        Letters, 1946. 1 folder.
        Holograph.
        Letters from Dutch children to American children in gratitude
           for American food relief in the Netherlands at the end of
           World War II.
        Gift, M. C. Vernon.

        Drawings by Dutch children for American children.

567. VEYSEY, VICTOR VINCENT, 1915- .
        Papers, 1960-1977. 121 ms. boxes.
        Member, California Legislature, 1963-1970; U.S. Representative
           from California, 1971-1975; Assistant Secretary of the
           Army, 1975-1977.
        Correspondence, speeches and writings, clippings, photographs,
           memoranda, and printed matter, relating to California and
           U.S. politics, government, and election campaigns and U.S.
           environmental and energy programs.
        May not be used without permission of V. V. Veysey.
        Gift, V. V. Veysey, 1977.

        Boxes 13, 34, 94, 98, and 109 -- Correspondence, reports,
           memoranda, and texts of speeches on education and labor.
        Box 66 -- Reports, notes, and articles on education of
           American Indians.

Boxes 68, 96, and 97 -- Reports and memoranda on higher
education.
Boxes 79-84, 87, and 104 -- Reports, memoranda, newspaper
clippings, correspondence, and articles on voucher system
of education and equal educational opportunity.
Box 99 -- Correspondence, reports, and notes relating to Youth
Conference, 1972-1973.

568. VICTOR, GEORGE.
Memoirs, n.d. "Odyssey from Russia." 1 folder.
Transcript (mimeographed).
Relates to emigration of G. Victor from Russia via Turkey and
western Europe to the U.S. around the time of the Russian
Civil War.

Section on life in Turkey and its traditional religious
schools.

569. VIETNAM WAR LETTERS, 1972. 1 folder.
Holograph.
Letters from East German elementary school students addressed
to Stanford University, opposing United States involvement
in the Vietnam War.

Notes, drawings, and newspaper clippings relating to German
students.

570. VISOIANU, CONSTANTIN, 1897- .
Papers (in Romanian, French, and English), 1937-1960.
5 ms. boxes.
Romanian Minister of Foreign Affairs, 1945-1946; President,
Romanian National Committee, Washington, D.C.
Correspondence, memoranda, reports, speeches, writings, and
photographs, relating to Romanian foreign relations,
political developments in Romania, and anticommunist emigre
activities.
Register.
During their lifetimes, access requires the written permission
of C. Visoianu or George Duca. In addition, Boxes 3-5 are
restricted until January 1, 2002.
Gift, C. Visoianu, 1976. Incremental gift, 1977.

Box 1 -- Pamphlet on persecution of religion in Romania with
article on propaganda against Catholicism.
Box 2 -- Book on suppression of human rights in Romania, with
section on propaganda against United Nations.

571. VOEGELIN, ERIC, 1901- .
        Papers, 1930-1974. 26 ms. boxes.
        German-American philosopher and political scientist.
        Correspondence, speeches and writings, reports, and memoranda,
            relating to international affairs and political science.
        Gift, E. Voegelin, 1975.

        Box 8 -- Bulletin and pamphlet on Thomas Aquinas College,
            relating to its academic regulations and Catholic liberal
            education, 1971.
        Box 22 -- Article on the fate of liberal education.

572. "VOICE OF DEMOCRACY" COMMITTEE.
        Sound recordings, 1948. 2 phonorecords.
        Promotional announcements and model radio broadcasts, relating
            to a contest for high school students for radio broadcast
            scripts on democracy in the U.S., sponsored by the U.S.
            Junior Chamber of Commerce, the National Association of
            Broadcasters, and the Radio Manufacturers Association.
            Includes posters.
        Gift, Federal Radio Education Committee, 1949.

573. VOLKOV, LEON, 1914-1974.
        Papers, 1948-1974. 7 ms. boxes.
        Lieutenant Colonel, Soviet Air Force, during World War II;
            editor and journalist for Newsweek magazine, 1953-1974;
            consultant on Soviet affairs to the U.S. Departments of
            State and Defense.
        Diaries, correspondence, speeches and writings, reports, press
            excerpts, clippings, and printed matter, relating to social
            and political conditions in Soviet Union, Soviet foreign
            policy, international politics, and Russian refugee life.
        Register.

        Box 1 -- Propaganda letter to Russian people against
            Bolshevism.
        Box 5 -- Article on Soviet Jews, with sections on their social
            conditions and education.

574. VOL'SKII, NIKOLAI VLADISLAVOVICH, 1879-1964.
        Papers (in Russian and English), 1908-1964. 10 ms. boxes,
            1 envelope.
        Russian revolutionary and author.
        Photographs, correspondence, writings, clippings, and reports,

relating to Russian revolutionary movements and emigre
life, Imperial Russian and Soviet agricultural and economic
policies, labor movements, Menshevism, and political events
in Russia.
Preliminary inventory.
Purchase, Vera Vol'skii, 1965. Purchase, International
Institute of Social History, 1976.

Box 1 -- Reports on Menshevism and propaganda of the
Revolutionary Government.

575. VON ARNOLD, ANTONINA R.
Study, 1937. "A Brief Study of the Russian Students in the
University of California." 1 folder.
Typescript.
American social worker. Relates to the adjustment of Russian
emigre students at the University of California, Berkeley,
to American university life.

Difficulties encountered by Russian emigres in San Francisco
Bay area and their adjustment to the new environment after
escaping terror of Soviets.

576. VON MOHRENSCHILDT, DIMITRI SERGIUS, 1902- .
Papers, 1917-1970. 4 ms. boxes.
American historian; editor, Russian Review.
Correspondence, writings, printed matter, and photographs,
relating to acquisition of Russian historical materials and
to the Russian Orthodox Church in the U.S. Includes
letters from Sergei A. Von Mohrenschildt, Russian military
historian and father of D. S. Von Mohrenschildt, describing
political and economic conditions in Poland under Soviet
and Lithuanian occupation, 1939-1940.
Register.
Gift, D. S. Von Mohrenschildt, 1971. Incremental gift, 1976.

Box 4 -- Article on Russian Naval Academy in Sevastopol
(1915-1917) and in Petrograd (1917-1918) entitled "A
Russian Emigre Student in Yale," 1922-1926.

577. VON WIEGAND, KARL HENRY, 1874-1961.
Papers (in English and German), 1911-1961. 88 ms. boxes,
6 binders (1 linear foot), 1 stack of oversize mounted
clippings (1 linear foot), 2 swords, 1 shield.
American journalist; Hearst Newspaper foreign correspondent,
1917-1961.

Correspondence, dispatches, writings, photographs, clippings, and printed matter, relating to European diplomacy and German politics between the world wars, the Sino-Japanese War, the European Theater in World War II, the Cold War, the postwar Middle Eastern situation, and U.S. foreign policy.
Purchase, estate of K. H. Von Wiegand, 1975.

Box 58 -- Pamphlets on Egypt under Colonel Nasser and education in that country.
Box 68 -- Pamphlet, in folder on India, with section on Islamic education and Islamic civilization.
Box 69 -- Issue of Indiagram, October 29, 1958, with section on Youth Festival in New Delhi, and text of address by Arnold Toynbee to McGill University students on some realities about Israel.

578. WALES, NYM, 1907- .
Papers, 1931-1954. 37 ms. boxes, 30 envelopes.
American journalist and writer; member, Board of Directors, American Committee in Aid of Chinese Industrial Cooperatives, 1941-1951.
Personal and collected correspondence, speeches and writings, news dispatches, interviews, reports, memoranda, organizational records, and photographs, relating to the Chinese Communists; the industrial cooperative movement, student movement, and labor movement in China; the Sian incident, 1936; the Sino-Japanese Conflict; and Chinese art and literature.
Register.
May not be used without permission of Helen Foster Snow (Nym Wales).
Purchase, Helen Foster Snow, 1958.

Boxes 11 and 12 -- Correspondence, notes, newspaper clippings, articles, and essays on Chinese Student Union and youth in China.
Boxes 13 and 14 -- Manifestos of American Student Union, Peiping Student Union, and Chinese universities.
Box 31 -- Articles and reports on education in China.

579. WARREN, GERALD LEE, 1930- .
Papers, 1968-1978. 244 ms. boxes, 1 oversize box, 5 binders.
Deputy Press Secretary to U.S. Presidents Richard M. Nixon and Gerald R. Ford, 1969-1975.
Correspondence, memoranda, reports, notes, press releases, press conference transcripts, press summaries, clippings,

189

and other printed matter, relating to U.S. foreign and
domestic policy, the Watergate affair, and the American
press.
Closed until 1984.
Deposit, G. L. Warren, 1980.

Boxes 6 and 111 -- Memoranda, reports, and newspaper clippings
on desegregation and public schools.
Box 30 -- Text of presidential address on the federal
responsibility to education, October 1972.
Boxes 45 and 71 -- Correspondence, notes, newspaper clippings,
and reports on student violence and campus unrest in U.S.
Boxes 48, 55, 88, and 209 -- Reports, memoranda, and notes on
White House and youth.
Box 67 -- Memoranda and reports on emergency school aid, 1971.
Boxes 134, 143, and 180 -- Memoranda, notes, and newspaper
clippings on education.

580. WATKINS, JAMES THOMAS, IV, 1907- .
Papers, 1945-1962. 18 ms. boxes. 2 microfilm reels,
1 envelope, 1 phonorecord.
American political scientist; Political Affairs Officer,
Military Government Headquarters, Okinawa, 1945-1946.
Correspondence, reports, and maps, relating to the Allied
military government in Okinawa following World War II and
to miscellaneous aspects of postwar international relations
and U.S. politics.
Preliminary inventory.
Gift, J. T. Watkins, IV, 1971. Subsequent increments.

Boxes 2 and 6 -- Notes and minutes of meetings on education.
Boxes 11-13 -- Reports on educational programs in Japan and
Ryukyus, 1950.
Box 18 -- Stanford University oral examination reports,
1933-1963.

581. WATKINS, RALPH JAMES, 1896- .
Papers, 1926-1978. 93-1/2 ms. boxes.
American economist.
Speeches and writings, studies, reports, memoranda,
correspondence, notes, and printed matter, relating to
economic planning in the U.S., Mexico, Ecuador, Egypt,
India, Taiwan, South Korea, Japan, and to Allied Civil
Affairs Administration in North Africa during World War II.
Preliminary inventory.
Gift, R. J. Watkins, 1980.

Box 11 --Reports by the United Nations Children's Fund,
   1972, with sections on children and their educational
   opportunities.
Box 66 -- Reports, notes, and charts on educational program in
   Taiwan.
Box 78 -- Report by the Pakistan Planning Commission, with
   section on education.

582. WATKINS, SUSAN E., COLLECTOR.
   Miscellany (in English and French), 1916-1921. 1/2 ms. box.
   Correspondence, postcards, leaflets and miscellanea, relating
      to civilian relief work in France during and after World
      War I, especially to the work of Fatherless Children of
      France.
   Gift, Mr. Watkins, 1967.

   Newspaper clippings relating to Red Cross and adoption of
      French orphans by Americans.

583. WEBSTER, JAMES BENJAMIN, 1879-1929.
   Papers, 1903-1931. 22 ms. boxes, 2 envelopes.
   American missionary in China.
   Diaries, correspondence, notebooks, writings, and photographs,
      relating to theology and to missionary activities and
      Christian education in China.
   Preliminary inventory.
   Gift, family of J. B. Webster, 1970. Incremental gift, 1973.

   Boxes 3-8 -- Correspondence and reports on religious
      education.
   Boxes 14 and 15 -- Reports on Chinese adolescent and student
      interests.
   Boxes 16-20 -- Notes on psychology and values of Christian
      education.
   Box 22 -- James Webster's writings on China and Christian
      education in that country.

584. WEGERER, ALFRED VON, 1880-1945.
   Writings (in English and German), 1941. 1 folder.
   German historian. Study (typewritten), entitled "From War to
      Peace," relating to the causes of World War II and
      prospects for peace; and photocopy of a memorandum
      (typewritten in German), relating to the proposed
      establishment of an Academy on War and Peace in connection
      with the Hoover Institution on War, Revolution and Peace.
   Gift, Ralph Lutz, 1943. Gift, Charles Burdick, 1976.

585. WEILER, HANS, 1934- .
        Collection (in German), 1963-1969. 1 ms. box.
        American educator; professor of education and political
            science, Stanford University, 1965- ; Director, Inter-
            national Institute of Educational Planning, UNESCO,
            1974-1977.
        West German secondary school official and student publications
            relating to education and student life.
        Gift, H. Weiler, 1980.

586. WEINBERGER, CASPAR W., 1917- .
        Papers, 1973-1975. 47 ms. boxes, 1 oversize box
            (1 linear foot).
        Counselor to the President of the U.S., 1973; Secretary of
            Health, Education and Welfare, 1973-1975; Secretary of
            Defense, 1981- .
        Correspondence, reports, and photographs, relating to American
            politics and to social welfare, health, and educational
            policy during the presidential administrations of Richard
            M. Nixon and Gerald R. Ford.
        Preliminary inventory.
        Consult the Archivist for restrictions.
        Deposit, C. W. Weinberger, 1977.

587. WEST, RALPH E.
        Papers, 1969-1977. 7-1/2 ms. boxes.
        Lieutenant Colonel, U.S. Marine Corps.
        Correspondence and clippings, relating to the Vietnam War, the
            Watergate affair, and U.S. and international politics.
        Gift, R. E. West, 1977.

        Box 1, Section a. -- Issue of The American Legion, July 1970,
            with articles on the United Nations' 25th birthday and the
            background of the tragedy at Kent State University.
        Box 1, Section b. -- Dan Smoot report entitled "Nationalizing
            Education," vol. 2, no. 4, January 25, 1965.

588. WEST INDIAN CONFERENCE, 2d, ST. THOMAS, VIRGIN ISLANDS, 1946.
        Report, 1946. 1 folder.
        Typescript (mimeographed).
        Report of the Drafting Committee of the second West Indian
            Conference. Includes transcript of an interview with
            Rexford G. Tugwell, Governor of Puerto Rico, relating to
            discussion at the conference of social and economic
            conditions in the West Indies.

        Sections on education in West Indies.

589. WESTERN COLLEGE CONGRESS, 1st, STANFORD UNIVERSITY, 1947.
        Records, 1947. 1 folder.
        Congress of college student leaders in the western U.S.
        Resolutions, agenda, and study papers, relating to the
            international situation and U.S. foreign policy.

        Reports on freedom of speech and peace in the Far East.

590. WESTERN REGIONAL CONFERENCE ON THE HOLOCAUST, 1st, SAN JOSE,
        1977.
        Proceedings, 1977. 9 phonotapes.
        Conference sponsored by the National Conference of Christians
            and Jews. Relates to the ancient, medieval, and modern
            origins of the Holocaust, its meaning for Western
            civilization, and the methodology for teaching about the
            Holocaust in schools and universities.
        Gift, Lillian Silberstein, 1977.

591. WHITE, GEOFFREY.
        Papers, 1939-1968. 9-1/2 ms. boxes.
        American Trotskyist leader.
        Correspondence, writings, reports, resolutions, minutes,
            discussion bulletins, and printed matter, relating to
            American Trotskyist politics, the Socialist Workers Party,
            and the formation of the Spartacist League. Includes a few
            items relating to the Communist Party of the U.S.A. and the
            Independent Socialist League.
        Gift, G. White, 1978.

        Box 4 -- Issue of The New Student, with articles on student
            economic needs and academic freedom, December 1947.
        Boxes 5-10 -- Numerous bulletins, with topics on youth and
            students.

592. WHITE HOUSE CONFERENCE ON CHILD HEALTH AND PROTECTION,
        WASHINGTON, D.C., 1930.
        Records, 1909-1950. 142-1/2 ms. boxes, 5 posters.
        Conference established by President Herbert Hoover to
            investigate child welfare in the U.S.
        Correspondence, reports, memoranda, expense statements, and
            pamphlets, relating to the physical and social condition of
            children in the U.S., the status of school health education
            and health service programs, and proposals for the
            promotion of child welfare. Includes reports of the
            American Child Health Association.
        Preliminary inventory.
        Gift, Ray Lyman Wilbur, 1933.

Box 13 -- Correspondence, leaflets, and reports relating to National Conference of Parents and Teachers and National Education Association.

Box 42 -- Correspondence and reports on education and training of parents.

Boxes 44 and 45 -- Correspondence, reports, and articles on schoolchildren and training of teachers.

Boxes 47 and 48 -- Correspondence and reports on youth outside home and school.

Boxes 63 and 104 -- Reports on health education in schools.

Boxes 72-74 and 76 -- Correspondence relating to the congress of parents and teachers of several states.

Box 124 -- Report on Philippine schools.

593. WILBUR, RAY LYMAN, 1875-1949.
Papers, 1908-1949. 121 ms. boxes, 11 posters, 3 albums.
American educator; U.S. Secretary of the Interior, 1929-1933; President, Stanford University, 1916-1943.
Correspondence, memoranda, reports, pamphlets, and miscellanea, relating to U.S. and world politics, development of natural resources in the U.S., and national health and other social problems.
Preliminary inventory.
Gift, R. L. Wilbur, 1933. Subsequent increments.

Box 12 -- Correspondence and memoranda on vocational education and French education.

Boxes 36, 37, 39, and 90 -- Correspondence, pamphlets, reports, leaflets, and memoranda on youth, foreign students, college students, and postwar education.

Box 40 -- Correspondence, memoranda, reports, and leaflets on education.

Boxes 58-64 -- Books, newspaper clippings, correspondence, reports, memoranda, and leaflets on Boy Scouts.

Boxes 85 and 86 -- Leaflets, correspondence, reports, and books on adult education.

Boxes 87-89 -- Reports, booklets, and pamphlets on social problems and education.

Box 113 -- Correspondence and reports on Student Army Training College.

594. WILLOUGHBY, CHARLES ANDREW, 1892-1972.
Papers, 1945-1961. 2 ms. boxes, 1 album, 1 envelope, 1 phonorecord, 1 framed certificate.
Major General, U.S. Army; Chief of Intelligence, U.S. Army Forces in the Far East, 1941-1951.
Drafts, reports, correspondence, printed matter, and newsletters relating to the World War II campaigns of General

Douglas MacArthur in the Pacific, the Richard Sorge
espionage case, the anticommunist movement in the U.S.,
Cold War defense needs of the U.S., and Japanese
rearmament.
Preliminary inventory.
Gift, C. A. Willoughby, 1961.

Box 2 -- Issues of American Mercury, with articles on teachers
and education.

595. WILSON, CAROL GREEN, 1892- .
Papers, 1918-1969. 14 ms. boxes.
American journalist and author.
Correspondence, writings, clippings, and other printed matter,
relating primarily to the life of Herbert Hoover. Includes
material used for research for the book by C. G. Wilson,
Herbert Hoover: A Challenge for Today.
Preliminary inventory.
Gift, C. G. Wilson, 1970.

Boxes 9 and 10 -- Bound volumes of The Stanford Illustrated
Review, 1918-1935, with articles on students, their
activities, and education.

596. WILSON, LAURENCE L., COLLECTOR.
Collection on the Philippines, 1942-1946. 1 ms. box.
Writings, leaflets, posters, and proclamations, relating to
conditions in the Japanese-occupied Philippines during
World War II and to the return of U.S. troops to the
Philippines in 1944-1945.
Gift, L. L. Wilson, 1945. Subsequent increments.

Typescript volumes with sections on war and youth. Report of
symposium by Malolos High School students on impact of
Japanese culture upon culture of the Philippines.

597. WISKOWSKI, WLODZIMIERZ, COLLECTOR.
Collection on Poland (in Polish), 1914-1919. 5 ms. boxes.
Writings, reports, memoranda, booklets, leaflets, magazines,
newspapers, memorials, and speeches, relating to political
conditions in Poland during World War I and the development
of Polish nationalism.
Register.
Purchase, W. Wiskowski, 1921.

Box 4 -- Pamphlet and articles on Polish education.

598. WISSMANN, HELLMUTH, 1884- .
        Writings (in German), 1939-1947. 1 folder.
        Typescript.
        Relates to national socialism in Germany, the role of
            propaganda, post-World War II German reparations, and plans
            for world peace.

599. WOLFE, BERTRAM DAVID, 1896-1977.
        Papers, 1903-1977. 150-1/2 ms. boxes. 2 card file boxes,
            1 oversize box, 6 microfilm reels, 4 phonotapes,
            19 envelopes.
        American historian; representative of the Communist Party,
            U.S.A., to the Communist International, 1928-1929; author
            of Three Who Made a Revolution (1948) and other works on
            communism.
        Writings, correspondence, notes, memoranda, clippings, other
            printed matter, photographs, and drawings, relating to
            Marxist doctrine, the international communist movement,
            communism in the Soviet Union and in the U.S., literature
            and art in the Soviet Union and in Mexico, and the Mexican
            artist Diego Rivera.
        Register.
        Gift, estate of B. D. Wolfe, 1977.

        Box 82 -- Newspaper clippings, notes, and articles on
            education in Soviet Union and U.S.
        Box 111 -- Articles and newspaper clippings on communist
            propaganda.
        Boxes 136 and 137 -- Newspaper clippings, newsletters, and
            pamphlets on U.S. student movements and student unrest.

600. WOLTERS, MARIA, 1866-1962.
        Papers, 1904-1959. 4 ms. boxes.
        American relief worker in Japan.
        Writings, correspondence, photographs, clippings, and
            memorabilia, relating to famine and earthquake relief and
            child welfare in Japan.
        Gift, M. Wolters, 1941. Subsequent increments.

        Some of the contents are in Japanese.
        Box 3 -- Booklet on the World's League of School Boys and
            Girls.

601. WOOD, HUGH BERNARD, 1909- .
        Papers (in Nepali and English), 1955-1971. 3 ms. boxes.
        American educator; educational adviser to the Nepali
            Government, 1954-1962.

Writings and printed matter, relating to education in Nepal
and India.
Gift, H. B. Wood, 1978.

Box 1 -- Books and articles on different aspects of education
in Nepal.
Box 2 -- Articles and writings on education in Nepal and
booklet related to education in India.
Box 3 -- Issues of Nepal's College of Education Quarterly.

602. WOOLLEY, BARRY LEE, 1947- .
History, 1974. "Adherents of Permanent Revolution: A History
of the Fourth (Trotskyist) International." 1/2 ms. box.
Typescript (photocopy).
Relates to the American and international Trotskyist
movements.
During his lifetime, access requires the written permission of
B. L. Woolley.
Purchase, B. L. Woolley, 1977.

Chapter 8 -- Sections on flood of youth into the movement,
stampede of adults out of the movement, and student
orientations.

603. WORLD BLACK AND AFRICAN FESTIVAL OF ARTS AND CULTURE,
2d, LAGOS, 1977.
Issuances, 1977. 1/2 ms. box.
Reports, newsletters, speeches, and informational material,
relating to African art.

Pamphlet on education and social life in Tanzania.

604. WORLD WAR II ALLIED PROPAGANDA, 1939-1945.
3-1/2 ms. boxes.
Pamphlets, leaflets, and reports, including propaganda
material in a variety of languages, distributed by Allied
forces in Western and Eastern Europe and Asia during World
War II. Includes a U.S. Psychological Warfare Division
report on leaflet operations in western Europe, 1945.

Box 4 -- Issues of Iranian bimonthly journal, with articles on
adult education and child training.

197

605. WORLD WAR II AXIS PROPAGANDA, 1939-1945.
       1 ms. box, 1 envelope.
       Printed.
       Axis propaganda, mostly German, distributed in Europe and Asia
          during World War II in various languages.

       Languages include English, French, Russian, Arabic, and Urdu.

606. WORLD WAR II -- BALKANS.
       Collection, 1941-1944. 1 ms. box.
       Studies, reports, handbooks, maps, photographs, diagrams, and
          printed matter, relating to political, economic, social,
          and military conditions in Albania, Bulgaria, Greece, and
          Yugoslavia and to the location of strategic power plants
          and industries in Yugoslavia. Includes two intelligence
          reports on the Cetnik and Partisan resistance movements in
          Yugoslavia prepared for Allied Military Headquarters,
          Balkans.

       Handbooks on Albania, Bulgaria, and Greece, with sections on
          education and welfare.

607. WORLD WAR II -- U.S. ARMED FORCES PAMPHLETS, 1941-1945.
       3 ms. boxes.
       Printed matter, including manuals and guidebooks issued by the
          U.S. Army and Navy, and pamphlets and guidebooks relating
          to the U.S. Armed Forces issued by commercial publishers
          during World War II. Collected separately by Willis Stork
          and Margaret Windsor.
       Preliminary inventory.
       Gift, M. Windsor, 1948. Gift, W. Stork, 1964.

       Guidebooks are related to social conditions, culture, and
          education of various countries.

608. YOUNG, ARTHUR N., 1890- .
       Papers, 1918-1961. 116 ms. boxes, 1 folder.
       American economist; Economic Adviser, U.S. Department of
          State, 1922-1928; Financial Adviser, Government of China
          and Central Bank of China, 1929-1946.
       Diary, correspondence, reports, studies, statistical
          summaries, financial statements, press releases, clippings,
          and ephemeral publications, relating to the European
          financial crisis following World War I, the work of the
          Reparations Commission in formulating the Dawes Plan in
          1924, and the economic and financial situation in China,
          1929-1946.

Register.
Materials are opened to users who sign a statement agreeing to
the conditions of use set down by A. N. Young.
Gift, A. N. Young, 1966. Subsequent increments.

Box 107 -- Booklets and chart relating to culture and
education in China.

609. YOUNG COMMUNIST LEAGUE OF THE U.S. COLLECTION, 1934-1949.
2 ms. boxes.
Leaflets, pamphlets, and mimeographed material, relating to
Young Communist League activities in San Francisco, the
Communist Party, U.S.A., election propaganda, labor
relations, trade unions, education, and the Spanish Civil
War.
Purchase, L. B. Magee, 1943. Subsequent increments.

Box 1 -- Manual entitled "The Model Congress of Youth."
Box 2 -- Pamphlet relating to Peoples' Educational Center.

610. YOUNG MEN'S CHRISTIAN ASSOCIATIONS.
Miscellaneous records, 1917-1920. 68 ms. boxes, 5 folios,
79 envelopes, 40 albums.
International social and charitable organization.
Clippings, printed matter, posters, and photographs, relating
to activities of the Young Men's Christian Association in
the United States and Europe during World War I.
Register.
Gift, World Alliance of Young Men's Christian Association,
1933.

Box 48 -- Notes relating to Army Educational Commission.
Box 52 -- Newspaper clippings relating to Educational
Department of American Expeditionary Forces University and
guidebook relating to American Expeditionary Forces
University in France, with section on College of Education.
Box 62 -- Poster by YMCA Educational Service relating to free
scholarships for ex-servicemen.

611. YUGOSLAVIA - STUDENT PROTEST MOVEMENT.
Collection (in Serbo-Croatian), 1968. 1 folder.
Photocopy.
Leaflets, circulars, and resolutions, issued by various
student groups, relating to student protest movements at

the University of Belgrade against social injustice,
inequality in higher education, and poor student living
conditions.
Gift, Roland V. Layton, Jr., 1976.

612. ZALAR, CHARLES.
Dissertation, 1958. "A Critical Study of Yugoslav Communism
with Special Regard to the Present Stage." 711 p.
Typescript.
Relates to communism in Yugoslavia. Ph.D. dissertation,
Georgetown Univeristy.

Sections on education, culture, and religion in Yugoslavia.

613. ZILBERMAN, BELLA N.
Papers, 1924-1959. 1/2 ms. box.
American peace advocate.
Writings, letters, and printed matter, relating to the plans
of B. N. Zilberman to bring about world peace.

614. ZORN COLLECTION. Ca. 1900-1930.
(In French, German, Italian, and English). 12 ms. boxes.
Printed.
Relates to international law, the League of Nations, questions
of war and peace, territorial disputes, and reparations.
Preliminary inventory.

Box 3, Folder G -- Booklet entitled "The League of Nations and
the Schools."

615. BELLQUIST, ERIC CYRIL, 1904-1979.
  Papers, 1920-1979. 163 ms. boxes, 2 oversize boxes, 2 card
    file boxes.
  American political scientist; U.S. Office of War Information
    official, 1943-1945; Chief, European Division, Office of
    International Information and Cultural Affairs, U.S.
    Department of State, 1945-1947.
  Reports, memoranda, writings, letters, clippings, serial
    issues, and printed matter, relating to politics in the
    U.S., Scandinavia, and elsewhere, American foreign policy,
    World War II and postwar propaganda, and public opinion
    information.

616. DAVIS, RUSSELL GERARD, 1922- .
  Papers, 1967-1979. 23 ms. boxes.
  American educator; consultant to the U.S. Agency for
    International Development and various foreign governments.
  Studies, reports, statistics, and memoranda, relating to
    education and economic development in underdeveloped
    countries.
  Gift, R. G. Davis, 1981.

617. ECKHARDT, WILLIAM, 1918- .
  Writings, 1965-1981. 1/2 ms. box.
  Director, Peace Research Laboratory, St. Louis, Missouri.
  Journal articles and reprints, relating to psychological,
    ideological and social sources of aggressiveness,
    militarism and war, and peace.

618. EDUCATIONAL RESEARCH COUNCIL OF AMERICA.
  Issuances, 1959-1977. 96 ms. boxes, 5 linear feet,
    41 motion picture reels.
  Educational research organization.
  Reports, textbooks, teachers' manuals, motion picture film,
    and other instructional materials, relating to elementary
    and secondary school education in the U.S.
  Gift, Educational Research Council, 1981.

619. EVANS, LUTHER HARRIS, 1902-1982.
  Conference summaries, 1949. 1 folder.

American educator; member, U.S. National Commission for the
United Nations Educational, Scientific and Cultural
Organization (UNESCO), 1946-1952 and 1959-1963;
Director-General, UNESCO, 1953-1958.
Relates to meetings of the U.S. delegation to the Third
Session of the UNESCO General Conference, 1948.

620. FAR EASTERN COMMISSION.
Records, 1946-1951. 5 ms. boxes.
Mimeograph.
Allied commission for supervision of the occupation of Japan.
Minutes, memoranda, and reports, relating to the occupation
of Japan after World War II.
Gift, U.S. Army Intelligence and Security Command, 1981.

621. GAMBLE, DAVID PERCY, COLLECTOR.
Collection, 1954-1976. 1/2 ms. box.
Serial issues, bulletins, posters, other printed matter, and
radio broadcast transcripts, relating to political and
economic conditions and education in Sierra Leone.
Gift, D. P. Gamble, 1981.

622. GERMANY (TERRITORY UNDER ALLIED OCCUPATION, 1945-1955, U.S.
ZONE). OFFICE OF MILITARY GOVERNMENT.
Miscellaneous records (in English and German), 1944-1950.
11 ms. boxes.
Correspondence, reports, memoranda, statistics, and indexes,
relating to American administration of occupied Germany
after World War II, especially to civilian relief,
economic conditions, housing, and denazification.

623. GERSHAM, CARL.
Papers, 1962-1978. 14 ms. boxes.
Executive Director, Social Democrats, U.S.A.
Speeches and writings, correspondence, minutes, resolutions,
discussion bulletins, and printed matter, relating to
socialist and radical movements in the U.S., the Young
People's Socialist League, and Social Democrats, U.S.A.
Gift, C. Gershman, 1981.

624. HALPERIN, SAMUEL, 1930- .
Papers, 1957-1981. 16 ms. boxes.
American educator and political scientist; Deputy Assistant
Secretary of Health, Education and Welfare for
Legislation, 1966-1969.

Speeches and writing, correspondence, legislation, memoranda, reports, studies, and printed matter, relating to federal aid to education in the U.S.
Gift, S. Halperin, 1981.

625. HUNTINGTON, GEORGE HERBERT, 1878-1953.
Diary, 1925. 1 folder.
Typescript.
American educator; professor, Robert College, Istanbul, Turkey, 1907-1937.
Relates to visit with royal family of Romania. Includes correspondence of Elizabeth Dodge Huntington Clarke, wife of G. H. Huntington, 1925-1955, relating to royal family of Romania.
Gift, Elspeth McClure Clark, 1981.

626. HUNTLEY, JAMES ROBERT, 1923- .
Miscellaneous papers, 1949-1981. 1 folder.
Executive Secretary, Atlantic Institute, 1960-1965.
Reports, resolutions, statements, and writings, relating to the foundation and activities of the Atlantic Institute, an international center to promote cultural exchange among the North Atlantic Treaty Organization countries.
Gift, J. R. Huntley, 1981.

627. HURD, PAUL DEHART, 1905- .
Report, 1981. "Science Education in the People's Republic of China." 44 pages.
Typescript (photocopy).
American educator; Faculty Fellow, U.S.-China Relations Program at Stanford University. Prepared for the National Science Foundation.
Gift, P. D. Hurd, 1981.

628. LINCOLN RENAISSANCE.
Miscellaneous records, 1977-1980. 1 folder.
Lincoln County, Ontario, organization of parents and taxpayers.

Correspondence, statements, brochures, and clippings, relating to educational issues in Canada, such as parental control and sex education.
Gift, Helen Gauvreau, 1981.

629. MOUSSAVI, FAKHREDDIN, 1940-   .
       Papers (in English and Persian), 1975-1980.
          1-1/2 ms. boxes.
       Iranian educator.
       Dissertation, other writings, serial issues, and clippings,
          relating to education in Iran, the Iranian revolution of
          1979, and political, social, and economic conditions in
          Iran.
       Gift, F. Moussavi, 1981.

630. NEWCOMBE, HANNA, 1922-   .
       Writings, 1968-1981. 1/2 ms. box.
       Canadian social scientist; coeditor, Peace Research Abstracts
          Journal, 1962-   .
       Studies, reprints, and journal articles, relating to peace,
          measurement of international tension, international
          organization, and voting patterns in the United Nations.
          Includes writings of Alan G. Newcombe and others.
       Gift, H. Newcombe, 1981.

631. PEOPLE OF AMERICA RESPONDING TO EDUCATIONAL NEEDS OF TODAY'S
          SOCIETY.
       Newsletters, 1978-1980. 1 folder.
       Mimeographed.
       American education information organization.
       Relates to educational policy in the U.S.
       Gift, Ruth Feld, 1981.

632. REICHSSCHRIFTTUMSKAMMER.
       Publications (in German), 1938-1942. 1/2 ms. box.
       Printed (photographic copy).
       German Government Chamber of Literature.
       Liste des Schaedlichen und Unerwuenschten Schrifttums (List
          of Harmful and Undesirable Literature), 1938, enumerating
          prohibited authors and books; and Schriftsteller-
          Verzeichnis (Register of Authors), 1942, listing approved
          writers.

633. SAUDI ARABIA. WIZARAT AL-MA'ARIF.
       Publications (in Arabic, English, and French), 1970-1980.
          1 ms. box.
       Saudi Arabian Ministry of Education.
       Reports and serial issues, relating to education in Saudi
          Arabia.
       Gift, Saudi Arabia Ministry of Education Data Center, 1981.

634. STANFORD, BARBARA DODDS, 1943- .
    Papers, 1968-1981. 1/2 ms. box.
    American educator and author.
    Writings, course outlines, and other teaching materials,
        relating to education for peace and conflict resolution.
    Gift, B. D. Stanford, 1981.

635. STODDARD, GEORGE DINSMORE, 1897- .
    Miscellaneous papers, 1946-1981. 3 ms. boxes.
    American educator; Chairman, U.S. Education Mission to Japan,
        1946.
    Memoirs, correspondence, speeches and writings, reports,
        memoranda, clippings, other printed matter, and
        photographs, relating to the U.S. Education Mission to
        Japan and to the subsequent development of Japanese
        education.

636. STONE, FRANK ANDREWS, 1929- .
    Papers, 1951-1981. 2 ms. boxes.
    American educator; Director, I. N. Thut World Education
        Center, University of Connecticut, 1971- .
    Speeches and writings, correspondence, bulletins, and
        reports, relating to international education in Turkey and
        to ethnic studies.
    Gift. F. A. Stone, 1981.

637. STROBRIDGE, WILLIAM S.
    History, n.d. "Golden Gate to Golden Horn: Camp Fremont,
        California, and the American Expedition to Siberia of
        1918." 70 pages.
    Mimeographed.
    Colonel, U.S. Army.
    Relates to the training of the 8th Division of the U.S. Army
        at Camp Fremont, California, prior to its departure for
        Siberia during the Russian Revolution.
    Gift, John K Caldwell, 1981.

638. THOMAS, LAWRENCE GREGG, 1909- .
    Papers, 1930-1981. 13 ms. boxes.
    American educator; professor of education, Stanford
        University, 1939-1974.
    Correspondence, writings, syllabi, lecture outlines, notes,
        and printed matter, relating mainly to the philosophy of
        education.
    Gift. L. G. Thomas, 1981.

639. THORPE, STEVE, COLLECTOR.
  Photographs, 1945-1948. 1 envelope.
  Depicts student demonstrations at Xinan Lianhe Daxue
   (Southwest Associated University), Kunming, China,
   protesting the killing of four students at the university
   by Kuomintang soldiers in 1945.
  Gift, S. Thorpe, 1981.

640. ULMER, LAURA M. WHITE.
  Diary, 1932-1938. 1/2 ms. box.
  Typewritten transcript.
  American missionary in China, 1924-1930 and 1932-1939.
  Relates to social conditions and medical missionary
   activities in China.
  Gift, Evelyn Ulmer, 1981.

NOTES ON PUBLISHED HOLDINGS ON EDUCATION AND SOCIETY
IN THE HOOVER INSTITUTION LIBRARY

The Hoover Institution holdings are separated into (1) archives
and (2) library materials. The Hanna Collection focuses on
archives, and this catalog is a guide to the six hundred nonprint
archival collections on education.

The scholar will also find at the Hoover Institution extensive
holdings of library materials that treat education and society.
The following is a general description of these holdings.

AFRICAN AND MIDDLE EAST LIBRARY

The basic strength of the Africa collection, one of the best in
the western United States, provides a wealth of resources on the
politics, economics, and history of Sub-Saharan Africa, including
the various countries' education policies and practices. The
Hoover Institution's excellent African colonial history
collections include accounts of European colonial education
policies and of missionary educational activities in publications
such as the Revue d'histoire des missions (Paris, 1924-1937),
TAM-TAM: Revue des etudiants catholiques africains (Paris, 1955,
1963-1970), Missionary Herald, American Board of Commissioners
for Foreign Missions (Boston, 1923-1944), Journal des missions
evangeliques (Paris, 1919-1928, 1937-1944), Zambesi Mission
Record (1898-1934), Le Christ au Gabon by Sister Marie-Germaine
(Louvain, 1931), L'Enseignement aux indigenes (Bruxelles,
Institut Colonial International, 1931), and L'Afrique Equatoriale
Francaise (Paris: Encyclopedie Maritime et Coloniale, 1950, which
contains a detailed account on mission education).

Contemporary educational policies, including political sociali-
zation efforts appear in publications such as Whirlwind Before
the Storm: The Origins and Development of the Uprising in Soweto,
by Alan Brooks; Education for Self-Reliance, by Anza Lema; and
The Conflict over What Is to Be Learned in Schools: History of
Curriculum Politics in Africa, by Stephen Heyneman. The last two
works deal with Tanzania's educational policies.

The important role of university students in national political
life is evidenced in publications such as the Report of the
University of Ibadan Commission of Inquiry into Disturbances on
the Campus, 1st February 1971; Report of the Commission of
Inquiry into Certain Matters Relating to the University of the
North (South Africa); and Report of the South Africa Commission
of Inquiry into Certain Organisations (including the National

Union of South African Students). Hoover Library has received for many years the publications of the National Union of South African Students.

The Institution holds collections on the issue of university investments in companies doing business in South African, with studies such as Dartmouth and Southern African Investments, Yale University Ad Hoc Committee on South African Investments Report to the Corporation, Sell the South African Stock: The Divestiture Struggle at Northwestern University, and University of California Investments: Racist or Responsible?

Periodicals on contemporary issues include Saso Newsletter, the journal of the South African Students' Organisation, which was the founder of the Black Consciousness Movement in South Africa; the black workers' rights newsletters--Isisebenzi, Abasebenzi, and Umanyano--published by white South African students; and Mvioni, the journal of Kivukoni College, Tanzania's ideological/party institute. The active role taken by African students abroad is reflected in such journals on contemporary Ethiopian politics as Resistance (National Union of Eritrean Students), Kara Wallabumaa (Union of Oromo Students in Europe), and Waldaansso (Oromo Students, Washington, D.C.).

Finally, Hoover Library and the Stanford University Library belong to CAMP (Cooperative Africana Microform Project), which gives them access, through interlibrary loan, to rich sources such as those on colonial/missionary education policies in the Church Missionary Society Records, 1800s-1914 (276 reels); the Joint International Missionary Council/Conference of British Missionary Societies Archives for Africa, 1910-1945; the Ghana Archive of the Basel Mission, 1829-1917 (170 reels); the Universities' Mission to Central Africa Documents, 1860s to early 1900s (39 reels); and the Council for World Mission Archives (incorporating the London Missionary Society), 1775-1940.

Consult: Peter Duignan, Curator
         Africa and Middle East Collection
Location: 201 Hoover Tower

CENTRAL AND WESTERN EUROPEAN LIBRARY

Traditionally, the library of the Hoover Institution has been interested in educational policies practiced in the various nations of Western Europe. The Hoover Library's catalog reflects this interest in the subject heading "Education" subdivided by nations, e.g. "Education - France." These books discuss educational policy and planning, but do not deal with educational methods and lesson plans. Of particular importance is the subject heading "Education and State," which in turn is subdivided by country, e.g. "Education and State - Germany." This section covers educational policy from World War I through Weimar and the Nazi state. Post-World War II developments of educational policies in the two Germanies are covered in the subject headings "Education and State-Germany, West" and "Education and State-Germany, East." For all of Western Europe the collection contains about 1,500 titles.

Added to these formally catalogued materials accessible through an author/title/subject approach, there are several special collections that, in some cases, have their own informal register. The "German Dissertation Collection" (12 linear feet) contains dissertations on a wide variety of academic subjects, completed in the period 1900-1933, and listed by author.

The "German Textbook Collection" (18 linear feet) contains text-books, from the Nazi period, for different age groups in the fields of civics, mathematics, German literature, and geography. Of great interest is the fact that a particular text book may be available in different editions for various school grades.

The "German Youth Movement Collection" (18 linear feet) has a register. The material deals with the pre-World War I and the Weimar youth movement, especially the "Wandervoegel," and a similar group in Switzerland. Periodical files from this collection have been integrated into the Serials catalog.

There is also a small Italian textbook collection (3 linear feet), which contains Italian textbooks issued in elementary schools in 1943, as well as textbooks issued for the same schools by Allied Military Government after the invasion of Sicily.

Special mention should be made of educational journals with a particular political tendency, which are integrated into the serials and newspaper files. For instance, the library holds a file of L'Ecole et la nation issued by the French Communist Party from 1936 to the present. For the German Democratic Republic, it holds Forum: Organ des Zentralrats der FDJ (Freie Deutsche Jugend) from 1961 to the present.

Consult: Agnes F. Peterson, Curator
          West European Collection
Location: 214 Hoover Tower

EAST ASIAN LIBRARY

Printed Japanese materials relating to education now total around 2,800 volumes. Most of these items cover higher educational developments and government policies toward education. The Institution has recently acquired 60 microfilm rolls describing the Meiji government's activities between 1870 and 1892 in building a modern educational system. The Institution has also another 200 rolls of educational statistics, for the period 1870 until the present, describing schools, enrollments, etc. We also have acquired educational histories for about 25 prefectures in Japan, roughly half of the total. Further, we have acquired a set of 36 volumes of science textbooks that replicate the early Meiji originals, which serve as an excellent illustration of how the Japanese administration, at that time, planned to catch up with the Western scientific community. Some materials on the education of Japanese minority groups and women have also been acquired over the past decade. We have now a very focused collection on Japanese educational history relating primarily to national educational policy and higher educational developments, especially at the prefectural level.

With respect to China and Taiwan, the Hoover Institution has a total of 3,660 volumes, of which around 1,200 pertain to elementary, secondary, higher, and vocational education and special educational activities and developments. We also have some 200 textbooks, many from Taiwan and some from the People's Republic of China, dating particularly from the 1960s and 1970s. Educational statistical materials from Taiwan are especially abundant. We have some 150 volumes on educational theory, many pertaining to the pre-1949 period. The collection is rich and variegated, with many primary types of materials.

Consult: Ramon Myers, Curator
          East Asian Collection
Location: 111 Lou Henry Hoover Building

EAST EUROPEAN LIBRARY

Since its founding, the libraries of the Hoover Institution have been acquiring printed materials dealing with education and society. Special efforts have been made to collect books, magazines, newspapers, and pamphlets from the Eastern European states, especially the Soviet Union.

In the field of education in the USSR and Eastern European countries, the Hoover library's holdings contain over 1,500 titles, of which 75 percent are Soviet materials. The following is an excerpt from a recent survey* of Hoover's East European Library describing the strength in the area of Russian and Soviet education:

> The collection has ample material documenting the Soviet government's struggle against backwardness and illiteracy in the country, including a unique collection of popular pamphlets used to promote mass education. These pamphlets (some 300 in number) deal with almost every phase of peasant life (health problems, child care, agriculture and cattle raising, cooking, and other matters) and form an unusual body of documentation on the struggle against backwardness in the countryside. (The pamphlets are listed in the library catalog under "Russian Mass Education Collection.")

> The progress of education in schools is also well documented in the collection, particularly for the 1920s and 1930s and after 1945. Teaching programs for schools of various levels, reports on educational projects, publications of the Pedagogical Academy and the Ministry (formerly Commissariat) of Education, and educational statistics illuminate past and current educational problems. The collection also contains many monographs and articles in specialized periodicals on various fields of education, dealing with the Soviet Union as a whole as well as with specific regions. The material also focuses attention on political indoctrination in schools of all levels. The Hoover Institution has almost complete sets of publications of the leading Soviet learned societies whose activities are closely related to the Institution's field of interest, including the Academy of Sciences of the USSR and its affiliates, as well as the Marx-Engels-Lenin Institute. In addition, the library has scattered publications of learned societies from various non-Russian republics.

---

*Joseph D. Dwyer, Russia, The Soviet Union & Eastern Europe: A Survey of Holdings at the Hoover Institution on War, Revolution and Peace. (Stanford: Hoover Press, 1980).

An important collection not mentioned in the quote above is
Hoover's collection of materials in minority Soviet languages.
The collection contains more than 500 volumes in such languages
as Tatar, Georgian, Armenian, Azeri, Mari, Mordvin, Chuvash, etc.
Most of these items are of an educational nature and were
published in the 1920s and 1930s. These titles are not
catalogued and any information regarding them should be sought
through the curatorial office.

There also exists a collection of Soviet textbooks (ca. 100
volumes), most of them recent, acquired to demonstrate the
effects of Soviet sociopolitical ideas on education. The
majority of these works are textbooks in the areas of the social
sciences and humanities.

Finally, among the vast files of the library's rich serial
resources are numerous titles of periodicals and newspapers
relating to education in Eastern Europe, especially the Soviet
Union. A few of the longer and more important runs are Narodnoe
Prosveshchenie (1928-1930, with some gaps), Kommunisticheskoe
Prosveshchenie (1922-1926, 1934-1936, nearly complete), Narodnoe
Obrazovanie (1946- present, nearly complete), Sovetskaia
Pedagogika (1938-1972, nearly complete, 1981-present), Vestnik
Akademii Nauk SSSR (1934-present, nearly complete), Prepodavanie
Istorii v Shkole (1949-1966, 1972-present), Politicheskoe
Samoobrazovanie (1957-present), and Vestnik Vysshei Shkoly
(1965-1970, 1981-present).

Consult: Joseph D. Dwyer, Deputy Curator
          East European Collection
Location: 206 Hoover Tower

LATIN AMERICA LIBRARY

The Hoover Institution's library resources in the Latin American
area pertaining to the subject of education and society may be
found as catalogued books and pamphlets and as newspapers and
journals.

The beginnings of the Latin American Library Collection date back
to the time of the Paris Peace Conference when Hoover
collectors of delegation propaganda obtained material from
representatives of six Central and South American governments.

Extensive holdings of catalogued monographs dealing with this
subject can be located under the various headings beginning with
the word "Education": for example, Education - (country);
Education and crime; Education and the state. Other important

subject headings are Communism and education; Communist education; Illiteracy; Military education; Naval education. The term "Propaganda" with its various subdivisions covers resources of outstanding richness.

Of international importance is the Hoover collection on Castro's Cuba. It contains an estimated 2,500 volumes dealing with economic, political, and social affairs and currently receives some 50 newspaper and periodical titles. One title, Bohemia, is held in a virtually complete run from 1917 to the present. The collection contains important documentation on the Cuban government's literacy campaign announced at the United Nations in October 1960 by Fidel Castro. Working with groups of twenty-five to fifty illiterates, some 280,000 teachers were trained in the use of the basic teaching manual. In addition to the teacher, each group had a leader and another member in charge of political orientation as the regime wanted people to be able to read its propaganda. It was asserted by the end of the campaign that illiteracy had been reduced to 3.9 percent, the smallest figure in the world, and in 1964, a UNESCO Mission reported that "the Campaign was not a miracle, but rather a difficult victory achieved through work, technique, and organization."

Another example of Hoover holdings on education in Latin America is the material dealing with the literacy training program (concientizacion, conscientizacao) developed by Pasulo Freire to support the political activity of newly literate persons in Brazil and Chile. Freire's work has become well known; some regard him as one of the world's greatest educators of recent times. Throughout Latin America, programs of education designed along his principles are knows to exist in Brazil, Chile, Guatemala, Bolivia, and among certain Chicano groups in the United States.

Consult: Joseph W. Bingaman, Curator
          Latin American Collection
Location: 203 Hoover Tower

NOTES ON HOLDINGS ON EDUCATION AND SOCIETY IN OTHER
STANFORD UNIVERSITY LIBRARIES

The "Stanford University Libraries," as the main library system
at Stanford, houses significant collections of educational
materials both in the main research complex, the Cecil H. Green
Library, and in the Cubberley Education Library, which serves the
Stanford School of Education. Of particular note are several
collections that may not be fully accessible through the standard
card catalog. These include collections of government documents,
which are especially well represented.

GOVERNMENT DOCUMENTS

UNITED STATES

All publications issued through the depository program of the
Government Printing Office, including Department of Education,
Bureau of Education, and Office of Education titles since 1867
are available. Included are annual reports, statistical
compilations, analyses, directories, research reports, and other
materials. The publications of component divisions of the agency
are also included.

All nondepository publications listed in the Monthly Catalog
of Government Publications since 1953 are available in
microformat. Additionally, a large number are duplicated in book
form.

Size of collection: 114 linear feet, excluding nineteenth
century.

Consult: Joan Loftus
Location: Cecil H. Green Library

ERIC   (Educational Resources Information Center)

All microfiche issued for general distribution are available.
These encompass all publications since 1967; the center also has
some material reaching back to the mid-1950s. All publications
are indexed by author and subject in Resources in Education.

Size of collection: 200,000 microfiche

Consult: Barbara M. Van Deventer
Location: Cubberly Education Library

UNESCO

The major part of the 7,000 publications issued by UNESCO for
general distribution are available in the Stanford University
Libraries. In addition, records of the General Conference from
the first session in 1946 to date are held. The summary records
of the Executive Board, as well as the documents in the main
series of the Executive Board (including reports of subsidiary
bodies such as commissions and committees) for sessions 8-20
(1948-1950), and sessions 42 to date (1955-   ) are held.

Size of collection: 63 linear feet

Consult: Carol Anne Turner
Location: Government Documents Department
          Cecil H. Green Library

FOREIGN GOVERNMENTS

Publications of foreign national governments are well represented
in the collections. These titles are fully catalogued and, since
1974, have been available on-line through the RLIN network
(Research Libraries Network of the Research Libraries Group RLG).
Of special note are titles relating to Western Europe, Latin
America, and Sub-Saharan Africa.

Size of collection: Substantial

Consult: David Rozkuszka
Location: Government Documents Department
          Cecil H. Green Library

216

CUBBERLY EDUCATION LIBRARY

Within the Stanford University Libraries, Cubberley Education
Library houses the major research collections in education, which
support the academic programs of the School of Education.

This library currently holds over 100,000 volumes of material in
paper and microformats. These collections relate both specifically to education and increasingly to broader areas in the
social sciences that interact with the literature of education.
The following fields of study are emphasized.

Philosophy of Education
Anthropology of Education
Educational Psychology
Counseling Psychology
Child Development and Early Education
Sociology of Education
History of Education
Design and Evaluation of Educational Progress
International Development Education
Social Sciences in Education
Higher Education
Bilingual/Bicultural Education
Educational Administration
Political Studies in Education
Economic Studies in Education
Moral Education
Nonformal Education
Adult Education
Mathematical Methods in Education

The geographic focus of the collections is the United States,
Great Britain, Western Europe, and all developing nations.
Emphasis is on materials in Western languages, and preference is
given to current titles, except in acquisition of titles per-
tinent to the history of education. There are no chronological
limitations to the collections.

There are several specialized collections in the library in
addition to the substantial collection of microfiche from the
Educational Resources Information Center (see ERIC, p. 216).
There are strong historical collections of college and university
catalogs from the late nineteenth century to the 1970s. Foreign
catalogs are still obtained selectively, and a microfiche
collection of catalogs replaces the need to collect domestic
catalogs. Textbooks from the nineteenth century onward were
collected until the 1970s, as were curriculum guides from the
early twentieth century. A microfiche collection carries this

collection forward. There is a collection of standard tests,
which do not circulate. Selected titles from domestic, foreign,
and international governmental organizations are collected. The
library holds all dissertations compiled by students in the
Stanford School of Education.

Consult: Barbara M. Van Deventer
Location: Cubberley Education Library

STANFORD UNIVERSITY ARCHIVES

As an eminent university and research center, Stanford University
has acknowledged a responsibility to the academic community and
the general public to provide information about its origins and
development since 1885 as well as its operation, including
problems and their solutions, and the activities of its many
community members. To meet this need, the Stanford University
Archives were established in 1965 as the official repository of
the historical record of the university, its founding family, and
its many units.

As a result, the University Archives provide the researcher in
the field of higher education with a wide variety of resources
regarding the planning and maintaining of a major American
private university and its impact on teaching and research in all
academic fields. The resources of the University Archives
presently include over six million manuscript items, 40,000
publications, 500 serial titles, and 60,000 photographic images.

Of special note are:

   Archival records of campus academic, administrative, and
   research offices, such as those of the schools of
   Education, Engineering, Humanities, and Sciences; of
   Departments such as History, Geology, and Physics; of
   the Offices of the President, Provost, Public Affairs,
   Finance, Facilities, Planning, Registrar, and Student
   Affairs; and of research units such as the W. W. Hansen
   Laboratories and the Stanford Center for Research and
   Development in Teaching.

   Student records, such as those of the Associated
   Students of Stanford University, as well as fraternal,
   honorary, social, and dramatic organizations.

Correspondence, diaries, research notes, and other unpublished papers of Stanford faculty, trustees, and major staff, such as John Casper Branner, William H. Cowley, Ellwood P. Cubberley, David Starr Jordan, Frederic E. Terman, Lewis M. Terman, and Ray Lyman Wilbur.

Student letters, diaries, scrapbooks, and photograph albums relating to undergraduate and graduate experiences.

The professional and personal papers of the university's founders, Leland and Jane Lathrop Stanford, and of those family members involved in the planning and building of the university.

Photographic images, from daguerreotypes of the Stanford family and architect's documents of the turn-of-the-century construction to color slides of the most recent "Big Game."

Maps, blueprints, and other architectural drawings of buildings as constructed and modified and of landscaping, including Frederick Law Olmsted's original campus plans.

Posters, prints, watercolors, lithographs, etchings, and other art-on-paper of Stanford subjects.

Publications of all formats produced on campus, such as yearbooks and directories, reports and surveys, pamphlets and promotional brochures, committee minutes, Stanford University Press publications, dissertations and theses completed by Stanford graduates, and off-campus publications about the university and its community members.

Description guides to individual archival and manuscript collections, as well as an author/title/subject card catalog and specialized catalogs to the various graphic materials, dissertations, and biographical materials, are available in the University Archives' reading room. The University Archives indexes the Stanford Daily (1891-   ), the Campus Report, the

Stanford Observer, and Alumni Almanac, and selected retrospective
serial publications. A descriptive listing of major collections,
Stanford University Archives: A Guide to Archival and Manuscript
Collections (1978) may be purchased by writing to the Department.

The University Archives welcomes qualified researchers to its
reading room in the Cecil H. Green Library. The reading room is
open Monday through Friday, 9 a.m. to 5 p.m.

Consult: Roxanne Nilan, University Archivist
Location: Cecil H. Green Library

INDEX TO GUIDE ENTRIES

Entry numbers, not page numbers, are used in the index.
The 1981 supplement, pages 201 through 206, are not
included in this index.

Place-names............................ 223

Topics................................. 231

Organizations.......................... 234

Personal names......................... 240

Afghanistan
    82 164 276

Africa (see also individual countries)
    58 68 82 116 129 144 195 196 235 276 279 324 332 336 342 368
    401 417

Albania
    73 466 550 606

Algeria
    22 144 215

Argentina
    176

Asia (see also individual countries)
    21 48 54 167 238 260 274 276 279 291 356 368 482 489

Australia
    71 82 262

Austria
     8 24 50 71 125 220 484

Bangladesh (East Pakistan)
    128 276 392

Belgium
     7 38 40 41 83 95 122 191 246 285 304

Biafra
    51

Bolivia
    109 403

Botswana
    368

Brazil
    109 198 276 403

Bulgaria
    466 606

Burma
     310 367

Cameroon
     217 276 443

Canada
      71 193 378 392 525

Chile
     109 198 403 524

China
        4   20   21   30   32   62   63   76   84   86   89 104 105 106 112 113
      123 131 150 190 197 209 234 262 265 269 273 276 289 291 307 310
      318 327 332 333 348 350 353 354 359 392 407 412 430 440 451 458
      467 487 510 524 531 536 537 550 578 583 608

Colombia
     109 198 403

Congo, the
     129 323 368

Cuba
     129 323 368

Cyprus
     230

Czechoslovakia
     326 332 370 466 499

Dominican Republic
     109 149

Ecuador
     198 403

Egypt
     241 252 577

El Salvador
     276

Eritrea
     312

Estonia
    393

Ethiopia
    260 276 323

Europe (see also individual countries)
     12 31 66 69 71 74 92 120 167 168 209 276 293 312 319 326
    519 605

Finland
    209 380

France
     67 79 96 118 125 143 178 180 185 186 233 283 372 468 472 481
    582 593

French Equatorial Africa
    196

Germany
     27 44 45 46 49 50 72 93 94 125 139 145 146 157 163 166
    168 171 175 198 201 205 206 207 208 209 210 211 212 222 223 224
    231 236 242 271 291 294 309 325 328 329 330 345 346 374 382 390
    429 434 450 452 456 481 488 500 530 569 585 598 605

Ghana
     68 136 276 336 501

Great Britain (see United Kingdom)

Greece
    226 466 515 606

Guatemala
     25 198

Honduras
    276

Hungary
    375 478 564

India
    276 315 332 526 577 601

Indochina
    506

Indonesia
    218 268 291 315

Iran
    18 103 241 276 332 473 556 604

Iraq
    18 241 563

Israel
    277 556

Italy
    125 192 325 402 411

Ivory Coast
    129 276

Jamaica
    276

Japan
    23 111 112 115 117 142 147 173 194 239 244 253 262 273 291 300
    305 310 311 325 392 394 467 475 477 479 482 510 516 519 525 529
    533 535 550 561 565 580 596 600

Kenya
    129 162 218 276 368

Korea
    125 130 202 262 276 284 310 365 375 396 436 460 535 546 550 565

Laos
    218

Latin America (see also individual countries)
    19 100 141 198 218 262 275 276 279 368 513

Latvia
    53 171 317 442 466 476

Liberia
    129

Malawi
    129 276

Malaysia
    276 343 392 490

Mauritania
    22

Mexico
    109 183 198 258 276 351 357 525 534

Middle East
    5 43 252 276 310 363 517 556

Morocco
    22 235 351

Mozambique
    3

Nepal
    164 601

Netherlands
    566

New Zealand
    71 378 405

Nigeria
    1 61 129 276 287 417

Norway
    175 256

Pakistan
    89 276

Palestine
    18 400

Panama
    19 351

Paraguay
    403

Peru
    109 351 403

Philippines
    2 48 62 89 240 244 253 276 373 395 479 529 592 596

Poland
    93 121 148 296 299 361 398 399 414 418 419 420 421 422
    423 424 425 434 597

Portugal
    351 427 513

Puerto Rico
    399 441

Rhodesia
    68 195

Romania
    313 463 464 466

Russia (U.S.S.R.)
    15 18 26 34 35 36 37 39 42 60 64 75 82 84 87 107
    120 124 134 137 138 139 157 169 177 179 181 216 229 239 247 255
    267 270 288 295 301 314 316 362 370 376 414 418 419 420 428 430
    434 435 437 445 448 465 469 471 472 492 493 494 504 519 521 528
    545 552 573 574 575 576 599

Saudi Arabia
    340

Scotland
    332

Senegal
    276

Singapore
    563

South Africa
    3 68 124 148 420 483 505 565

South America (see also individual countries)
    100 368 483

Spain
355 513

Sri Lanka
276

Sweden
66 71

Syria
6

Taiwan
123 300 310 358 392 439 482 581

Tanzania
276 291 378 480

Thailand
276 291 367 480

Tibet
14

Tunisia
22 235

Turkey
54 77 133 236 252 302 351 375 408 540 543 486 568

Uganda
276 334 342

United Kingdom
5 82 171 192 222 223 225 339 342 507 518 550

United States

9	10	11	12	13	16	17	19	21	28	29	30	31	38	43	47
55	57	66	70	71	74	77	79	80	81	82	85	86	87	33	97
98	99	101	102	108	109	110	114	115	118	119	126	128	140	141	147
151	152	153	154	155	156	158	159	160	161	163	164	165	166	167	170
172	173	174	175	176	177	178	179	182	183	184	188	189	190	194	197
200	204	213	214	218	221	227	228	231	233	235	240	243	234	249	250
253	254	255	257	260	263	258	259	262	266	273	274	278	282	280	281
283	286	288	290	291	292	298	301	303	306	310	311	320	321	331	332
337	338	341	347	350	352	360	364	372	377	379	380	381	383	384	388
404	410	413	415	426	431	432	433	454	457	462	467	470	474	479	493

United States (continued)
    495 496 497 498 502 503 504 508 509 512 514 518 522 523 525 527
    532 534 535 536 538 539 544 547 548 549 550 551 553 554 555 556
    557 558 559 560 562 563 567 571 572 579 580 586 587 591 592 593
    594 595 599 607 609 610

Upper Volta
    276

Uruguay
    351 403

Venezuela
    91 109 276 351 403

Vietnam
    56 97 125 218 251 367 385 447 541

Western Samoa
    378

West Indies
    588

Yugoslavia (Serbia)
    154 192 199 238 466

Zaire
    323

Zambia
    129

TOPICS

Academic freedom
    335 364 504 591

Audiovisual education
    12 128 150 161 183 199 241 266 276 342 416 445 467 486 525 532
    535

Colleges and universities
      2   3   9 12 19 20 21 25 29 43 44 45 46 52 54 55
     59 62 66 77 79 84 85 86 89 91 99 107 108 109 120 121
    129 132 139 142 152 158 161 163 166 174 178 179 181 182 183 190
    193 197 209 213 218 225 227 234 244 250 255 258 259 260 262 268
    273 283 289 290 292 299 307 309 310 319 320 321 328 335 338 354
    355 364 365 367 370 375 386 391 397 399 402 408 411 412 414 422
    440 450 451 453 456 457 463 467 474 478 482 487 488 499 500 503
    504 511 518 523 526 533 536 537 544 562 571 575 578 580 587 593
    595 601 611

Communism and education
     39 43 66 94 108 109 159 161 179 310 314 332 335 376 382 384
    509 563

Comparative education
    82 128 139 405

Economic development and education
    174 188 260 335 350

Educational reform
    86 220 276 290 331 416 488 516 535

Educators
      7 90 120 188 243 248 157 377 389 395 527

Elementary education
     29 33 35 68 72 89 111 129 164 184 192 198 216 290 295 313
    337 340 341 384 395 449 490 541 563 567

Fascism and education
    204 402

Government educational policy
     70 86 152 161 184 214 221 303 341 347 360 392 462 488 497 532
    579 581 586 587

231

TOPICS (continued)

Health and welfare
   6   11   31   34   48   64   66   69   71   87   95 100 110 118 121 122
 134 144 148 165 180 184 200 209 212 238 245 256 269 277 281 283
 285 299 304 311 312 322 325 332 352 372 379 380 384 385 396 397
 406 415 417 418 420 422 434 442 454 477 489 492 494 497 515 530
 531 549 551 552 555 559 566 581 582 586 592 593 604 606

Higher education
  24   28   32   33   40   66   82   89 111 114 129 145 158 161 164 166
 176 184 209 216 262 270 272 278 290 295 303 314 341 347 379 384
 395 416 449 453 454 478 488 508 518 536 541 556 567 611

International education
   4   55   62   86 113 127 128 161 163 164 184 237 240 260 262 264
 276 291 297 298 368 378 381 397 405 470 508 513 542

Literacy (adult education or nonformal education)
  89 129 184 198 218 233 261 276 291 368 473 508 542 548 550 556
 563 593 604

Military education
  28   36   47   57 101 110 133 177 178 210 225 253 280 288 381 414
 428 477 497 502 547 549 557 558 562 576 593 610

Military occupation and education
   5   23   74 157 171 212 244 328 432 434 479 481 484 516 535 548
 561 596

Peace education
  19 236 291 292 323 476 485 584 613 614

Private education
 161 176 184 273

Propaganda and indoctrination
   2   9   18   27   30   37   41   49   54   56   97 104 106 109 125 154
 160 163 166 168 173 175 177 194 203 204 205 222 223 224 230 232
 235 236 251 253 255 261 266 271 281 282 310 311 314 318 325 326
 332 343 375 384 387 393 397 398 407 425 428 435 436 437 439 444
 459 461 472 496 502 507 510 514 521 523 529 530 545 546 550 552
 560 563 565 570 573 574 598 599 604 605 609

Race relations and education
   3   70   82 124 262 383 386 421 433 454 497 525 532 567 573 579
 590

Religion and education
    12 20 21 29 30 32 54 61 62 63 76 82 84 89 102 105
    115 116 117 131 139 142 144 148 150 180 195 197 198 215 217 219
    236 250 265 269 273 289 298 302 307 319 328 342 353 354 373 390
    394 420 438 440 443 451 457 458 469 475 487 528 561 568 571 577
    583

Secondary education
    1   19 50 56 68 72 89 111 114 120 129 161 164 166 184 192
    216 234 266 273 278 290 295 313 337 340 341 384 395 449 489 490
    508 541 563 567 585

Social and political reform and education
    56 103 200 201 274 291 524

Student organizations and youth
    9   10 11 13 15 16 19 21 22 24 26 32 40 44 45 46
    51 52 60 62 65 66 67 73 80 89 94 98 108 109 120 121
    122 123 124 126 131 132 134 135 136 138 140 143 146 147 149 151
    153 154 155 156 158 159 161 163 166 171 175 176 179 181 182 184
    185 186 188 191 192 198 207 208 209 216 218 221 225 230 231 236
    244 249 255 259 262 263 276 279 281 284 288 289 290 291 292 293
    294 295 296 297 302 309 310 311 312 313 316 319 320 321 323 329
    331 332 335 337 344 345 350 361 362 364 369 374 380 381 383 384
    386 392 398 399 402 404 410 413 420 424 425 426 427 428 429 433
    447 448 454 456 467 469 471 475 483 493 495 497 501 512 513 514
    520 521 522 526 532 535 538 541 542 544 545 550 555 556 565 567
    569 575 576 577 578 579 583 585 591 592 593 596 599 600 602 609
    610 611

Teacher education
    77 82 161 202 252 254 258 396 460 467 523 532 589 592 601

Textbooks and curricula
    9   33 54 89 95 110 119 137 166 173 179 190 203 210 254 262
    273 286 301 305 332 364 366 391 405 432 471 484 487 490 502 532
    550 557 558 565 590

Vocational education
    152 172 184 254 341 347 433 541 593

Women and education
    54 66 161 172 209 238 274 289 365 375 404 408 455 482 485 530
    535 562

ORGANIZATIONS
(Educational institutions not included)

Afro-Asian Educational Exchange, Inc., 467
Allgemeiner Studentenausschuss, 374
American First Committee, 10
American Afro-Asian Educational Exchange, Inc., 163, 350
American-Asian Educational Exchange, 335, 350
American Association for Economic Education, 335
American Association of School Administrators, 164
American Association of Teachers of Slavic and Eastern
    Languages, 295
American Association of University Women, 274
American Children's Fund, 11
American Committee on United Europe, 13
American Committee to Keep Biafra Alive, St. Louis Chapter, 12
American Council for Educational Development, 276
American Council on Education, 516
American Emergency Committee for Tibetan Refugees, 14
American Expeditionary Force in France, 178
American Federation of Teachers, 331
American Friends Service Committee, 26, 119, 147, 189
American Institute of Patriotic Education, 335
American Law Institute Committee to Encourage Discussion of
    Essential Human Rights, 170
American Red Cross, 37, 87, 100, 138, 158, 380, 582
American Relief Administration, 34, 69, 441
American Youth Congress, 126
Army War College, 428, 502
Association for the Advancement of International
    Education, 164
Association of Allied Professors and Lecturers in Great
    Britain, 397

Bees of America, 38
Belgian American Educational Foundation, 40, 264
Belorussian Liberation Front (London), 42
Berlin, Freie Universitaet, 44; Allgemeiner
    Studentenausschuss, 45
Biafra Students Association in the Americas, 51
Borden Merit Award Committee, 59
Boy Scouts, 11, 126, 197, 369, 541, 545
Brooklyn Women's War Relief Committee, 38

California Congress of Parents and Teachers, 381
Central and Eastern European Planning Board (New York), 92
Centralny Komitet dla Spraw Szkolnych i Oswiatowych
    (Polish refugee organization), 93
Chinese-American Educational Association, 430

234

Citizens Committee for a Free Cuba, 109
Citizens Committee for Reorganization of the Executive Branch of
    Government, 110
Commission for Polish Relief, 121
Commission for Relief in Belgium, 7, 29, 69, 83, 95
Commission for Relief in Belgium (1940-1945), 122
Committee for Free Asia, 123
Committee to Frame a World Constitution, 233
Communist Party of South Africa, 124, 125
Conference of the Institutions for the Scientific Study of
    International Affairs (Milan, 1932), 127
Constantinople Women's College, 408
C.R.B. Educational Foundation, 304

Deutsche Forrschungsgemeinschaft, 145
Deutsche Kongress-Zentrale, 209
Dom Polskich Dzieci (Oudtshoorn, South Africa), 148

EOKA (Greek underground organization), 230
Ethnogeographic Board (Washington, D.C.), 167

Far Western Slavic Conference (Stanford University, 1959), 169
Fight for Freedom Committee, 175
First Boy Scout International Jamboree (London, England,
    1920), 369
France, Commissariat General a la Famille, 180
Free Society Association, 182
Friends, Society of, American Friends Service Committee,
    Civilian Public Service, 189
Frontwacht, 191

General Headquarters of Supreme Commander for the Allied
    Powers, 23
George Peabody College for Teachers (Nashville, Tenn.), 202
German American Bund, 204
German National People's Party, 72
Germany, Deutsche Kongress-Zentrale, 209
Germany, Reichssicherheitshauptamt, Sicherheitsdienst, 210
Girl Scouts, 11, 158
Great Britain, Foreign Office: Political Intelligence
    Department, 223; Wellington House, 224

Henry Ford Peace Expedition, 485
Herbert Hoover Oral History Program, 248
Hoover Institution on War, Revolution and Peace, 158; Program on
    Overseas Development, 260; Revolution and the Development of
    International Relations Project, 261

Institute of Pacific Relations: American Council, 273;
    San Francisco Bay Region Division, 274
Institut fuer Politische Wissenschaft, 46
Institution of Current World Affairs, 272
Institut zur Studium der Judenfrage, 271
Inter-American Conference, 6th (Havana, 1928), 275
International Congress of Women, 485
International Federation of Free Teachers Union, 331
International Institute for Adult Literacy Methods, 473
International Institute for Educational Planning, 129
International Institute of Intellectual Cooperation of the League
    of Nations, 127
International Police Academy, 323
International Political Science Association, 5th World Congress
    (Paris, 1961), 277
International Refugee Organization (IRO), 71
International Socialists, 278
International Union of Students, 279

Japanese American Citizens League, 147
Jungsozialisten, 294

League of Red Cross Societies, 322

Makerere University, 342
Malayan Communist Party, 343
Marburger Hochschulgespraeche, 346
Marvin Liebman Associates, 69
Michigan, Legislature, Joint Committee on Reorganization of State
    Government, 360

National Catholic Educational Association, 298
National Christian Council of China, 265
National Citizens Committee to Save Education, 77
National Committee for World Literacy Program, 473
National Committee on Food for the Small Democracies, 380
National Conference of Parents and Teachers, 592
National Council for Prevention of War, Western Office (San
    Francisco), 381
National-Demokratische Partei Deutschlands (East Germany), 382
National Education Association, 264, 592
National Japanese American Student Relocation Council, 383
National Schools Committee for Economic Education, 350
National Russian Students' Christian Association in the U.S.A., 362
National War College, 553
News Research Service, (Los Angeles), 387
Nigerian Union of Teachers, 1

Organization of American Relief, 31
Overseas Educational Service, 1, 129

Paderewski Testimonial Fund, 59
Pan-African Congress, 6th (Dar es Salaam, Tanzania, 1974), 401
Paris Peace Conference, 1919, U.S. Division of Territorial,
    Economic and Political Intelligence, 403
Peace Corps, 19, 62, 89, 235, 501
Peoples' Educational Center, 609
Petrograd Children's Colony, 64
Philippine Public School Teachers' Association, 240
Poland, Konsulat Generalny, New York, 419
Poland, Konsulat Generalny, Pretoria - 420
Poland, Ministerstwo Prac Kongresowych (Ministry of Preparatory
    Work Concerning the Peace Conference, Polish Government-in-Exile,
    London), 421
Poland, Ministerstwo Spraw Kongresowych (Ministry of the Interior,
    Polish Government-in-Exile, London), 422
Polish Grey Samaritans, 423
Polish Information Service (New York), 424
Polish Research Information Center (New York), 425
President's Research Committee on Social Trends, 431
Protestant Episcopal Church, U.S.A., 438
Protesting Committee Against the U.S. Marines' Violence, 439

Radio Free Europe/Radio Liberty, 445
Rand Corporation, 218, 447
Rockefeller Foundation, 239
Romanian National Committee (Washington, D.C.), 463
Russia, Departament Politsii, Zagranichnaia Agentura, Paris
    (Russian Imperial Secret Police, Okhrana, Paris office), 471
Russia, Posol'stvo, Russian Embassy (France), 472
Russian Naval Academy, 576

Santo Tomas Internment Camp, 479
Secret Army Organization, 366
Stanford University, 158, 509, 510, 511
Students for a Democratic Society, 156, 522
Survey of Race Relations, 525

Teacher Education Research Center, 254
Terramare Office, (Berlin), 530
Tsing Hua Alumni Association, 537
Tule Lake War Relocation Authority Center (Calif.), 539
Turkish Wilsonian League, 540

United Nations, 177, 237, 243, 391, 491, 563, 587

United Nations Association of the United States of America, San Francisco Chapter, 542

United Nations Children's Fund, 581

United Nations Educational, Scientific and Cultural Organization (UNESCO), 42, 66, 88, 128, 155, 161, 166, 177, 264, 332, 335, 405, 416, 470, 482, 491, 563

United Nations Relief and Rehabilitation Administration (UNRAA), 71, 543; China Office, 544

United Nations Social and Economic Commission on Child Welfare in Greece, 515

U.S. American Relief Administration, Russian Operations, 545

U.S. Armed Forces, 607

U.S. Army Air Forces, 47, 74, 97

U.S. Army, Far East Command, Psychological Warfare Branch, 546

U.S. Army Infantry School (Ft. Benning, Georgia), 547

U.S. Army School for Military Government and Administration, New York, 2nd Section, Group V, 548

U.S. Army, Third Army, General Staff, G-2, 549

U.S. Central Bureau of Planning and Statistics, 200

U.S. Civil Affairs Training School (Stanford University), 550

U.S. Commission on Organization of the Executive Branch of the Government, 551

U.S. Department of Education, 441

U.S. Department of State, Office of External Research, 552

U.S. National Emergency Council, 554

U.S. National Resources Planning Board, Youth Section, 555

U.S. National Student Association, International Commission, 556

U.S. Naval Academy, 57, 101, 497

U.S. Naval Air Combat Intelligence School (Quonset Pt., Rhode Island) 557

U.S. Naval Reserve, 558

U.S. Office of Civilian Defense, 559

U.S. Office of War Information, 496, 560

U.S. Provost-Marshal-General's Bureau, Military Government Division Training Branch, 561

U.S. South Africa Leadership Exchange Program, 505

U.S. War Department Committee on Education and Special Training, 562

West Indian Conference, 2d (St. Thomas, Virgin Islands, 1946), 588

Western College Congress, 1st (Stanford University, 1947), 589

Western Interstate Commission for Higher Education, 454

Western Regional Conference on the Holocaust, 1st (San Jose, California, 1977), 590

Workers' Educational Association, 397

World Black and African Festival of Arts and Culture, 2d (Lagos, 1977), 603

Young Americans for Freedom, 153
Young Communist League of the U.S., 609
Young Men's Christian Association, 76, 120, 178, 288, 610
Young Women's Christian Association, 289, 458

Abernethy, David B., 1
Adams, Herbert B., 54
Adams, Marie, 2
Aitchison, Bruce, 5
Allen, Benjamin Shannon, 7
Almond, Nina, 8
Altrocchi, Rudolph, 9
Anders, Wladylsaw, 18
Applegarth, John S., 19
Argelander, Frank, 20
Arnold, Julean Herbert, 21
Ashford, Douglas E., 22
Asker, Aski Bir, 133
Ayau, Manuel F., 25

Babb, Nancy, 26
Bade, Wilfrid Albert Karl, 27
Bailey, Thomas Andrew, 28
Baker, George Barr, 29
Ballantine, Joseph William, 30
Bane, Suda Lorena, 31
Barbour, George Brown, 32
Barker, Burt Brown, 33
Barringer, Thomas G., 34
Basily, Nicolas Alexandrovich de, 35
Bastunov, Vladimir J., 36
Batsell, Walter Russell, 37
Bekeart, Laura Helene, 39
Benes, Edward, 257
Bennett, A. E., 43
Berman, Geoffrey, 47
Bernadino, Vitaliano, 48
Berndt, Alfred-Ingemar, 49
Bernfeld, Siegfried, 50
Bienen, Henry, 52
Bilmanis, Alfred, 53
Bisbee, Eleanor, 54
Blackwelder, Eliot, 55
Bohannan, Charles T. R., 56
Bolander, Louis H., 57
Bond, Marshall, 58
Botkine, Serge, 60
Bowen, Thomas Jefferson, 61
Boynton, Charles Luther, 62
Brady, R. F., 63
Bramhall, Burle, 64
Breshko-Breshkovskaia, Ekaterina, 65

Brodin, Nils-Eric, 66
Brody, General, 67
Brokensha, David Warwick, 68
Brown, Walter Lyman, 69
Brownell, Samuel Miller, 70
Brownlee, Aleta, 71
Brunton, Delbert, 72
Bunescu, Alexander D., 73
Bunn, John, 74
Bunyan, James, 75
Burgess, J. Stewart, 76
Burgess, Stella F., 76
Burgess, Warren Randolph, 77
Burnham, Frederick Russell, 78
Burr, Myron Carlos, 79
Busterud, John Arman, 80
Butler, Charles Terry, 81
Butts, R. Freeman, 82

Calder, Alonzo Bland, 84
Caldwell, John Kenneth, 85
Caldwell, Oliver Johnson, 86
Campbell, Hannah Brian, 87
Carr, William G., 88
Carson, Arthur Leroy, 89
Carter, Gwendolen, 90
Casas, Armengol Miguel, 91
Cerf, Jay H., 94
Chadbourn, Philip H., 95
Chadbourn, William H., 95
Chaigneau, Victor-Louis, 96
Chandler, Robert W., 97
Chang, Hsin-hai, 98
Chapin, Leland T., 99
Chapman, Frank Michler, 100
Chappel, Church Allen, 101
Cherington, Reed B., 103
Childs, James Rives, 103
Christian, Sutton, 106
Christoff, Peter K., 107
Church, Michael P., 108
Clapp, Frances Benton, 111
Clark, Erik, 112
Clark, Grover, 113
Clarke, Bruce C., 114
Clarke, Harold A., 114
Clarke, Ione Clement, 115

Clarke, William H., 116
Clement, Ernest Wilson, 115
Cobb, John B., 117
Cofer, Mrs. Leland E., 118
Cole, Betty, 119
Colton, Ethan Theodore, 120
Conwell, Russell H., 377
Coombs, Philip Hall, 128, 276
Cowan, Laian Gray, 129
Crampton, Frank Asbury, 130
Cross, Rowland McLean, 131
Cutler, Richard L., 132

Dagdeviren, Hidayet, 133
Dallin, Alexander, 134
Danielpol, Dumitru, 135
Danquah, Joseph Boakye, 136
David, Paul T., 555
Davis, Richard Hallock, 137
Davis, Robert E., 138
Day, George Martin, 139
Decker, Benton W., 140
De Conde, Alexander, 141
De Forest, Charlotte B., 142
Delage, Jean, 143
Delavignette, Robert Louis, 144
Dodge, Alice Sinclair, 147
Domke, Paul C., 150
Donohoe, Christine, 151
Donovan, James Britt, 152
Dowd, Patrick, 153
Dragnich, Alex N., 154
Draper, Theodore, 155
Dumbacher, Joseph, 156
Dunner, Joseph H., 157
Dyer, Susan Louise, 158

Egbert, Donald Drew, 159
Eliel, Paul, 160
Elliott, William Yandel, 161
Eltse, Ruth Ricci, 162
Emmet, Christopher Temple, Jr., 164
Engleman, Finis Ewig, 164
Enke, Stephen, 165
Epstein, Julius, 166

Farrand, Stephen M., 170
Feldmans, Jules, 171
Feliz, Frank E., 172
Fellers, Bonner Frank, 173
Fertig, Lawrence, 174
Finn, Chester E., Jr. , 176
Fisher, Harold Henry, 177
Flint, Rebecca, 178
Fotitch, Konstantin, 179
Frederiksen, O. J., 181
Freeman, Joseph, 183
Freeman, Roger Adolf, 184
Freud, Sigmund, 257
Friedland, William H., 187
Friedman, Milton, 188
Frillmann, Paul William, 190
Froebel, Friedrich, 389
Furlong, Charles Wellington, 192

Gadsby, Henry Franklin, 198
Gahagan, G. William, 194
Gann, Louis Henry, 195
Gardinier, David E., 196
Garside, Bettis Alston, 197
Gauld, Charles Anderson, 198
Gavrilovic, Milan, 199
Gay, Edwin Francis, 200
Geiger, Theodor, 201
George, Rosemary, 203
Ghazali (Iman), 54
Gitlow, Benjamin, 214
Godard, Yves Jean Antoine Noel, 215
Golder, Frank Alfred, 216
Good, Albert I., 217
Goodman, Allan Erwin, 218
Graham, Malbone Watson, 219
Grant, Donald, 220
Gray, Edward Rutherford, 221
Gregory, Thomas C., 227
Grey, Ben, 228
Grimm, David Davidovich, 229
Grivas, George, 230
Grossman, Kurt Richard, 231
Grzybowski, Kazimierz, 232
Guerard, Albert Leon, 233
Gunn, Selskar M., 234

Hall, Luella J., 235
Hallgarten, George Wolfgang Felix, 236
Hallgarten, Katherine Drew, 237
Halpern, Joel M., 238
Hamilton, Maxwell McGaughey, 239
Hanna, Paul Robert, 240, 291, 555
Harley, Paul T., 555
Harris, Christina Phelps, 241
Harris, David, 242
Harris, Herbert, 243
Hastings, William, 244
Hatfield, Mark Odom, 245
Hayden, Tom, 156
Healy, James Augustine, 246
Heitman, Sidney, 247
Herbits, Stephen E., 249
Herron, George Davis, 250
Herz, Martin Florian, 251
Heyworth-Dunne, James D., 252
Hiestand, John, 253
High, Sidney C., Jr., 254
Hilger, Frances E., 255
Hill, Margaret E., 256
Hill, Paul Albert, 257
Hill, Robert C., 258
Himmler, Heinrich, 330
Hoover, Herbert Clark, 69, 158, 245, 248, 259, 263
Hoover, Lou Henry, 158
Hornbeck, Stanley Kuhl, 262
Hudson, Ray M., 263
Hunt, Edward Eyre, 264
Huston, Jay Calvin, 265
Hutchins, Robert M., 188
Hutchinson, John Raymond, 266

Iliff, John L., 267
Inglis, John, 269
Inglis, Theodora, 269
Innis, Harold Adams, 270
Irvine, Dallas D., 280
Irwin, William Henry, 281

Jackson, Florence, 283
Jacobs, Joseph Earle, 28
Jacobs-Pauwels, F. Marguerite, 285
Jelinek, James John, 286
Jenkins, George D., 287

PERSONAL NAMES (continued)

Jenny, Arnold E., 288
Job, Martha, 289
Jones, Hardin B., 290
Jones, Howard Palfrey, 291
Jordan, David Staar, 292
Juenger, Ernst, 293

Karcz, George F., 295
Karski, Jan, 296
Katz, Friedrich, 297
Kefauver, Grayson Neikirk, 298
Kellogg, Vernon Lyman, 299
Kerr, George H., 300
Kerr, Margaret Ann, 301
Key, Kerim Kami, 302
Kilpatrick, Wylie, 303
Kirby, Gustavus T., 304
Kitagawa, Kay I., 305
Kittredge, Tracy Barrett, 306
Knowlton, Lucerne H., 307
Koch, Howard, Jr., 308
Koenigs, Folkmar, 309
Kohlberg, Alfred, 310
Kolbe, James, 385
Kramer, Howard D., 311
Kramer, Jack, 312
Krupenskii, Aleksandr Nikolaevich, 313
Kwiatkowski, Antoni Wincenty, 314

Larsen, E. S., 315
Laserson, Maurice, 316
Lau, Kenneth, 318
Launay, Jacques de, 319
LaVarre, William, 320
Lea, Ethel, 430
Lea, Homer, 430
Lawrence, John Hundale, 321
Lefever, Ernest Warren, 323
Lemarchand, Rene, 324
Lerner, Daniel, 325
Lettrich, Joseph, 326
Liebknecht, Karl, 316
Liebman, Marvin, 350
Lindgren-Utsi, Ethel John, 327
Lochner, Louis Paul, 328
Loewa, Joachim, 329
Loewenberg, Peter, 330

Lowenthal, Alfred Max, 331
Lovestone, Jay, 332
Lowdermilk, Walter Clay, 333
Lowenkopf, Martin, 334
Lowman, Myers G., 335
Lubeck, Paul, 336
Lundeen, Ernest, 337
Lutz, Ralph Haswell, 8, 31
Lyle, Annie G., 338

McCarran, Sister Margaret Patricia, 339
McConnell, Philip C., 340
McGrath, Earl James, 341
MacArthur, Douglas, 529
MacNeil, Eleanor, 289
Marawske, Max, 345
Marland, Sidney Percy, Jr., 347
Marlowe, Sanford Stratton, 348
Marquardt, Frederic S., 349
Mason, John Brown, 351
Mathews, Forrest David, 352
Matthews, Harold S., 353
Mattox, Elmer L., 354
Maurin, Joaquin, 355
Mayers, Henry, 357
Mayo, Sebastian, 357
Mei, I-ch'i, 358
Melrose, Paul C., 359
Mikolajczyk, Stanislaw, 361
Mitchell, Anna V. S., 362
Mitchell, Richard Paul, 363
Moley, Raymond, 364
Monagan, Walter E., Jr., 365
Monday, Mark, 366
Monroe, Paul, 403
Montgomery, John Dickey, 367
Moore, Franklin, 368
Moore, William C., 369
Moran, Hugh Anderson, 370
Moreland, William Dawson, Jr., 371
Mosher, Clelia Duel, 372
Munger, Henry W., 373
Munro, Dana Carleton, 375
Muraveiskii, S., 376
Murphy, Robert Daniel, 377
Murra, Wilbur Fim, 378

PERSONAL NAMES (continued)

Nambara, Shigeru, 516
Nathan, Richard P., 379
Naylor, Robert, 385
Niederpruem, William J., 389
Niemoeller, Martin, 390
Norton, Robert, 391
Nossal, Frederick, 392

Oiderman, M., 393
Olds, Charles Burnell, 394
Orata, Pedro T., 395
Orion, Walter Harold, 396
Osusky, Stefan, 397

Paderewski, Ignacy Jan, 398, 399
Panunzio, Constantine Maria, 402
Park, Alice, 404
Parkyn, George William, 405
Parmelee, Ruth A., 406
Pastuhov, Vladimir D., 407
Patrick, Mary Mills, 408
Peck, Willys Ruggles, 409
Pennington, Levi T., 410
Perry, W. L., 411
Peterkin, Wilbur J., 412
Phillips, Ethel G., 413
Platonov, Valerian Platonovich, 414
Platt, Phillip Skinner, 415
Platt, William James, 416
Plotnicov, Leonard, 417
Pool, Ithiel de Sola, 426
Possony, Stefan Thomas, 428
Potulicki, Michal, 429
Powers, Joshua B., 430
Preston, Archibald E., 432
Price, Raymond Kissam, Jr., 433
Pronin, Dimitri, 434
Pruitt, Ida, 440
Pusta, Kaarel Robert, 442

Quinn, Frederick, 443

Raemaekers, Louis, 446
Raymond, Edward A., 448
Reagan, Ronald, 449
Redlich, Fritz, 450

Reed, Alice C., 451
Reeves, Floyd W., 555
Rhodes, Cecil John, 453
Ricardo-Campbell, Rita, 454
Richardson, Grace, 455
Richter, Harald, 456
Rieffel, Aristide, 457
Rietveld, Harriet, 458
Rixford, Mary C., 459
Robb, Felix C., 460
Robinson, Jacob, 461
Robnett, George Washington, 462
Roosevelt, Franklin D., 166
Rostovtseff, Fedor, 465
Roucek, Joseph Slabey, 466
Rowe, David Nelson, 467
Ruark, Arthur Edward, 468
Ruhl, Arthur, 469
Russell, Mrs. Henry Potter, 470
Ryan, John W., 473
Ryan, Paul B., 474

Sakharov, Andrei, 494
Salisbury, Laurence E., 475
Salnais, Voldemars, 476
Sams, Crawford F., 477
Samsonow, Michael S., 478
Satorn, Pinyo, 480
Scapini, Georges, 481
Schenck, Hubert Gregory, 482
Schneider, Elizabeth, 483
Scholly, Nora, 484
Schwimmer, Rosika, 485
Scipio, Lynn A., 486
Scott, Roderick, 487
Seabury, Paul, 488
Serebrennikov, Ivan Innokentievich, 489
Seymour, J. Matt, 49
Sharp, Walter Rice, 491
Shaw, George Bernard, 257
Sheiman, Boris, 492
Shishmanian, John Amar, 493
Shockley, William Bradford , 494
Shriver, Harry C., 496
Shoup, David Monroe, 495
Shultz, George Pratt, 497
Simmons, Robert Glenmore, 498

Slavik, Juraj, 499
Sljivar, Vojislav, 500
Smith, Eddie, 501
Smith, Ralph C., 502
Smith, Ralph Elbertson, 503
Solow, Herbert, 504
Sprouse, Philip D., 506
Squires, Duane, 507
Staley, Eugene , 508
Starr, Clarence T., 514
Stavrianos, Leften Stavros, 515
Sterling, J. E. Wallace, 516
Stevens, Harley C., 517
Stockton, Gilchrist Baker, 518
Story, Russell McCulloch, 519
Strong, Sydney, 520
Struve, Peter B., 521
Sullivan, Mark, 523
Sung, Tzu-wen, 524

Talbot, Phillips, 526
Tarr, Curtis W., 527
Tarsaidze, Alexandre Georgievich, 528
Telesco, Lee, 529
Thelander, Hulda Evelyn, 531
Thomas, Donald Roff, 532
Thompson, Dorothy, 151
Torres Quintero, M. Gregorio, 534
Trainor, Joseph C., 535
Treat, Payson J., 536
Tuck, William Hallam, 538
Turner, Robert F., 541

Utley, Freda, 563

Vambery, Rusztem, 564
Vatcher, William Henry, Jr., 565
Vernon, Manfred C., 566
Veysey, Victor Vincent, 567
Victor, George, 568
Visoianu, Constantin, 570
Voegelin, Eric, 571
Volkov, Leon, 573
Vol'skii, Nikolai Vladislavovich, 574
Von Arnold, Antonina R., 575
Von Mohrenschildt, Dimitri Sergius, 576
Von Wiegand, Karl Henry, 577

Wales, Nym, 578
Wallace, Mike, 188
Warren, Gerald Lee, 579
Watkins, James Thomas, IV, 580
Watkins, Ralph James, 581
Watkins, Susan E., 582
Webster, James Benjamin, 583
Wegerer, Alfred von, 584
Weiler, Hans, 585
Weinberger, Caspar W., 586
West, Ralph E., 587
White, Geoffrey, 591
Wilbur, Ray Lyman, 593
Willoughby, Charles Andrew, 594
Wilson, Carol Green, 595
Wilson, Laurence L., 596
Wilson, Woodrow, 257
Wiskowski, Wlodzimierz, 597
Wissmann, Hellmuth, 598
Wolfe, Bertram David, 599
Wolters, Maria, 600
Wood, Hugh Bernard, 601
Woolley, Barry Lee, 602

Young, Arthur N., 608
Young, Carl, 257
Yucel, Hassan Ali, 133

Zalar, Charles, 612
Ziberman, Bella N., 613